ROADTRIP A

A Sports Fan's Guide to

Route 66

IMBRIFEX
BOOKS

ROADTRIP AMERICA

A Sports Fan's Guide to

Route 66

Ron Clements

IMBRIFEX BOOKS

IMBRIFEX BOOKS
8275 S. Eastern Avenue, Suite 200
Las Vegas, NV 89123, USA

IMBRIFEX.
BOOKS

Editors: Vicki Adang & Patricia Clements
Book and Cover Designer: Sue Campbell
Maps: Chris Erichsen
Author Photo: John Harrington
All cover and interior photos by the author except as noted on page 344.

Library of Congress Cataloging-in-Publication Data:

Names: Clements, Ron, 1974- author.
Title: A sports fan's guide to Route 66 / Ron Clements.
Other titles: Route 66

Description: Las Vegas, NV : Imbrifex Books, [2021] | Series: Roadtrip

America | Includes index. | Summary: "In this groundbreaking new book,
sports writer and lifelong sports fan Ron Clements goes beyond nostalgic

buildings and classic cars to highlight historic sports venues, storied
sports professionals, and current sports events along the Mother Road"--
Provided by publisher.

Identifiers: LCCN 2021013748 (print) | LCCN 2021013749 (ebook) |
ISBN 9781945501739 (paperback) | ISBN 9781945501746 (ebook)
Subjects: LCSH: Sports--United States. | United States Highway 66.
Classification: LCC GV583 .C54 2021 (print) | LCC GV583 (ebook) | DDC
796.0973--dc23

LC record available at https://lccn.loc.gov/2021013748

LC ebook record available at https://lccn.loc.gov/2021013749

First Edition: August 2021
Printed in Canada

Get Your Balls, Bats,
and Sticks on Route 66!

Contents

INTRODUCTION: What This Book Is All About

MANY BOOKS HAVE BEEN WRITTEN ABOUT ROUTE 66, THE 2,400-MILE HISTORIC highway that stretches from Chicago to Los Angeles. Most of those books focus on travel tips about where to eat or sleep and the nostalgic locations along what John Steinbeck in his classic 1939 novel, *The Grapes of Wrath*, called the Mother Road. Route 66 is an iconic part of American culture, and people travel from across the world to drive the historic byway and experience something uniquely American.

But what if some of those visitors want to check out NBA, NHL, or MLB games? See some minor league baseball? Watch a NASCAR or drag-racing event? Experience Texas high school football under the Friday night lights? Watch some college football, basketball, or baseball? If you really want to get your kicks on Route 66, why not see some soccer or rugby? All of this is covered in *A Sports Fan's Guide to Route 66*. This book is for the people who have driven past a high school, college, or professional stadium and thought, "I wonder what it's like to see a game there."

Connecting Route 66 and sports may seem counter to the road's folksy, hometown reputation. "When you think about Route 66, you think about everyone sharing the unique experiences up and down the entire highway," California Historic Route 66 Association President Scott Piotrowski said of sports and the Mother Road. "You think of mom-and-pop motels with the neon glowing. Sports is not that. Sports is the 'us-versus-them' mentality.... It's not something that by nature gets tied together with 66."

But if you look deeper, you'll find at the heart of Route 66 the same thing that's at the heart of every town and city: community. "Most books about the Mother Road focus on how things were—a noble calling to be sure," said Texas Old Route 66 Association President Nick Gerlich. "But while they examine obscure alignments, historical artifacts, and even the mighty people of the road, they overlook one of the most unifying activities along its 2,400 miles. From high school to the highest level of professionals, sports provide the cement that keeps communities glued and coming out for the spectacle of it all. It is no different along 66."

No Shortage of Places to Visit

Along Route 66, you'll find mainstream sports like baseball, football, and basketball, but also a bit of the obscure. Outdoorsmen who might want to catch their own dinner as they camp can find hunting and fishing spots along the route. Want to get in a round of golf along the Mother Road? *A Sports Fan's Guide to Route 66* will tell you where courses are along the highway and give you an idea of the cost as well.

Some nostalgic Route 66 sites—gas stations, eateries, murals, and motels—are mentioned, but in the context of their proximity to a sporting event or venue. Several schools, gymnasiums, and stadiums along Route 66 are on the National Register of Historic Places.

A Sports Fan's Guide to Route 66 not only takes you to various sporting events and explains what the atmosphere is like at those venues but also features interviews. You'll hear from the Chicago Blackhawks team historian, the track president at Chicagoland Speedway, various coaches and athletics directors at the high school and college levels, media members connected with cities and teams, as well as pro athletes like LeBron James.

What You'll Find in the Book

Whether you're doing all or part of Route 66, this is your comprehensive guide to sports along the highway. The book begins where the Mother Road does, in Chicago, and travels west to Santa Monica, California, where Route 66 comes to an end. Most venues are within 5 miles of the present-day route; those that are farther out are well worth the visit if you have time to spare. Places of interest are printed in bold to help you identify potential stops during your travels. Addresses are listed at the end of each chapter.

At the beginning of each chapter is a state map with the alignment of Route

66 that I used while working on this book. Icons on each of the eight state maps indicate where some of the venues that are mentioned in the text can be found. Not every sporting venue or place of historical significance that I wrote about are found on these maps, but I have included a variety so you can navigate to the ones I've highlighted. On the inside front cover is a map that shows the entire highway path of Route 66, along with some of the sports locations identified in greater detail in this book.

I hope you enjoy *A Sports Fan's Guide to Route 66,* the first sports-related book about America's Main Street, and that it inspires you to go see a game or two along the world's most famous road.

February 2021

Ron Clements

ILLINOIS

The Illinois segment of Route 66 may not be as scenic as the portion that runs through the fabled landscape of the American Southwest, but it has a little bit of everything for travelers. Beginning and ending in major cities, the 301 miles through the Land of Lincoln are dotted with small towns that embrace their Route 66 heritage. You'll also find a lot of sports diversity with NFL, NBA, NHL, and MLB teams, as well as auto and horse racing tracks in addition to a slew of high school and collegiate sports along the way.

CHICAGO

Chicago is one of just 12 U.S. cities to have at least one team in each of the four major North American professional sports leagues, but only two play near Route 66. Major League Baseball's Cubs make their home at venerable Wrigley Field, but it's 7 miles north of the Route 66 starting point. The White Sox are at Guaranteed Rate Field 5 miles to the south. The NFL's Bears are a little closer, 2 miles south of the Chicago Art Institute at Soldier Field. But the home of the NBA's Bulls and NHL's Blackhawks is **United Center**, and it's only two blocks off the Adams Street portion of Route 66.

With your starting point on South Michigan Avenue in front of the Chicago Art Institute, head west down Adams Street about 3 miles before hanging a right on Damen Avenue. Before you even get to Monroe Street one block north, you'll see United Center towering over Madison Street.

Larger-than-life United Center

The first impression you get as you approach United Center is that it's enormous. With a spectator capacity of more than 22,000 for sporting events, United Center is the largest NHL and NBA arena. Because of its size, it's also a popular venue for NCAA events and a regular host for the Big Ten men's basketball tournament in March.

United Center opened in 1994 and replaced the old Chicago Stadium, which opened in 1929. The Blackhawks were the first tenants of Chicago Stadium, with the Bulls moving in for the 1967–68 NBA season. Known as "The Madhouse on Madison," Chicago Stadium could cram 18,000 people into tight seats and steep rows and was known as the loudest arena in the NHL and NBA. Blackhawks team historian Bob Verdi said United Center is the new "Madhouse on Madison," except with "suites and dessert trays."

"One of the theories is that the noise at the old Chicago Stadium, one of

Route 66 begins at the Chicago Art Institute at the Corner of Michigan Avenue and Adams Street.

the great old buildings, would never translate across the street to United Center, which is about three times as large," Verdi said. "But there's no lack of atmosphere at the United Center."

Jordan and the Bulls' Kingdom

Two decades—the 1990s and the 2010s—were especially exuberant at United Center. Michael Jordan led the Bulls to three straight NBA championships twice. Chicago claimed the NBA crown from 1991 to 1993 and again from 1996 to 1998. The gap between the three-peats occurred when Jordan stepped away from basketball for two seasons to pursue a baseball career with the Chicago White Sox. Jordan never rose above Double A and returned to the Bulls in 1995.

"Michael Jordan helped build that building," Verdi said. "There's no doubt about it."

A 12-foot statue of a soaring "Air Jordan," known as "The Spirit," was unveiled in 1994 outside the arena, but was moved into the United Center atrium in 2015. It's now a popular meeting spot for fans before finding their seats. The atrium is lined with shops, cafes, ticket offices, and bars with "His Airness" in the center of the 190,000-square-foot space. Even for the casual sports fan, United Center is a can't-miss experience.

"You can go to a game at any of these arenas now, never see a minute of the game, and still have a great time," Verdi said. "It's not just a game; it's an event."

The Bulls and Blackhawks do a wonderful job of paying tribute to the franchises' respective histories. Photos, plaques, and signs line the concourses on every level. Banners of each team's retired numbers as well as their championship banners are draped from the ceiling—Bulls on one end, Blackhawks at the other.

Blackhawk wins through the decades

Like the Bulls, the Blackhawks have won six championships. While the Bulls won all six of their titles in a single decade, the Stanley Cup championships are spread across more than 80 years. The Blackhawks won their first title in 1934—the club's seventh season of existence when the NHL had just 10 teams. Another championship followed in 1938 and again in 1961 with Hall of Famers Stan Mikita, Al Arbour, and

A statue of Michael Jordan soaring over an opponent is in the atrium of United Center.

Bobby Hull leading the way. The Blackhawks didn't win another Cup until the 2009–10 season, but won two more in 2013 and 2015.

Mikita and Hull are immortalized with bronze statues outside of United Center. The 7-foot-tall bronze sculptures, unveiled in 2011, show the two in full color with red sweaters and leggings, sticks in their hands, and skating in still-motion atop 5-foot-tall black granite pedestals.

The Blackhawks were one of the NHL's "Original Six"—along with the Toronto Maple Leafs, Boston Bruins, Detroit Red Wings, Montreal Canadiens, and New York Rangers. Verdi said that distinction is still recognized by today's young players.

"We all assume the millennials don't have an appreciation for what came before them, but for some reason, the 'Original Six' is implanted in the new players," Verdi said. "If you're a 25-year-old and you get traded here or to the Toronto Maple Leafs, that's a big deal."

Verdi said ending the 49-year championship drought in 2010 was similar to when the Hawks ended their 23-year drought in 1961.

"When Bobby Hull and Stan Mikita arrived in the late '50s, it kind of rescued the Blackhawks from a dark period," Verdi said. "They were drawing nobody and played neutral-site games because the crowds were so bad. They played in St. Louis, Omaha, Indianapolis, and Minneapolis.

"At one time, the situation was so bad, the NHL talked about moving the Blackhawks to St. Louis. But obviously it never happened."

Winning fixes everything, and Verdi said the Blackhawks now have one of the best game environments in the NHL. Since 2008, the alternative rock song "Chelsea Dagger" by the Fratellis has been played after each Blackhawks goal and victory.

Banners of each team's retired numbers as well as their championship banners are draped from the United Center ceiling—Bulls on one end; Blackhawks on the other.

A club level view of a Chicago Blackhawks game in 2019.

"You've got standing-room-only crowds," Verdi said. "They've made the in-game experience and presentation really spectacular."

It doesn't get much better than when the Blackhawks are playing the St. Louis Blues because of the cities' natural sports rivalry. When the Blues entered the NHL in 1967 as an expansion team, they went to three consecutive Stanley Cup Finals with a roster full of former Blackhawks players led by Arbour. Verdi said United Center is "very intense" and "rocking" when the Blues and Blackhawks face off.

Before seeing a game at United Center, you can have dinner at historic **Berghoff Restaurant** on Adams. If you're staying in Chicago for the night after a game, grab breakfast at **Lou Mitchell's** on Jackson on your way out of the Windy City.

HINSDALE

From Interstate 290 in Chicago, rejoin Route 66 at Harlem Avenue and head south 4 miles to Joliet Road. Joliet Road winds through the villages of Lyons and McCook before intersecting with 55th Street. Located just 3 miles west of where Route 66 splits from 55th Street and turns south onto Brainard Avenue in Countryside is the Hinsdale high school with more state championships than any other school in Illinois.

The gymnasium at **Hinsdale Central** is impressive with banners for the 103 state championships (through 2020) in the 31 sports in which the Red Devils compete. The entirety of the gym is encircled with banners from each of the school's state titles. The school's most prosperous sports are tennis and swimming, which won a combined 70 titles from 1955 to 2019. Central set a state record with state championships in eight events during the 2014–15 school year.

"We're in an area where both [tennis and swimming] are very popular with parents and the community itself, so the kids get involved at an early age," said Dan Jones, Hinsdale Central's athletics director. "We have a lot

Hinsdale Central's swim program is one of the best in the nation, and the Red Devils have equally impressive facilities.

of clubs in the area that give lessons. We have three swim clubs that feed into our school."

Olympic gold medalists John Kinsella and John Murphy came out of the Central swim program, and Olympian Robert Nieman was also a Red Devils swimmer. The Central tennis program helped Marty Riessen become a professional player. Former Chicago White Sox owner Bill Veeck, who was inducted into the Baseball Hall of Fame in 1991, also attended the school when it was simply known as Hinsdale Township High School.

The Red Devils' primary rival is Lyons Township High School, 4 miles northeast on Brainard Avenue in LaGrange.

"It's a heated rivalry in every sport," Jones said of the Central-Lyons rivalry. He added that basketball and football games are standing-room-only events when the two schools face off. "It's heated, but competitive. There isn't a lot of tomfoolery. There is some good-natured ribbing and pretty good student chants."

Central and Downers Grove North also have a friendly rivalry, and the two teams have played for "the Old Oaken Bucket" every year since 1935. The scores from each of the games are written on the bucket and its wooden pedestal.

The gymnasium at Hinsdale Central is truly impressive with banners for the 103 state championships (through 2019) in the thirty-one sports in which the Red Devils compete. The entirety of the gym is encircled with banners from each of the school state titles.

When it comes to big-time high school sports in Illinois, it really doesn't get any bigger than Hinsdale Central. Three miles due south from Central is the iconic **Dell Rhea's Chicken Basket** on Route 66, which again merges with Interstate 55 along Highway 83. Six miles later, take Exit 268 for Joliet Road and head west for 3 miles until you connect with Illinois Highway 53.

ROMEOVILLE

Traveling south on Highway 53 will take you through Romeoville, a town originally named Romeo while Joliet was called Juliet as a tribute to the tragic Shakespeare lovers. The current names were adopted in 1845, when Joliet was renamed to honor French explorer Louis Jolliet. **Romeoville High School** sports teams have not been the most competitive, but the community has produced former NFL players Oliver Gibson and Byron Stingily; former NHL goalie Gerald Coleman; and professional wrestler Robert Anthony, who is also known as Egotistico Fantastico.

Lewis University

The Chicago suburb is also home to **Lewis University**, a Catholic school that competes at the NCAA Division II level in each of its 23 sports with the exception of men's volleyball. The Flyers have a solid Division I volleyball program that started in 1994 and defeated BYU in 2003 to win a national championship.

"At a time when there really weren't a lot of men's volleyball programs in the Midwest outside of Ohio State, Illinois, and Ball State, Chicago has always been a hotbed of volleyball," said Luke Rinne, the director of athletic communications at Lewis.

When Lewis defeated Southern California in 2019, a Los Angeles newspaper noted that USC's enrollment was more than the entire population of Romeoville. The paper wasn't wrong. USC has an undergraduate enrollment of 44,000, and Romeoville has a population of 39,000.

Volleyball is king at Lewis, and you may want to take in a match before or after having some fried chicken at **The White Fence Farm**.

JOLIET

Route 66 may begin in Chicago, but the essence of what Route 66 is—a road full of nostalgia and Americana—really starts in Joliet. The city, which is home to a minor league baseball team, NASCAR track, and high school on the National Historic Register, largely identifies itself with the Mother Road.

"Route 66 is a big part of the town," said Curt Herron, a longtime sports columnist with the *Joliet Herald*. "Joliet is the first big town you get to if you're coming from Chicago. Joliet has always been a very important transportation hub with the steel and industries they had here. And then, along the route, you really don't run into any bigger towns until you get to Bloomington-Normal.

"Route 66 is a unique chapter of Americana," Herron added. "Any town that can associate with that should be proud of it and highlight the strengths of the community. There's a lot of pride here. It's who we are. That's the history of this whole area, being on a main thoroughfare. This whole county is as vibrant as it's ever been."

The Joliet area has an abundance of limestone, which is why many of the city's buildings were built using the yellow material. The famous **Joliet Correctional Center**, which closed in 2002 and is now open to tourists, is perhaps the best example of the limestone construction. The prison has been featured in various movies and television shows—most notably *The Blues Brothers* in 1980, the 2006 comedy film *Let's Go To Prison*, and the Fox television crime drama *Prison Break*.

The historic Joliet prison has been used in movies and television shows.

Joliet Central High School

About a mile from the prison is **Joliet Central High School**, which was originally the lone public high school in Joliet. It is now one of three high schools (two public, one private) in the city of 150,000. The sprawling four-story, castle-like complex has layers of limestone bricks used in its original construction in 1901.

The school has expanded eight times to meet the needs of a growing community, and each addition was constructed using the same limestone. But as much as limestone means to Joliet, the steel industry helped build the city. For this reason, the Central sports teams are known as the Steelmen.

Several professional athletes have come out of the Steelmen sports programs, most notably former Major League Baseball player Jesse Barfield, who led Joliet Central to a state runner-up finish in 1975. R&B singer Lionel Richie was a standout tennis player for the Joliet East Kingsmen. Joliet East was the third public high school in Joliet and was in existence from 1964 to 1983 before merging with Joliet Central.

Joliet Central's castle-like original building is on the National Register of Historic Places.

Folks in Illinois take their basketball seriously. The Illinois High School Association (IHSA) was the first to coin the term "March Madness" back in 1939. The IHSA had trademarked the phrase by 1973. However, it failed to adequately defend the trademark, and it was officially registered by the NCAA in 1986.

Although the boys' basketball program may have just one state title, the Steelmen

Joliet Central's 3,000-seat gymnasium has hosted more IHSA playoff games than any other venue in the state.

are regular playoff participants. The Steelmen play in a spacious gymnasium that has hosted more IHSA postseason games than any other arena in the state.

The primary seating area holds about 3,000 spectators, and a balcony that encircles the gym floor used to provide a bird's-eye view of games for overflow crowds. On the baseline walls and in the center of the floor is the Steelmen logo, a metal figure leaning forward with its head facing the floor.

The Steelman was created for the 1933 World's Fair in Chicago. The Steelman is a 500-pound sculpture called *Science Advancing Mankind* and is constructed of what is believed to be white bronze. It was designed by former Joliet Township student Louise Lentz Woodruff, who donated the

The Joliet Steelman was unveiled at the 1933 World's Fair in Chicago.

statue to her high school alma mater in 1935. The Joliet Township athletics teams took the Steelmen name the following year. The statue is on display near the principal's office and stands on a base constructed of marble slabs and stainless steel.

Joliet Catholic Academy and University of Saint Francis

While Central has had some success in various sports, the most successful Joliet high school is **Joliet Catholic Academy**. Playing their home games at **Joliet Memorial Stadium**, the Hilltoppers have won 14 state football championships—the most of any other school in the state. Since Illinois began a state football tournament in 1974, Joliet Catholic has been a participant 42 times through the 2019–20 school year. The baseball team has won a trio of state titles, and the volleyball team won four state championships from 2003 to 2010.

With 10,000 seats, Joliet Memorial Stadium hosts football and soccer games for Joliet Catholic and the **University of St. Francis**, which competes at the NAIA level. The St. Francis Saints baseball team shares **DuPage Medical Group Field**, formerly known as Route 66 Stadium, with the Joliet Slammers of the independent Frontier League.

Herron, the *Joliet Herald* sports columnist, noted that the strongest Saints sports are basketball and volleyball. That said, St. Francis has two NAIA national championships, and neither are in basketball or volleyball. The baseball team captured a national title in 1993 under Gordie Gillespie, and the men's cross country squad claimed a national championship in 2012. When Gillespie, who died at the age of 88 in 2015, retired in 2011, he was the all-time winningest college baseball coach at any level with 1,893 victories. He also coached football at Joliet Catholic and basketball at Lewis.

Sounds of the Steelmen

While Joliet Central's sports teams have been up and down, one constant at any Steelmen football or basketball game is the school's renowned band. The high school band was started by A. R. McAllister in 1912 with 12 students playing secondhand instruments, but it has gradually risen to international prominence.

McAllister helped found the National Band Association, and his group of musicians drew praise from famed military conductor John Philip Sousa. The Joliet Area Historical Museum has a large corner display dedicated to the original Joliet Township marching and pep bands.

The old Joliet Township marching band gained national recognition and that tradition continues today at Joliet Central.

Joliet Slammers

"Slammers" is a perfect name for a city widely known for its famous prison. The ball club played its first season in 2011, replacing the Joliet Jackhammers of the Northern League as tenants at what was then called Silver Cross Field.

A Jackhammers display at the **Joliet Area Historical Museum and Route 66 Welcome Center** includes several items used in their inaugural season of 2002 in addition to a team photo and game program from that year.

When the Jackhammers folded after nine seasons, the Slammers moved in and won the Frontier League championship in their first season. Another Frontier League title was bestowed in 2018.

A downtown sign still directed visitors to Route 66 Stadium in 2019. A statue of a leaping ball player adorns the top of a colorful column at the towering entrance. The stadium formerly known as Route 66 Stadium also hosts the annual IHSA state baseball tournament.

A display recognizing the defunct Joliet Jackhammers baseball team is on the second floor of the Joliet Area Historical Museum.

Fast cars and the Blues

Before leaving Joliet, you may want to take in a show at the historic **Rialto Square Theatre** and say hello to "Joliet" Jake Blues at the Joliet Area Historical Museum. A replica of the car used by Jake and his brother, Elwood, can be seen at the **Route 66 Food N Fuel** truck stop south of the city on Highway 53. The "Bluesmobile" rests atop a 20-foot pole, and a sign with the famous quote from the movie about the car with a "cop car motor" is at ground level. The "hit it" quote is on a wall inside the gas station. It's a popular stop along Route 66.

Across the highway from the truck stop is **Chicagoland Speedway and Route 66 Raceway**. Herron described the speedway complex as "fascinating." The Route 66 NHRA Nationals and NASCAR's Chicagoland 400 provide a financial windfall for the community every summer.

Route 66 Raceway opened in 1998 with the mile-and-a-half-long speedway following

Before leaving town, see a show at Joliet's historic Rialto Square Theatre, which opened in 1926.

in 2001. An oval dirt track near the drag strip is also part of the Route 66 racing complex. Building the complex on Route 66 was serendipitous. The original investors included a farmer who owned a piece of land southwest of Joliet. While placing the tracks along the Mother Road may not have been intentional, the ownership group has embraced its Route 66 presence.

"It adds to the character and nostalgia of our facility," said Scott Paddock, a former Notre Dame basketball player who has been the track president since 2011. "This was the Mother Road. The really true, authentic starting point is in Joliet."

Kevin Harvick won the first two Chicagoland 400 races, but Tony Stewart had three victories from 2004 to 2011 for the most wins at the track through 2019. Kyle Busch (2008, 2018) and Martin Truex Jr. (2016–17) have also won the event twice.

In addition to NHRA and NASCAR events, the speedway hosted IndyCar races from 2001 to 2011. Three of the closest finishes in IndyCar history took place at Chicagoland, including the closest finish ever in 2002 with Sam Hornish Jr. edging Al Unser Jr. by 0.0024 second. The first IndyCar driver to celebrate in Victory Lane was Denver native Jaques Lazier. Scottish driver Dario Franchitti was the last IndyCar victor at Chicagoland.

Chicagoland Speedway hosts an annual NASCAR race and is also home to the Route 66 Raceway drag strip.

Paddock said Route 66 Raceway isn't just a couple of drag strips with some bleachers. It's built like a stadium with acoustics designed to allow spectators to be immersed in the races with a "full-body sensory experience."

When champion Top Fuel dragster Antron Brown first visited Route 66 Raceway, he said he imagined the feeling the gladiators must have had in the ancient days when arriving at the Colosseum to do battle for the first time.

"That's what he thought the first time he saw the magnitude and scale of this beautiful masterpiece," Paddock recalled. "No one had ever seen anything like it in the drag-racing community. Route 66 Raceway is considered the gold standard" in the drag-racing community, Paddock said. "No expense was spared when they built this place, and it's still best in class."

As a spectator, Paddock said seeing a nitromethane fuel dragster go from 0 to over 300 miles per hour in under 4 seconds will "shake you to the core."

"The drivers will tell you it's what astronauts feel during liftoff of the space shuttle," Paddock said. "It's really, really cool."

Route 66 Raceway is rarely dormant from April through October. When it's not taken over by the NHRA, it hosts other drag-racing events—including for the television series *Street Outlaws*—swap meets, trade and car shows, import shows, nostalgia events with vintage cars, concerts, and even a "race your ride" promotion. "Race your ride" was created to encourage people to bring their personal vehicles to the raceway instead of drag racing on city streets.

Paddock said the raceway has "programming pretty much every weekend," and employees have given impromptu tours.

"We'll get people who are just driving down Route 66 and stop unannounced for pictures or tours," Paddock said. "And they're from all over the world."

If someone from another country "pops in," Paddock said his staff tries to "give them a good memory" by showing them around the campus instead of simply turning them away. That said, scheduling a tour ahead of time is preferred.

WILMINGTON

Wilmington is a town of 5,700 people nestled between the Kankakee River and Forked Creek. Fishing and kayaking on the Kankakee River are popular summer activities.

On your way south from Joliet, you can get a little hiking in along Highway 53 at the **Midewin National Tallgrass Prairie**. The prairie, which used to be home to the Joliet Army Ammunition Plant, is now used as a conservation area for a herd of American bison. The prairie has several trails on which to hike, bike, or run past the old ammunition bunkers. About a mile north of the entrance on Highway 53 is the **Abraham Lincoln National Cemetery**. Two miles to the south you'll find the famous **Gemini Giant** at the **Launching Pad** in Wilmington.

The Gemini Giant at Wilmington's Launching Pad is the first of several "Muffler Man" statues along Route 66.

The Giant is the first of several "Muffler Man" statues you'll see along Route 66. The "Muffler Men" are moulded fiberglass figures about 20 feet tall with arms positioned to hold large "mufflers" or other items used to promote roadside businesses. The walls of the diner adjacent to the Gemini Giant are decked out in a Route 66 motif. A small guitar museum is in a room behind the kitchen. The Launching Pad, which reopened in 2019 after years of neglect, is best known for its Chicago-style hot dog. After you enjoy that hot dog and peruse the gift shop and museum, check out the historic **Mar Theatre**. The Mar is a two-screen movie theater that opened in 1937 and is still in operation today. Wilmington is the hometown of former Washington Nationals pitcher Tanner Roark, who led Wilmington High School to IHSA baseball championships in 2003 and 2005.

The next three towns you pass through are Dwight, Odell, and Cayuga. Former NFL tight end Clay Harbor was a three-sport athlete at Dwight, earning four letters in football, basketball, and track. Pro Football Hall of Famer Mac Speedie was born in Odell.

PONTIAC

Pontiac, 42 miles southwest of Wilmington, is a city that fully embraces its place along Route 66. Numerous signs and murals pay tribute to the historic Mother Road. The **Route 66 Association of Illinois** is in downtown Pontiac, where Howard Street and Main Street intersect, across from City Hall. You can peruse a handful of other museums in Pontiac, where many of the buildings are adorned with murals that represent days of yesteryear.

The **Pontiac-Oakland Automobile Museum** on Mill Street is a popular stop for car enthusiasts and features a few race cars, including the first-ever Pontiac race car. Next to that 1926 Pontiac is a 1966 GTO Tin Indian, which was driven by Larry "Doc" Dixon, who was undefeated as an NHRA champion in 1966.

Route 66 isn't the only historic thing in Pontiac. Between Christmas and New Year's Day, the town of 12,000 people is home to the nation's oldest high school holiday basketball tournament. The tournament began in 1926, and the **Pontiac High School** gymnasium has hosted some of the best high school basketball teams from Illinois.

Pontiac has one of the most photographed Route 66 murals along the Mother Road.

"If it was just another basketball tournament, I wouldn't do it," said tournament director Jim Drengwitz, who retired as principal of Pontiac High in 2007 but decided to continue running the tournament. "Anyone can run a basketball tournament, but this tournament is special. It's a huge community event. This tournament is second to none."

Drengwitz said finding teams for the 16-team tournament isn't a problem because he's constantly fielding calls from schools that want in. Even out-of-state teams from Iowa, Missouri, and Nebraska have called Drengwitz. But he's kept it an all-Illinois tournament and believes he gets the best teams the state has to offer.

The tournament had some of its biggest crowds from 2010 to 2012 when Jabari Parker was playing at Chicago Simeon. Parker was one of the top high school players in the country, and Simeon was ranked number one nationally. Parker was such a huge draw that basketball fans traveled to Pontiac from as far as Toronto just to see him play in person.

"People ask me why I brought Simeon in because they win it a lot, and I tell them, when Tiger Woods was winning all those golf tournaments, everyone wanted to see Tiger, but they also got to see all of the other guys," Drengwitz said. "Tiger was good for the others.

"That's what people want to see. They want to see the big dog. That's the way we look at it with our tournament."

Parker and Simeon coach Robert Smith led the Wolverines to four straight state championships before Parker went to Duke University for one season. He was a first-round pick of the Milwaukee Bucks in the 2014 NBA Draft.

Other future NBA players have competed on the colorful Pontiac gym floor. Derrick Rose, who also attended Simeon and was the 2011 NBA MVP, was the Pontiac tournament MVP in 2005 and 2006. NBA journeyman Iman Shumpert suited up for Oak Park and River Forest High School from 2005 to 2008. Others have been Frank Williams from Peoria Manual, who was Illinois's Mr. Basketball in 1998 and the Pontiac MVP in 1997; former Utah Jazz player and 2000 Pontiac tourney MVP Roger Powell, who attended Joliet Central; Lockport alumnus and 2001 Pontiac MVP Alando Tucker, who was the 2007 Big Ten player of the year at Wisconsin before spending four seasons with the Phoenix Suns and Minnesota Timberwolves; former

San Antonio Spurs player Brandon Paul, who was the state's Mr. Basketball in 2009; and former Portland Trail Blazers center Cliff Alexander, who was the national prep player of the year for Chicago Curie in 2014 and the 2013 Pontiac tournament MVP.

If you're not traveling Route 66 in late December and find yourself in Pontiac in the fall, you might want to spend a Friday evening watching the Indians football team. Pontiac is a regular playoff qualifier and won a state championship in 1993.

LEXINGTON

Three small towns are between Pontiac and Normal—Chenoa, Lexington, and Towanda—but only Lexington still has a high school. Lexington is home to the **Route 66 Memory Lane**, always a popular attraction for travelers. It's also home to the **David Hyatt Van Dolah House**, or The Castle, on Route 66. Built in 1898, The Castle is on the National Historic Register. Across the street from The Castle is a sign that boasts the athletic achievements of **Lexington High School**. Those include a state baseball title in 1990 and a state track championship in 2018. The football team is a regular playoff participant among Illinois's small schools. The Minutemen program produced NFL quarterback Alex Tanney, who was part of eight NFL teams from 2012 to 2020.

BLOOMINGTON-NORMAL

Route 66 is known for its oddities, but you'll find at least one normal thing in Illinois about 130 miles south of Chicago. The city of Normal and its sister community of Bloomington contain several Route 66 stops. Normal is also home to **Illinois State University**, which has a strong athletics program. The college is the state's oldest, and the city's name was taken from the school. ISU was founded in 1857 as Illinois State Normal University—a "normal" school is one that focuses on training teachers.

Illinois State is the first of several NCAA Division I universities on Route

The campus of Illinois State University in Normal is right on Route 66.

66. The Redbirds built a strong basketball reputation in the 1990s when they qualified for the NCAA Tournament three times as the Missouri Valley Conference champions.

ISU is regularly competitive in both men's and women's basketball. The men made the NCAA Tournament six times from 1983 through 1998, and the women danced five times between 1983 and 2008. ISU athletics director Larry Lyons called **Redbird Arena** "an iconic building" and "one of the great environments in college basketball."

The 10,000-seat arena with a white domed roof has superb vantage sight lines from the lower and upper bowls. The student section, known as "Red Alert," is almost always a rowdy bunch.

Redbird Arena also hosts the women's volleyball team, which has won six Valley championships, and the annual IHSA volleyball and girls' basketball tournaments. It's also been home to the state wrestling and cheerleading events.

Outside of the arena is statuary of former coach Will Robinson and star ISU guard Doug Collins, who played eight seasons in the NBA before going into coaching. Collins was a four-time All-Star as a player and then coached the NBA All-Star Game in 1997 while leading the Detroit Pistons.

Redbird Arena at Illinois State offers one of the country's best environments for college basketball.

Fun at Hancock Stadium

Adjacent to Redbird Arena is **Hancock Stadium**, the facade of which faces Route 66. Tulsa's H. A. Chapman Stadium is the only other Division I football stadium located directly on Route 66. One end zone has a wide concourse with party tents called "field level suites." The Kaufman Football Building is at the other. A berm in one corner of the Kaufman end zone allows fans

Fans standing on a small berm behind the end zone corner can get a great view of the action.

to stand just a few feet from the field to watch the action.

The NCAA has two subdivisions for Division I football—Football Bowl Subdivision, or FBS, (formerly I-A) is the top level with the Football Championship Subdivision, or FCS (formerly I-AA), just beneath it. Illinois State has become one of the better FCS programs in the country, consistently ranking in the top 10. The 2014 team reached the FCS national championship game before losing to powerhouse North Dakota State. The Redbirds football program has sent players like Estus Hood, Laurent Robinson, James Robinson, Devontae Harris, Shelby Harris, Nate Palmer, and James O'Shaughnessy to the NFL.

Illinois State University's sports teams enjoy excellent support. Part of the local support stems from ISU's participation in community events like Normal's annual Lincoln's Festival on Route 66 every July. ISU athletics director Lyons, who grew up in Pontiac, understands the importance of the Mother Road and wants the university represented at most Route 66 events.

"Route 66 winds through Normal and went right through uptown," Lyons said. "There's an affinity for Route 66 here, particularly with the campus because it goes right through here.

"Route 66 is in our blood and culture. It's Midwestern culture and Midwestern hospitality."

Other ISU sports

The Illinois State baseball program has produced MLB players Paul DeJong, Dave Bergman, and Buzz Capra. The Redbirds softball team produced All-American pitcher Margie Wright, who got into coaching after her playing career was over and skippered her alma mater from 1980 to 1985 before leaving for Fresno State. She led the Bulldogs to a national championship in 1998.

The Illinois State campus has its own golf course that hosts the IHSA golf tournament and has hosted various NCAA championship events. **Weibring Golf Club**, named after professional golfer and ISU alumnus D. A. Weibring, is open to the public when not in use by the school. Lyons said the course "came out of a cornfield," but is now one of the best college courses in the country.

Nurturing ball players—and corn

Summer travelers can also see some minor league baseball in Normal at one of the most unique venues in the country. The Corn Crib is home to the Normal CornBelters, a collegiate wood-bat summer baseball team that plays in the Prospect League. There are two notable aspects of this stadium. The ballpark was built so that the entrance lines up with home plate, thus affording incoming fans with one of the best views of the park. Jonathan Cole, who was the principal designer of the ballboark said "We purposefully split the press box on the main concourse to allow for unobstructed views to the playing field. No matter what ticket you've purchased, everyone attending a game has the opportunity to experience what most consider the best seat in the house." And the corn you purchase at the concession stand is grown right at the ballpark. Rows of corn stalks are along the fences down the right- and left-field concourses and the batter's eye in center field is a mini corn field.

The CornBelters were founded in 2009 as an independent minor league team in the Frontier League, the same league as the Joliet Slammers. Former

Center field is a mini corn field at the Corn Crib Stadium in Normal, Illinois

MLB player and manager Hal Lanier was initially tasked with leading the CornBelters, who won a division title in 2015. The costs of operating a professional team eventually became too costly with waning attendance. Normal opted out of the Frontier League after the 2018 season. Instead of a 96-game schedule in the Frontier League, the CornBelters now have a 60-game slate from May to August with amateur players.

The Prospect League, which has sent about 200 players to Major League Baseball since it was founded in 1963, has another team on Route 66. The Springfield Sliders reside in the Illinois state capital, just a few blocks east of Peoria Road and 2 miles from the capitol. Notable Prospect League alumni are Gary Gaetti, Ryan Howard, Jon Papelbon, Dan Quisenberry, Tanner Roark, and Hall of Famer Mike Schmidt.

The original Steak 'n Shake was in Bloomington but is now a Monical's Pizza. And, speaking of pizza, the first pizza place in Central Illinois was **Lucca Grill**, which opened in 1936 and is still in operation today. So, before or after a game, grab a pie and some beverages in Bloomington-Normal. After leaving the Twin Cities of Illinois, you can pick up some syrup at **Funks Grove Pure Maple Sirup Farm**, just north of McLean.

ATLANTA

Whether you have 15 minutes, an hour, or an entire day in Atlanta, you will see plenty of Route 66 landmarks. The town of 1,700 relies on Route 66 tourism as its primary industry. Most restaurants and shops have some sort of Route 66 signage. The famous **Bunyon Giant**, holding an enormous hot dog, is across the street from the Palms Grill Cafe, which closed in 2020 due to the coronavirus pandemic. The 1950s-style diner had a baseball-themed pinball machine that was more than 80 years old but could still be played. One of Atlanta's biggest draws is the **J. H. Hawes Grain Elevator Museum** and its Wabash boxcar. The **Atlanta Route 66 Inn and Colaw Rooming House** will rent you a room for the night if you lose track of time playing vintage video games at the **Atlanta Route 66 Arcade Museum**.

LINCOLN

Ten miles southwest of Atlanta is the city of Lincoln, where Route 66 passed directly through downtown from 1926 to 1978. There isn't a single person more represented along the Illinois stretch of Route 66 than Abraham Lincoln. The 16th president of the United States has a statue in Pontiac, another in Atlanta, a couple more in Lincoln, and several in Springfield. The city of Lincoln was named for him during an 1853 ceremony he attended. Lincoln would not be president for another seven years, but the town bears his name because he helped establish the fledgling community along the newly laid Chicago & Mississippi Railroad. After squeezing some watermelon juice on the ground to christen the new village, legend says Honest Abe humbly remarked, "Nothing bearing the name of Lincoln ever amounted to much."

Lincoln College

Today several things besides statues bear the name of Lincoln. The Illinois city of 14,000 is also home to the first college with his appellation. **Lincoln College** was founded in 1865, two months before the president's assassination. The Lincoln Lynx compete at the NAIA level and field more than 20 intercollegiate sports.

Lincoln has been a men's basketball and wrestling power at the NAIA level. The Lynx basketball team won national championships in 2010 and 2011. Before becoming a four-year school, Lincoln College was a regular National Junior College Athletic Association (NJCAA) tournament participant and was the national runner-up in 1981. That program helped propel Kevin Gamble to the NBA, via the University of Iowa.

The wrestling program, which won NJCAA national championships in 1989 and 1991, helped produce UFC fighters Matt Hughes and Corey Anderson.

There is plenty of Abraham Lincoln-related history to see in "his" city, but also some decent amateur athletics to watch while you're there. Lincoln is also the hometown of former MLB player Kevin Seitzer, a two-time All-Star with the Kansas City Royals and Milwaukee Brewers. From Lincoln, Route 66 runs parallel to Interstate 55 through the communities of Broadwell, Elkhart, and Williamsville before merging with I-55 just north of Illinois's capital city.

SPRINGFIELD

About 30 miles south of the town that bears his name is the city that made Abraham Lincoln famous. Route 66 visitors interested in Lincoln have plenty to see in Springfield. Sites include the **Lincoln Home**, now a historic site managed by the National Park Service; the **Lincoln Presidential Library and Museum**; the **Illinois State Capitol**, where Lincoln delivered his famous "House Divided" speech and where his body lay in state for a day before he was buried at **Oak Ridge Cemetery** on Monument Avenue; and numerous statues of the late president scattered throughout the city.

University of Illinois at Springfield

One of those statues is on the campus of the **University of Illinois at Springfield**, where the Prairie Stars athletics teams compete at the NCAA Division II level in the Great Lakes Valley Conference (GLVC). Lincoln's image is all over the UIS campus, and his statue is adjacent to the center quad. The beardless young lawyer with hat in hand is a popular photo backdrop for visitors and even for the Prairie Stars athletes.

UIS competes in 17 sports—8 men's and 9 women's. Since moving from NAIA to NCAA Division II in 2010, the school's teams have been increasingly more competitive. The 2018–19 school year was particularly solid, with the softball and baseball teams both winning GLVC championships and hosting NCAA regionals. The women's volleyball team also won a conference title to qualify for the NCAA tourney. Both the women's and men's track teams had individual conference champs. The women's golf club and men's soccer team are NCAA Tournament regulars.

"That's great for an athletics program. You usually don't see programs make that kind of leap," said UIS deputy athletics director Roy Brown. "It's a rising program—pun intended. We're the Prairie Stars, and we're rising. We're nowhere near the apex or pinnacle, but every year, we're showing more progress."

The Abraham Lincoln Presidential Museum is a must-see when in Springfield.

The men's soccer club, which plays at **Kiwanis Stadium**, has enjoyed success dating back to its NAIA days. The Prairie Stars won three NAIA national championships between 1986 and 1993, with a national runner-up finish in 1998.

The connection to Abraham Lincoln isn't lost at the ticket office, where general admission tickets for basketball games at **The Recreation and Athletic Center (TRAC)** are just $5. Kids age 12 and under get in free to all UIS sporting events.

Even if you're not interested in seeing a sporting event at UIS, a stroll around the lush campus is worth the time. There is also a performing arts center with a year-round schedule of plays and concerts. The theater is just a few yards from the Lincoln statue.

"Being here is special because of the history of the city and the type of history with Abraham Lincoln," UIS deputy athletics director Roy Brown said. "It's pretty cool, and we've certainly tried to capitalize on that historical context."

Though Brown is originally from Louisiana, he knows what Route 66 means to the city.

"It's iconic. It's Americana," he said. "You may not know the exact route of Route 66, but you know the song. It's cool that we can point to signs here and say, 'Hey, this is the original route.'"

Home to Illinois's winningest high school football coach

Just about a mile off Old Route 66 in Springfield, you will find a football stadium named for the winningest high school football coach in the state of Illinois.

Ken Leonard, who is the head football coach and athletics director at **Sacred Heart-Griffin High School**, has won more than 400 games since 1980.

"Football and sports have been part of my life since I was a kid. I always knew what I wanted to be," said Leonard, who was inducted into the Illinois High School Football Coaches Hall of Fame in 2006. "I've been blessed to do something I've had a passion for over 40 years. I love it. Even the bad times."

Leonard became head coach at Sacred Heart-Griffin in 1984 and has since won five state championships. His first state title in 2005 remains his favorite because it was with a team "that nobody thought would be the first state champions."

That team had only 10 seniors, a contributing factor to the Cyclones repeating as 5A state champs in 2006 and winning a 6A title in 2008. Two more 5A crowns came in 2013 and 2014. SHG placed second in 1995, 2003, and 2016 under Leonard.

As successful as Leonard has been at Sacred Heart-Griffin, his son, Derek, has enjoyed even bigger success at Rochester High School, which is 8 miles southeast of downtown Springfield. Derek Leonard has been at Rochester since 2005 and won seven of eight 4A state titles from 2010 to 2017. Derek Leonard led Rochester to a 5A crown in 2019.

Sacred Heart Griffin coach Ken Leonard stands in front of the scoreboard at the field named in his honor.

When the elder Leonard picked up his 375th career victory in 2018 to become the state's winningest coach, it came at Derek's expense with a 45–6 SHG victory. The annual "Leonard Bowl" has become a standing-room-only event when the two Central State Eight Conference teams get together.

Because of the success he's had at SHG, the school renamed the football field in his honor in 2017. And nearly every milestone during his career has been within 10 miles of the Mother Road.

"I grew up on Route 66 in Chenoa, and I've been coaching on Route 66 ever since," said Leonard, who played football at Illinois State. "It's my heritage. I've been a part of (Route 66) my whole life. I'm a true-blooded Route 66 guy."

Some of Leonard's former players have wound up in the NFL. Receivers Eric Peterman and Malik Turner, defensive tackle-turned-UFC fighter Matt Mitrione, and NFL assistant coach Brendan Daly all developed their skills at Sacred Heart-Griffin. Other SHG alumni include former Chicago Cubs pitcher Ryan O'Malley and 2016 Olympic swimmer Ryan Held.

Springfield's links

A pair of Springfield golf courses not far from Route 66 can satisfy your fix. The **Rail Golf Course** is on the north side of town off Peoria Road, and **Piper Glen Golf & Social Club** is south of the city on Highway 4.

LITCHFIELD

Driving the early alignment of Route 66 instead of what is now the I-55 corridor will take you 41 miles down State Highway 4 and through the small towns of Chatham, Auburn, Virden, Girard, Carlinville, and Gillespie.

Back on the I-55 corridor of Route 66, the next stop is Litchfield. The **Ariston Cafe** in Litchfield is a historic Route 66 landmark. The place hasn't changed much since it opened in 1935 and today offers a wide-ranging menu and a full bar. Dozens of visitors every day take advantage of the opportunity to stand behind the bar for a photo or two, taken by the friendly staff at the stalwart restaurant that was added to the National Historic Register in 2006.

Across the street from the Ariston Cafe is the **Litchfield Museum and Route 66 Welcome Center**. The museum is a great place to visit for those wanting to learn more about the area. It also features several sports-related items and displays.

One of the first things you see when you walk through the doors is a poster recognizing Litchfield as the hometown of Baseball Hall of Famer Ray Schalk. Known as the best defensive catcher of his era, Schalk helped

The Litchfield Museum and Route 66 Welcome Center is directly across the street from the historic Ariston Cafe.

the Chicago White Sox win the 1917 World Series, but he was also a member of the infamous Black Sox team of 1919. A glass display honoring Schalk's MLB career includes a biography and an image of his Hall of Fame plaque. Litchfield was also home to former MLB player Jackie Mayo, who spent six seasons with the Philadelphia Phillies and was part of the 1950 World Series team that lost to the New York Yankees.

One of the biggest employers in Litchfield is **Schutt Sports**, which produces a variety of sports equipment, primarily football helmets, and has its own display in the museum. The company began in 1918 and built basketball hoops, but it designed the first football facemask in 1935. It is still a big basketball hoop manufacturer with its equipment used by the Philadelphia 76ers, collegiately by the Southeastern and Missouri Valley conferences, and by the Illinois High School Association.

The museum includes a display about Schutt, which also provides equipment to **Litchfield High School**. The school's Purple Panthers also have a section in the museum.

After eating a meal at the Ariston Cafe, taking a stroll through Litchfield's history is worth at least an hour of your time. If you're traveling between April and September, be sure to check what's playing at the **Skyview Drive-In Theater**.

ST. LOUIS METRO EAST

Before you get to the St. Louis metro area, you'll drive through the towns of Mount Olive and Staunton. Be sure to check out Mount Olive's **Mother Jones Monument** to honor labor union organizer Mary Harris Jones, and **Henry's Rabbit Ranch** in Staunton. Route 66 splits into multiple spurs as you enter St. Louis, but no matter the alignment you take, there is plenty to do and see along the way.

Whether you take the **Chain of Rocks Bridge** route through Edwardsville and Granite City, the 1940–77 alignment that routes you through Collinsville and East St. Louis before crossing over the Martin Luther King Memorial Bridge, or stay on I-55 to I-44 and pick up Route 66 on Chouteau Avenue in St. Louis, high school, college, and professional sports dot the byways.

Because St. Louis is one of the major metro areas along Route 66, the recommendation here is to plan an extended stay to take in all the city and the surrounding area have to offer.

EDWARDSVILLE

As largely a bedroom community for St. Louis, Edwardsville doesn't have the industry to lure would-be residents to the city. But 25,000 people live in the St. Louis Metro East city, drawn there by a public school that has a goal to compete with the plethora of private schools on the Missouri side of the Mississippi River. **Edwardsville High School** holds its own, thanks to amenities on par with those costly private institutions; it even has a uniform and merchandising deal with Under Armour.

"There was a vision for the school," athletics director Alex Fox said. "A lot of that was brought in by our superintendent (Dr. Ed Hightower, 1996–2015). He had a vision that athletics was going to be the centerpiece to draw people into the community. He started with the facilities ... and tried to create a college environment at a public high school."

The result has been a school that is competitive in just about every sport, with a multitude of state championships, including a baseball title in 2019.

The school also ranks as one of the state's best in academics.

Although the football stadium isn't quite what you'd see in Oklahoma or Texas, its entrance is similar to that of a college venue with a decorative arch over a wide pathway that leads visitors to the grandstand. Edwardsville's other sports facilities are better than what you'd find at most public schools. That includes an Olympic-class aquatic center that also houses a dedicated wrestling facility.

Edwardsville coaches and alumni

After building unmatched facilities, the next step was finding the right coaches to lead the teams. Fox again credited Hightower, who "went out and got the best coaches who were available at the time." EHS hired multiple coaches who went on to get inducted into various halls of fame.

The sun sets before a 2019 Edwardsville High School football game.

"We went out and got all these coaches, and success followed," Fox said. "The winning just happens if you get everything in place. That was the vision, and they took the facilities to a different level."

That success has included numerous state championships in several programs that helped produce multiple professional athletes.

Edwardsville basketball alumni include Harlem Globetrotters owner Mannie Jackson and former NBA All-Star Don Ohl. The large EHS gymnasium is named after Jackson and former coach Joe Lucco, who led the Tigers to state championship appearances in 1954 and 1956. Jackson was on the 1956 team before playing at the University of Illinois and joining the Globetrotters.

Excellence attracts fans

Neither a chilly October night nor a St. Louis Cardinals playoff game across the Mississippi River can keep Tigers fans away on homecoming night. The home bleachers are consistently packed with alumni, parents, and a rowdy student section. When winter arrives, Lucco-Jackson Gym is almost always full for basketball games, especially when the Tigers play regional rivals like Alton and East St. Louis.

The Tigers reached the playoffs every year from 2011 through 2019. Morris Bradshaw, a two-time Super Bowl champion with the Oakland Raiders, was a product of the Edwardsville football program.

Former Anheuser-Busch and Coca-Cola executive Chuck Fruit was a swimming aficionado and made a generous donation to the Edwardsville school district before his death in 2008. The donation went toward the construction of Edwardsville's Chuck Fruit Aquatic Center, which is home to the Tigers program plus year-round events with the local YMCA, USA Swimming, and Special Olympics.

The Tigers golf teams play their home matches at **Oak Brook Golf Club** free of charge, thanks to club pro Mike Suhre. The 27-hole course on Fruit Road is open to the public and boasts "the highest quality golf experience for the lowest possible fee" on its website.

No matter the sport, Edwardsville is one spot along Route 66 to see quality high school athletics.

"Our facilities are second to none, and our staff is second to none," Fox said. "The generosity of the community to get us where we are ... a lot of what we have is because of donations ... It's a blessing to have what we have."

Southern Illinois University Edwardsville

Old Route 66 follows Highway 157 through Edwardsville and separates the Edwardsville High School campus from that of **Southern Illinois University Edwardsville**. SIUE was founded in 1957, and its Cougars began competing collegiately at the NCAA Division II level in 1967. Women's sports were added in 1972, and SIUE began its transition to Division I in 2008. Now in the Ohio Valley Conference, SIUE has struggled to win, but athletics director Tim Hall is confident it will happen.

"We're a relatively young university, but from an institutional perspective, the success SIUE has had belies its youth," said Hall. "Athletically, we're still a fledgling program.

"It's important for basketball to be successful. This area is starved for a winner and wants to rally around a program that can be successful."

The school's first basketball coach was former NBA player Harry Gallatin, who was a seven-time All-Star in the 1950s and a 1991 Basketball Hall of Fame inductee.

Though SIUE's basketball success has been slow-developing, visitors to the **Vadalabene Center** can see some of the best college basketball players in the country. When Murray State visited SIUE in January 2019, Racers guard Ja Morant scored 40 points during a record-setting season that led to him to being selected with the second pick of the 2019 NBA Draft.

Gallatin was also the men's golf coach for 24 years, and the team's practice facility is named for him. He led the team to NCAA Division II championships 19 times with six top-10 finishes. SIUE calls Gateway National Golf Links in nearby Madison its home course.

Soccer: SIUE's strength

Soccer is king at SIUE. While all other sports competed at the Division II level until 2008, the Cougars footballers have been Division I competitors since 1973. National Soccer Hall of Fame coach Bob Guelker, who left Saint

Louis University to start the SIUE program in 1966, led the Cougars to 14 Division I tournaments. They were national runners-up in 1975 and national champions in 1979. Another national title followed in 1982. Before the move to Division I, the Cougars won the 1972 Division II title. SIUE reluctantly dropped back down to Division II in 1996 and remained there until 2013. SIUE returned to the Division I tournament in 2014 and remains one of the strongest soccer programs in the country.

SIUE has close soccer ties to St. Louis—the most notable of which is the Twellman family, who are soccer royalty and have their roots at SIUE. Brothers Mike, Tim, and Tom Twellman are all members of the SIUE Athletics Hall of Fame. Mike Twellman helped lead SIUE to its 1979 national championship before playing professionally. Tom Twellman played soccer for the Cougars but also led the SIUE baseball team to four NCAA tournament appearances before a three-year professional baseball stint with the Houston Astros. Tim was the team's leading scorer in 1975 and later played professionally. Tim's son, Taylor, was a star player at Saint Louis University High School from 1995 to 1998 before becoming an All-American at the University of Maryland. He played professionally in Major League Soccer and was a member of the United States Men's National Team.

GRANITE CITY

Should you decide to take the 1930–40 spur of Route 66 that takes you to the old **Chain of Rocks Bridge**, you will skirt the north end of Granite City. The original 1926 alignment goes south through the city on Nameoki Road to Madison Avenue.

Granite City High School, located at the Nameoki-Madison intersection, has a pretty rich sports tradition with some famous alumni. The most notable is Kevin Greene, who was a 1980 graduate of Granite City South before spending 15 seasons in the NFL. He helped the Pittsburgh Steelers reach Super Bowl XXX and was on the coaching staff for the Green Bay Packers team that won Super Bowl XLV. When he retired after the 1999 season, his 160 career sacks ranked third all-time. Greene was inducted into the Pro

The Chain of Rocks Bridge spans the Mississippi River between Illinois and Missouri.

Football Hall of Fame in 2016. Greene is also a member of the Granite City Sports Hall of Fame, and the high school football field is named in his honor. Greene was only 58 years old when he died suddenly on Dec. 21, 2020.

Kevin Greene Field at Granite City High School is part of an athletic complex that includes a soccer pitch called Gene Baker Field. Baker coached the Granite City boys' soccer team from 1973 to 1999 and took over the girls' team in 1988. His boys' teams won nine state championships, while the girls had three top-four finishes under Baker. Former professional players Steve Trittschuh and Ruben Mendoza came out of the Granite City program. The girls' team won a state title in 2011 under Skip Birdsong and remains one of the stronger soccer programs in the region.

Between the Greene and Baker fields is a statue recognizing the old Granite City North Steelers teams from 1973 to 1983. Granite City used to be a bustling steel town, and although the industry isn't as prominent as it once was, Granite City Works is still one of the largest employers in the community. When the steel industry was healthier, Granite City was a thriving city of 41,000 people. About 29,000 people now live in Granite City, and a decline in high school sports competitiveness has coincided with the decline in population.

The exception would be the wrestling program, which is the winningest in the state. The late Bill Schmitt won 589 dual meets while leading the Warriors from 1950 to 1988. He coached four individual state champs, won 26 sectional titles, and had 15 top-10 finishes at the state tournament. Like Greene and Baker, Schmitt is a member of the Granite City Sports Hall of Fame, but he is also in the Illinois Wrestling Coaches and Officials Association Hall of Fame. The Warriors wrestlers are still regular state tournament participants, and Memorial Gym can get packed for matches, especially against Southwestern Conference rivals.

Other notable alumni from Granite City include Basketball Hall of Famer Andy Phillip, who led the Warriors to their lone state championship in 1940, and former MLB player Dal Maxvill, who spent 10-plus seasons with the St. Louis Cardinals and won four World Series championships.

COLLINSVILLE

Home to the "world's largest catsup bottle" and the annual horseradish festival, Collinsville is a city of 25,000 people and rich with history. The post-1940 alignment of Route 66 follows Highway 159 south from I-55 to Collinsville Road, which then heads west. Along Collinsville Road is the Cahokia Mounds State Historic Site, which covers 2,200 acres and includes about 80 burial mounds from an ancient settlement that is believed to have been North America's first city. **Collinsville High School** is 5 miles east, and the sports teams are called the Kahoks to pay homage to the ancient civilization.

Although the Kahoks football program isn't great, it did produce Pro Football Hall of Famer George Musso. The real Friday night draw in autumn is Collinsville's stellar marching band. The Marching Kahoks have won multiple regional contests and are among the best bands in Illinois with their visually stunning performances at **Kahok Stadium**.

Aside from Musso, arguably the school's most famous athlete, other Collinsville alumni include MLB players Hoot Evers, Art Fletcher, Terry Moore, Ken Oberkfell, and Tanner

Collinsville is most famous for its world's largest "Catsup" bottle.

Houck; professional soccer player Joe Reiniger; Olympic gold medalist swimmer Tom Jager; former NBA players Tom Parker and Charlie Kraak; and former college basketball coach Kevin Stallings.

The most famous Collinsville grad isn't from the sports world; it's R.E.M. lead singer Michael Stipe. So while you're cruising through Collinsville, feel free to check out the high school to see a game or two, and the band, but make sure you're jamming out to "It's the End of the World As We Know It," "Man on the Moon," "Losing My Religion," "Shiny Happy People," and "What's the Frequency, Kenneth" as you drive down the road.

Play horse hooky for a day

There are a handful of major horse tracks along Route 66, and the first you'll see traveling from east to west is **Fairmount Park**. Located 2 miles east of the historic Cahokia Mounds and right off I-255, Fairmount Park has been around since 1925. It is one of just three tracks in Illinois and the only one outside the Chicago area.

From March to September, the mile-long oval dirt track hosts more than 90 racing events with more than 700 races. The track offers off-track betting with myriad televisions to follow races at other tracks; boxing and UFC fights; and college and professional games. More than 120 booths exist at the track to place bets on the on-site races.

Horses are held in beautifully maintained stables at Fairmount Park before racing.

The grandstand includes suites that are ideal for groups and allow spectators to follow a race in a controlled environment. Most spectators prefer to stand near the track, and that standing-room crowd brings the overall capacity up to 12,000. A large HD screen on the infield stands to the left of green scoreboards that post race results. Bets are placed throughout the day as the odds continue to change. Even when the track isn't hosting races, tellers are still taking bets, and the bar and grill is open.

The track was approved in 2019 to add a casino that will include several slot machines as well as table games like blackjack, craps, and roulette, but not poker. Breaking ground on the new racino was expected to happen in 2021.

One of the track's more popular events is "Horse Hooky" every Tuesday from March to September. The races begin at 1 p.m. with general admission just $1.50. Twelve-ounce draft beers are only $1.50 in the grandstand with $1 hot dogs and sodas.

Great price for a round of golf

A public golf course appropriately named **Indian Mounds Golf Course** is a mile west of its namesake state historic site and national historic landmark. Golfers can play 18 holes for under $20, cart included, on the course designed by Dave Murray and Jan Freilberg. The signature hole is number seven, a 183-yard, par 3 that requires a tee shot to the peninsula green. The executive course features 5 par 4s and 13 par 3s ranging from 100 to 227 yards.

MADISON

Just before you cross over the Mississippi River into Missouri, you'll go past the **World Wide Technology Raceway at Gateway**. The Gateway property is 6 miles from downtown St. Louis and easily accessible from the freeway just before I-55 splits with I-70 but merges with I-64.

Gateway was a regular stop on the NASCAR Nationwide (now Xfinity) Series from 1997 to 2010 and is still an annual stop for NASCAR's truck series. The IndyCar Series visits Gateway for a 500-kilometer race every

August. The 2018 IndyCar race was the fastest ever at Gateway, with just two cautions and an average speed of 155.644 miles per hour and Australian Will Power winning.

The draw of the drag strip

Although NASCAR and IndyCar races are held at the speedway, the drag strip is the raceway's primary draw. The NHRA has been an annual tenant at Gateway every year but one since the track opened in 1997. The lone exception was 2011 after both tracks closed in 2010. The drag strip reopened in 2012 with the speedway resuming operations for the 2014 NASCAR season. The NHRA takes over Gateway every fall—in either late September or early October—and is part of the circuit's "Countdown to the Championship."

Track owner and CEO Curtis Francois deserves credit for convincing the

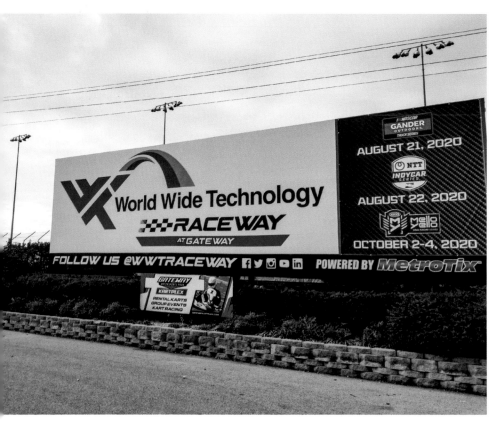

Auto racing fans can get their fix at World Wide Technology Raceway near St. Louis.

NHRA, NASCAR, and IndyCar to return to Gateway. Francois, a St. Louis real-estate magnate and former race car driver, spent $20 million to renovate the raceway.

"They were two weeks away from taking the grandstands down and selling them. Curtis said we can't let this happen," said John Bisci, the director of public relations at World Wide Technology Raceway. "He used a lot of his own money and had to write the big check. Then it started to grow. When he was able to prove the NHRA was viable, he went to NASCAR and said we can make the truck race work here. Then he got IndyCar to come back."

The track's resurgence led to development around the speedway with local landowners offering to sell property to Francois. World Wide Technology Raceway also acquired **Gateway National Golf Links**, which is on the north side of the tracks off Highway 203. Gateway National calls itself "the most challenging golf course in St. Louis."

A building at Turn One of World Wide Technology Raceway houses suites and a large press box.

EAST ST. LOUIS

When Route 66 was at its peak, East St. Louis was a bustling city with more than 80,000 residents. The second half of the 20th century was not kind to East St. Louis, with several businesses moving operations elsewhere. The city deteriorated, and many of its once grand buildings have fallen into disrepair. That includes the Historic Majestic Theatre on Route 66.

Now a city of only 27,000 people, East St. Louis is often associated with crime and poverty. But it's also home to one of the most successful high school football programs in the country. The **East St. Louis High School** Flyers "live, breathe, eat, and sleep" football under coach Darren Sunkett, who took over the program in 2002. Sunkett led the Flyers to 7A state titles in 2008 and 2016 with a 6A championship in 2019. The winning culture dates back to 1974, when East St. Louis was the state runner-up in the inaugural IHSA football tournament. The Flyers won their first of nine state championships in 1979 under Bob Shannon. The program has produced several NFL players, including Hall of Famer Kellen Winslow and three-time Pro Bowler Bryan Cox.

Football isn't the only sport to watch in East St. Louis, dubbed the "City of Champions." Lincoln High School, which merged with East St. Louis Senior High in 1998, won a state championship in girls' basketball in 1980, boys' basketball titles in 1982 and 1987–89, boys' track in 1973 and 1982–86, and girls' track 14 times from 1978 to 1993. East St. Louis Senior High has its own girls' state track championships in 2008, 2011, and 2019. The East St. Louis boys claimed 12 state track championships between 1975 and 2019. It's only appropriate that the city that produced Olympic legend Jackie Joyner-Kersee would be so strong in track-and-field. Other Olympic gold medalists to come out of East St. Louis are Al Joyner and Dawn Harper-Nelson.

East St. Louis High School won its first boys' basketball title in 2019. The Flyers hoops program helped propel Darius Miles to the NBA. Former NBA player LaPhonso Ellis led Lincoln's 1987 and '88 state championship teams.

Baseball Hall of Famer Hank Bauer was from East St. Louis, and 1958 Cy Young Award winner and World Series MVP Bob Turley was an East St. Louis High School graduate. Tennis Hall of Famer Jimmy Connors also attended

East St. Louis High School.

East St. Louis may not be a town you'd want to spend a lot of time in, but if you want to be able to say you saw a future sports star while they were in high school, you might want to check out a football or basketball game or a track-and-field meet before crossing the Mississippi River into St. Louis.

Major fun at Sauget's minor league stadium

Abutting East St. Louis to the south is the tiny town of Sauget, which has a minor league baseball team. The Gateway Grizzles play in the independent Frontier League that includes the Joliet Slammers. **GCS Ballpark** is just minutes off Route 66 and famous for its wacky food options like a Krispy Kreme cheeseburger. The 8,000-seat stadium offers a view of downtown St. Louis and the Gateway Arch.

"Fans can interact with players and yell at the umpires because you're so close," said Grizzlies team photographer Paul Baillargeon. "And for

GCS Ballpark in Sauget is minutes from downtown St. Louis and is a fun atmosphere to watch minor league baseball.

entertainment, you can't beat it because we do games between innings that are goofy and stupid. I've also seen kids run out to the parking lot for foul balls and leave with 10 or 12 baseballs. If you've never caught a ball at a Major League game, try a minor league game because I think that is everyone's ultimate goal."

Illinois Route 66 Points of Interest

THE ART INSTITUTE OF CHICAGO – 111 S. Michigan Ave., Chicago, IL 60603

BERGHOFF RESTAURANT – 17 W. Adams St., Chicago, IL 60603

LOU MITCHELL'S – 565 W. Jackson Blvd., Chicago, IL 60661

UNITED CENTER – 1901 W. Madison St., Chicago, IL 60612

HINSDALE CENTRAL HIGH SCHOOL – 5500 S. Grant St., Hinsdale, IL 60521

DELL RHEA'S CHICKEN BASKET – 645 Joliet Road, Willowbrook, IL 60527

ROMEOVILLE HIGH SCHOOL – 100 N. Independence Blvd., Romeoville, IL 60446

LEWIS UNIVERSITY – 1 University Pkwy., Romeoville, IL 60446

THE WHITE FENCE FARM – 1376 Joliet Road, Romeoville, IL 60446

JOLIET CORRECTIONAL CENTER – 1125 Collins St., Joliet, IL 60432

JOLIET CENTRAL HIGH SCHOOL – 201 E Jefferson St., Joliet, IL 60432

JOLIET CATHOLIC ACADEMY – 1200 N Larkin Ave., Joliet, IL 60435

JOLIET MEMORIAL STADIUM – 3000 W. Jefferson St., Joliet, IL 60435

UNIVERSITY OF ST. FRANCIS – 500 Wilcox St., Joliet, IL 60435

DUPAGE MEDICAL GROUP FIELD – 1 Mayor Art Schultz Drive, Joliet, IL 60432

JOLIET AREA HISTORICAL MUSEUM AND ROUTE 66 WELCOME CENTER – 204 N. Ottawa St., Joliet, IL 60432

RIALTO SQUARE THEATRE – 102 N. Chicago St., Joliet, IL 60432

ROUTE 66 FOOD N FUEL – 2401 S. Chicago St., Joliet, IL 60436

CHICAGOLAND SPEEDWAY AND ROUTE 66 RACEWAY – 500 Speedway Blvd., Joliet, IL 60433

MIDEWIN NATIONAL TALLGRASS PRAIRIE – 30239 IL 53, Wilmington, IL 60481

LAUNCHING PAD DRIVE-IN/GEMINI GIANT – 810 E. Baltimore St., Wilmington, IL 60481

MAR THEATRE – 121 S. Main St., Wilmington, IL 60481

ROUTE 66 ASSOCIATION OF ILLINOIS – 110 W. Howard St., Pontiac, IL 61764

PONTIAC HIGH SCHOOL – 1100 E. Indiana Ave., Pontiac, IL 61764

PONTIAC – Pontiac-Oakland Automobile Museum – 205 N. Mill St., Pontiac, IL 61764

ROUTE 66 MEMORY LANE – Parade Road, Lexington, IL 61753

DAVID HYATT VAN DOLAH HOUSE – 10 N. Spencer St, Lexington, IL 61753

LEXINGTON HIGH SCHOOL – 100 E. Wall St., Lexington, IL 61753

HANCOCK STADIUM – N. Main St., Normal, IL 61761

REDBIRD ARENA – 702 W. College Ave., Normal, IL 61761

WEIBRING GOLF CLUB – 800 Gregory St., Normal, IL 61761

THE CORN CRIB – 1000 W. Raab Road, Normal, IL 61761

THE LUCCA GRILL – 116 E. Market St., Bloomington, IL 61701

FUNKS GROVE PURE MAPLE SIRUP FARM – 5257 Old Rte. 66 McLean, IL 61754

PAUL BUNYON GIANT STATUE – 112 S.W. Arch St., Atlanta, IL 61723

J. H. HAWES GRAIN ELEVATOR MUSEUM – 293 S.W. 2nd St., Atlanta, IL 61723

ATLANTA ROUTE 66 INN AND COLAW ROOMING HOUSE – 204 N.W. Vine St., Atlanta, IL 61723

ATLANTA ROUTE 66 ARCADE MUSEUM – 108 S.W. Arch St., Atlanta, IL 61723

LINCOLN COLLEGE – 300 Keokuk St., Lincoln, IL 62656

LINCOLN HOME – 413 S. 8th St., Springfield, IL 62701

ABRAHAM LINCOLN PRESIDENTIAL LIBRARY AND MUSEUM – 212 N. 6th St., Springfield, IL 62701

ILLINOIS STATE CAPITOL – 401 S. 2nd St., Springfield, IL 62701

OAK RIDGE CEMETERY – 1441 Monument Ave., Springfield, IL 62702

UNIVERSITY OF ILLINOIS SPRINGFIELD – Richard Wright Drive, Springfield, IL 62703

SACRED HEART-GRIFFIN HIGH SCHOOL – 1200 W. Washington St., Springfield, IL 62702

THE RAIL GOLF COURSE – 1400 S. Club House Drive, Springfield, IL 62707

PIPER GLEN GOLF & SOCIAL CLUB – 7112 Piper Glen Drive, Springfield, IL 62711

THE ARISTON CAFE – 413 Old Rte. 66 N, Litchfield, IL 62056

LITCHFIELD MUSEUM AND ROUTE 66 WELCOME CENTER – 334 Historic Old Route 66 North, Litchfield, IL 62056

SCHUTT SPORTS – 710 Industrial Drive, Litchfield, IL 62056

LITCHFIELD HIGH SCHOOL – 1705 N. State St., Litchfield, IL 62056

SKYVIEW DRIVE-IN THEATER – 1500 Old Rte. 66 N, Litchfield, IL 62056

MOTHER JONES MONUMENT – 22160 Old Reservoir Road, Mt. Olive, IL 62069

HENRY'S RABBIT RANCH – 1107 Historic Old Rte. 66, Staunton, IL 62088

CHAIN OF ROCKS BRIDGE – 4205 Chain of Rocks Road, Granite City, IL 62040

GRANITE CITY HIGH SCHOOL – 3101 Madison Ave., Granite City, IL 62040

EDWARDSVILLE HIGH SCHOOL – 6161 Center Grove Rd., Edwardsville, IL 62025

SOUTHERN ILLINOIS UNIVERSITY EDWARDSVILLE – 1 Hairpin Drive, Edwardsville, IL 62026

OAK BROOK GOLF CLUB – 9157 Fruit Road, Edwardsville, IL 62025

COLLINSVILLE HIGH SCHOOL – 2201 S. Morrison Ave., Collinsville, IL 62234

FAIRMOUNT PARK – 9301 Collinsville Road, Collinsville, IL 62234

CAHOKIA MOUNDS STATE HISTORIC SITE – 30 Ramey St., Collinsville, IL 62234

WORLD WIDE TECHNOLOGY RACEWAY AT GATEWAY – 700 Raceway Blvd., Madison, IL 62060

GATEWAY NATIONAL GOLF LINKS – 18 Golf Drive #1677, Madison, IL 62060

INDIAN MOUNDS GOLF COURSE – 3500 Kingshighway, East St. Louis, IL 62201

EAST ST. LOUIS HIGH SCHOOL – 4901 State St., East St. Louis, IL 62205

GCS BALLPARK – 2301 Grizzlie Bear Blvd., Sauget, IL 62206

MISSOURI

The Missouri stretch of Route 66 has a little bit of everything for any sports fan. The Show-Me State's 301 Mother Road miles have professional teams, a pair of NCAA Division I universities, multiple D-II schools, elite high school teams, and a handful of golf courses along the way.

After you've seen what there is to see in Missouri, take a bit of time to explore the high schools in the three towns that lie along Route 66 in Kansas. This stretch is only 13 miles long—about half the distance of a marathon.

MISSOURI

IOWA

ROADTRIP AMERICA

100 miles
100 km

MISSOURI

Fort Madison   Macomb

Kirksville

ILLINOIS

Quincy

Jacksonville

Hannibal

Moberly

Marshall

Columbia

Kansas City

Warrensburg   Sedalia

Jefferson City

St Louis

Busch Stadium

Lafayette High School

Enterprise Center

Historic Route 66

Meramec Caverns

Cuba Saddle Club Arena

Waynesville High School

Rolla

Munger Moss Motel

Lebanon   Allgood-Bailey Stadium

Fort Leonard Wood

Uranus Fudge Factory & General Store

Farmington

Webb City High School

Hammons Field   **Springfield**

Strafford High School

Joplin

Joe Becker Memorial Stadium

Missouri Sports Hall of Fame

Joplin High School

West Plains

Poplar Bluff

Rogers

Fayetteville

Oakville

Jonesboro

ARKANSAS

Fort Smith

Conway

Memphis

Little Rock

ST. LOUIS

The one thing people most associate with the city of St. Louis is the **Gateway Arch**. The 630-foot Arch is the most recognizable structure people traveling Route 66 will see, and there are three major sports venues within walking distance from it.

Just to the north is **The Dome at America's Center**, where the St. Louis Rams played from 1995 to 2015. It was also home to the St. Louis BattleHawks of the XFL in 2020. The Dome, with a seating capacity near 70,000, isn't just used for sports. It has hosted concerts by the Rolling Stones, U2, the Backstreet Boys, Metallica, One Direction, Beyoncé, Guns N' Roses, Taylor Swift, and Garth Brooks.

To the south is **Busch Stadium**, home to the iconic Cardinals of Major League Baseball. A couple of blocks west of Busch Stadium on Clark Street is **Enterprise Center**, home to the 2019 Stanley Cup champion St. Louis

The Gateway Arch can be seen from Busch Stadium as part of the St. Louis skyline.

Blues. The **World Chess Hall of Fame** is also in St. Louis, located near Forest Park on Maryland Avenue in the Central West End. The Chess Hall has hosted the renowned Sinquefield Cup annually since 2013.

St. Louis is definitely a baseball town and the Cardinals are the kings. Busch Stadium is their palace.

The luck and draw of Busch Stadiums

The crown jewel of St. Louis sports is baseball, and the Cardinals are the pride of the city, thanks to their 11 World Series championships—and another eight National League pennants and World Series appearances.

The current Busch Stadium is actually the third Busch Stadium the Cardinals have called home. From 1920 to 1966 they played at Sportsman's Park, which was renamed Busch Stadium in 1953 when the club was purchased by Anheuser-Busch president August (Gussie) Busch Jr. The first downtown Busch Stadium—or Busch II—opened in 1966 and hosted both the baseball Cardinals and the NFL's St. Louis Cardinals, who moved to Arizona in 1988.

The baseball Cardinals began the 1966 season at Sportsman's Park but moved into Busch II in May 1966. They won the World Series in 1967, their first full season in their new venue. History repeated itself in 2006, when the current Busch Stadium opened and the Cardinals won their 10th World Series. The Cardinals added another World Series title in 2011 and went back to the Series in 2013, losing to the Boston Red Sox.

Busch III is impossible to miss when you enter St. Louis along the Interstate 70/55/64 corridor. The stadium is right along the I-44 junction and nearly touches the elevated I-64 bridge through downtown. The stadium, which has a capacity of 45,000, was built with upper decks that stopped in left and right field to allow fans a view of the Gateway Arch and the **Old Courthouse** beyond center field. Those views are now obstructed by a condominium tower built at the Cardinals-owned **Ballpark Village** on Clark Street. Ballpark Village houses several eateries as well as a giant sports bar with huge television screens. Also located inside the complex is the **Cardinals Hall of Fame**, which traces the franchise's storied history back to 1881. In the stairwell leading up to the hall entrance is a huge Stan Musial mural made of Rubik's Cubes.

Busch Stadium is a fun place to watch a baseball game, whether you're in the multitude of luxury suites, the club areas that have unique food options, or the standing-room-only areas. Fans can enjoy live music before games in Ford Plaza in the main concourse or on the Budweiser Terrace in the 300 level down the right-field line. The **Bowtie Bar at the Left Field Porch** is one of the few concessions areas in baseball that serves alcohol during the entirety of a game. While most concessions stands stop alcohol sales after the seventh-inning stretch, the Bowtie Bar will sell beer in the 14th inning of a 14-inning game.

Then there are Cardinals fans, who have been branded the "Best Fans in Baseball." Because baseball is the city's lifeblood, most Cardinals fans are knowledgeable about the game and friendly to opposing fans. The Cardinals also do a wonderful job of paying tribute to the team's storied past. Not only are the franchise's retired numbers on display beneath the center-field scoreboard, pictures of those players and managers—as well as Gussie Busch and legendary broadcaster Jack Buck—are at field level on the left-field wall.

One of those Hall of Famers on the wall is Stan Musial, who is considered the greatest Cardinals player of all time. There are two statues of Musial outside Busch Stadium. One stands among a group of small bronze figures outside the team store at the corner of Clark and Eighth Street. The other is a 20-foot statue outside the Third Base Gate on Eighth Street. It was unveiled in 1968 and greeted fans at the previous Busch Stadium. Today it's a popular meeting spot for fans, and the phrase "Meet me at Stan" is a common expression used in St. Louis. The statue is surrounded by 3,630 sidewalk bricks. The number of bricks is split evenly at the statue's center to correspond with the even distribution of 1,815 hits Musial collected in home and road games. Other bricks in the sidewalk on either side of the stadium list significant events in franchise history. A stroll around Busch Stadium really is like a walk through baseball history.

The Blues have soul—and Towel Man

ESPN's Nick Wagoner, an Edwardsville, Illinois, native who graduated from the University of Missouri, understands how important sports are to the city of St. Louis. He was employed by the Rams as a writer before getting hired by ESPN to cover the team during their final three seasons in St. Louis. After the Blues won the 2019 Stanley Cup, Wagoner wrote, "If the Cardinals are the heart of the city, the Blues are its soul."

The Blues were an expansion team in 1967 and reached the Stanley Cup Final in each of their first three seasons. They lost each time because what is now the Western Conference was essentially expansion teams that couldn't compete with the more-established teams east of the Mississippi River.

The Blues' early success generated excitement for the city's new team. That excitement still exists and was amplified in 2019 when the Blues went on a remarkable run to win the franchise's first-ever Stanley Cup. Enterprise Center, with a seating capacity of just over 18,000, can have an electric atmosphere, and fans remain engaged. One of those fans is Ron Baechle, who has been a Blues season-ticket holder since the 1989–90 season and is better known as the "Towel Man."

Just down the street from Busch Stadium is Enterprise Center, home to the NHL's St. Louis Blues.

Baechle, a St. Louis native who owns an advertising agency, stands at the edge of his upper-level section after each Blues goal and waves a small towel before counting the number of goals the Blues have in the game. As he lifts the corresponding number of fingers, the thousands of fans in attendance shout the numbers. It's fun and as simple as 1-2-3.

Baechle's "Towel Man" persona began in 1989 when he and some friends drove to Peoria, Illinois, to see the Rivermen play an International Hockey League (IHL) game while future Blues players Tony Twist and Kelly Chase were on the team. Baechle noticed a Rivermen fan waving a towel after each home team score while fans counted the number of goals. One of Baechle's friends suggested he bring the towel waving back to St. Louis.

Baechle was not yet a Blues season-ticket holder, but at the next game he attended, he told the people in his section what he had planned for

The St. Louis Blues won their first Stanley Cup in 2019.

Blues goals. His fellow fans played along, and eventually a tradition was born—though not without a few hiccups.

"The first towels I brought were bath towels, and they were too big. I was hitting people in the head with it, and they were getting mad," Baechle said. "They were calling me names, called me an idiot, told me to sit down. I guess I wasn't smart enough to figure it out."

By the time the Blues moved into what is now Enterprise Center in 1994, Baechle was a season-ticket holder, and his "Towel Man" alter ego took off. He is now a fixture at Blues games and is asked to pose for photos and sign autographs before the game and between periods. The Blues began showing Baechle on the arena videoboard when they moved into their current venue.

From humble beginnings, the Blues' "Towel Man" is now a local celebrity and even has sponsors for the towels he tosses to fans.

Baechle has had season tickets in Section 314 since Enterprise Center opened. Sitting in a section number that matches the city's area code is purely coincidence. He's never been tempted to move down to a better section as his local fame grew; Baechle prefers to be with the "diehard fans in the upper level."

"If anyone told me it would turn into this, I'd tell them they were crazy," said Baechle, who hasn't missed a game since 2014. "But I get to be associated with goals, fun, and winning, and I'm good with that. I'm a fan just like the next guy.

"Someone once asked me how long I'll do this, and I said, 'As long as I'm having fun with it. I'll keep doing it until it's not fun anymore.'"

Just know that if you ask Baechle to name his favorite player, he prepared a response in 2011 that includes the names of several Blues.

"I wish I had a (Scott) *Nichol* for every time somebody asked me that," Baechle began. "I (Kris) *Russell* with this (Jaroslav) *Halák*. Use your (B. J.) *Crombeen* here; let me (David) *Backes* up a little and just for the (Brian) *Elliott*, let's say it's (Carlo) *Colaiacovo* ... (Jason) *Arnott*. I guess you thought I was (Vladimir) *Sobotka* say (David) *Perron*. I could say (Alex) *Pietrangelo*, and then maybe feel like a (Roman) *Polák*. If you (Kevin) *Shattenkirk*'s place, you'd have (Alexander) *Steen* that one coming. (T. J.) *Oshie*! I forgot about (Patrik) *Berglund* and (Andy) *McDonald*. How about I just be a good (Chris) *Stewart* and say (Jamie) *Langenbrunner*? So, if you (Ian) *Cole* me (Barrett) *Jackman*, that'd be a (Chris) *Porter*-line decision. Hot (Matt) *D'Agostini*. Would you (Ryan) *Reaves* me alone if I said (Kent) *Huskins*? Let's just say there's a little *Hitch* (Ken Hitchcock) in my favorite coach."

When the Blues aren't on the ice, the NCAA takes advantage of St. Louis's centralized location and awards it hosting duties for various competitions. While The Dome has hosted the 2005 Final Four and numerous NCAA basketball regionals, Enterprise Center is the most popular location used by the NCAA. It hosted the NCAA Division I wrestling championships in 2000, 2004, 2005, 2008, 2009, 2012, 2015, 2017, and again in 2021.

It has hosted the Missouri Valley Conference men's basketball tournament every March since 1995. The tournament, dubbed "Arch Madness," is regarded as one of the most fan-friendly NCAA conference tourneys in the country.

SLU's strength is soccer

A mile and a half west of Enterprise Center is **Chaifetz Arena**, the basketball home of the **Saint Louis University** (SLU) Billikens. The 10,600-seat arena abuts the rest of SLU's athletic fields and is at the corner of Market Street and Compton Avenue, just two blocks north of Chouteau Avenue, which was the original alignment of Route 66.

The Billikens have a solid basketball program with five NCAA Tournament appearances between 2000 and 2019. Basketball Hall of Famer Ed Macauley is the best player to come out of the SLU program, but Bob Ferry, Anthony Bonner, Larry Hughes, and Willie Reed also had multiyear NBA careers. Bonner, a St. Louis native, is SLU's all-time leader in points, rebounds, and steals.

The SLU baseball team, which reached the College World Series in 1965, has produced several MLB players and made its eighth NCAA Tournament appearance in 2018.

As solid as the Billikens baseball and basketball programs are, SLU's best program is men's soccer. The Billikens won 10 national championships between 1959 and 1973. The 10 national titles are an NCAA best, as are SLU's 48 NCAA Tournament appearances between 1959 and 2014.

The Saint Louis University pep band is one of the best you'll see at a college basketball game.

The SLU women have made the NCAA Tournament four times since the program was founded in 1996. Both the Billikens men and women play at **Hermann Stadium**, which is located just behind Chaifetz Arena and seats 6,500. It's named after former soccer executive Bob Hermann, who is also the namesake of the award that goes to the best college men's and women's soccer players in the nation.

Hermann Stadium is a regular host for various NCAA events and hosted the 2006 College Cup.

The SLU soccer program has produced multiple U.S. National and professional players. Bosnian pros Vedad Ibišević and Dado Hamzagić also played collegiately at SLU. Former New York Jets placekicker Pat Leahy played on three of SLU's national championship teams and was inducted into the Billiken Hall of Fame in 1994. He was enshrined in the Missouri Sports Hall of Fame in Springfield in 2007.

Before seeing a Billikens game, be sure to grab a meal at nearby **Pappy's Smokehouse**, which is famous for its barbecue and stays open until that day's food is sold out. Lunch lines on the weekends usually wrap around the block.

Once you get back on Chouteau and head west, Highway 100 turns into Manchester at The Grove neighborhood, which is chock-full of bars and restaurants, as well as **Urban Chestnut Brewery and Bierhall**. No matter which alignment of Route 66 you take through St. Louis, make sure you get a frozen custard "concrete" at **Ted Drewes** on Chippewa Street and eat at **Spencer's Grill** in Kirkwood, where NFL player Jeremy Maclin was a standout athlete for the **Kirkwood High School** Pioneers.

MAPLEWOOD

After cruising through The Grove, you'll leave the St. Louis city limits with a seamless transition to the municipality of Maplewood. The original Route 66 cuts right through downtown Maplewood, which is also packed with bars and restaurants and home to **Schlafly Bottleworks**. Schlafly is a great place to enjoy some craft beers and food while watching games on the multiple televisions around the bar.

One of the more popular sports bars in downtown Maplewood is **The Post**, which has a wall of TVs to supplement those attached to the ceiling. The Post has a variety of food and beverage options and is always full of fans on autumn Saturdays for college football, Sundays for the NFL, for Monday Night Football, and of course, for St. Louis Cardinals and Blues games.

On the western edge of downtown Maplewood is an athletic field that sits between Route 66 and **Maplewood-Richmond Heights (MRH) High School**. The school has been in the same three-story brick building since it was built in 1929.

Maplewood-Richmond Heights High School is directly on the original alignment of Route 66. Below: The small Maplewood-Richmond Heights gymnasium can get packed and loud for Blue Devils basketball games.

The field was once used for football, but MRH dropped the sport in 2015 due to a lack of players. The Blue Devils had enjoyed football success with a state semifinal appearance in 2007 and a championship game berth in 2010. Former University of Missouri quarterback Paul Christman, who was inducted into the College Football Hall of Fame in 1956 and played for the Chicago Cardinals and Green Bay Packers from 1945 to 1950, is one notable Maplewood alumnus.

Soccer replaced football for the MRH annual homecoming game, and the Blue Devils soccer team responded by winning a school-best 20 games and reaching the 2015 district title game before losing to top-ranked John Burroughs. The MRH baseball team also had a resurgence in 2014 and 2015, winning consecutive district titles for the first time since 1963.

Basketball is king at MRH, which won state championships in 2008 and 2009. Maplewood also reached the state Final Four in 1941, '55, '64, and '88. The tiny MRH gym, also used by the MRH volleyball and wrestling teams, is usually packed with standing-room-only crowds filling the facility's lone set of blue bleachers. MRH used to be a wrestling power with consecutive state championships from 1941 to 1946 sandwiched between a pair of second-place finishes, and another state championship in 1973. Both track teams are always competitive, and the MRH girls won a state crown in 1990, while the Blue Devils boys won three straight state titles from 2009 to 2011.

WILDWOOD TO PACIFIC

St. Louis high schools have produced many professional athletes, most notably Baseball Hall of Famer Yogi Berra. Other Hall of Famers to call St. Louis home during their youth have been baseball star James "Cool Papa" Bell; former Baltimore Orioles manager Earl Weaver; tennis stars Butch Buchholz, Doris Hart, and Chuck McKinley; and golfer Judy Rankin.

More recent sports stars include NFL players Trent Green, Jeremy Maclin, Sheldon Richardson, Ezekiel Elliott, and Markus Golden; NBA players Larry Hughes, David Lee, and Bradley Beal; and NHL players Chris Wideman and Patrick Maroon.

But only one high school has produced a trio of All-Star caliber players in one sport. MLB players David Freese, Ryan Howard, and Luke Voit all attended **Lafayette High School** in Wildwood.

Freese became a hometown hero in 2011 when he helped lead the Cardinals to their 11th World Series championship. Freese, who retired after the 2019 season, was the 2011 National League Championship Series and World Series MVP and an All-Star in 2012. Howard was a three-time All-Star for the Philadelphia Phillies and the 2006 National League MVP. Voit played for the Cardinals in 2017 and 2018 before he was traded to the New York Yankees.

Even before it was sending players to the big leagues, Lafayette had a rich baseball tradition with a trio of state championships from 1970 to 1972. The 2016 Lancers team set a state record by sending 22 batters to the plate in a single inning that saw 14 consecutive batters reach base against Eureka.

"It's definitely something we celebrate and share," said Lafayette activities director Jonathan Sumner, who has been at the school since 2009 and the

AD since 2019. "There's a lot of pride and support for baseball.

"We've had three high-level players come out of the program in a short period of time. It's pretty rare to have that type of talent in one sport."

As good as the Lafayette boys have been on the diamond, the girls are even better. The Lancers softball program won eight state championships between 1978 and 2007.

"There are high expectations all around for academics and athletics," Sumner said. "The culture is just there."

A stroll through the halls of Lafayette High School during a basketball game will take you by a display of jerseys worn by many former Lancers athletes who have gone on to play professionally or on a U.S. National team.

While Wildwood is along the original Route 66 corridor of Highway 100, some travelers may choose to follow Interstate 44. **Route 66 State Park** is off of I-44 in Eureka and offers abundant hiking and biking trails. The park is popular with bird-watchers and those who want to fish in the Meramec River.

Also just off I-44 is Pacific's **Red Cedar Inn**, which closed in 2005. It was a popular dining spot for MLB players like Bob Klinger, Dizzy Dean, and Ted Williams in its heyday, and the city of Pacific is intent on turning the restaurant into a museum.

SULLIVAN

When driving east to west on Route 66, you will see more than 30 billboards for **Meramec Caverns**, located near Stanton. The signs begin around Springfield, Illinois, and a few of the advertisements are even painted on barn roofs. The Caverns are one of the more famous Route 66 landmarks and worth the stop.

With a campground along the Meramec River, the Caverns are a good spot to hike or take a kayak or canoe out on the river. Canoes are available to rent on-site, and buses take you 6 miles up the river so you can casually float downstream back to the campground. Although the river is great for floating, it's shallow, so it's not ideal for fishing.

The nearby town of Sullivan was home to professional bowler Elvin

Mesger, who once held the world record for most perfect games with 27. Three of those came on June 10, 1967, with another four over the next three weeks.

Sullivan was also home to baseball Hall of Famer "Sunny" Jim Bottomley, who set a Major League Baseball record for the most RBI (runs batted in) in a single game with 12 while playing for the St. Louis Cardinals in 1924. It's a record that was tied by former Cardinals player Mark Whiten in 1993 but still stands. After he retired, Bottomley lived next to a ball field in Sullivan and would give local kids baseball equipment. Bottomley died in 1959, and he and his wife of 26 years are buried in Sullivan's **International Order of Odd Fellows Cemetery**.

Sullivan Golf Club is less than 2 miles east of the route. The 6,174-yard course opened in 1954 as a nine-hole course, but it has been a full 18-hole course since 1991. It was purchased by the city in 2018 and is now a public course with tall trees lining Bermuda fairways that lead to undulated bent grass greens. Fees are very affordable at about $20 per person.

The Bourbon water tower is often photographed by Route 66 travelers, but it is full of water—not bourbon.

BOURBON

One of the more popular Route 66 photo opportunities is at the **Bourbon Water Tower**, which is 9 miles down the road from Sullivan. Though the large metal reservoir may have "Bourbon" written on it, it is indeed full of water and not Kentucky whiskey. When you're done taking selfies, cross over Interstate 44 on Pine Street and turn right to stay on Route 66.

That will take you right past **Bourbon High School**, where you can't miss the bright blue track that circles the athletic field used by the Warhawks soccer teams. If there's a soccer match on the pitch or a track meet occurring, you might want to stop for a bit.

CUBA

Keep heading west on Route 66, which is well-marked, to reach Cuba—also known as Route 66's "Mural City." The town of 3,300 people has dozens of murals on various buildings along the Mother Road. The city was founded in 1857 and now has eight buildings listed on the National Register of Historic Places. Among those buildings is the **Cuba High School Annex**, which was built in 1934 to augment the high school that opened in 1904. The annex now houses the **Crawford County Historical Society Museum**. The rectangular two-story brick building was added to the historic register in 2013 and was last used as part of the school in the early 1960s. The current **Cuba High School** opened in 1996.

The Cuba Wildcats won their lone state championship in 1992 when the boys' cross-country team placed first in Jefferson City. Cuba's teams in the more popular sports—football, basketball, and baseball—are competitive but haven't had much postseason success.

The big draw for sports fans in Cuba would be the rodeo. The Ozark Rodeo Association (ORA) hosts a pair of marquee events at **Cuba Saddle Club Arena**. The first takes place in either May or June, depending on the year,

The world's largest rocking chair is at the Fanning 66 Outpost, just west of Cuba.

while the other is in September. ORA president Aaron Tilley said these are "family-based rodeos" with cowboys and cowgirls from as young as 4 years old competing for cash.

"They're spending more than they're making, but they're having a blast," said Tilley, a former bull rider who married a calf roper; now the couple has children who do rodeo events.

There is good turnout for the two ORA events in Cuba, but it's not quite as big as the Championship Bull Riding event every July at the **Crawford County Fair**, which is right off Route 66.

Cuba has the first of many rodeo arenas along Route 66. They are most abundant in Missouri, Oklahoma, Texas, New Mexico, and Arizona from Cuba to Williams. The National Federation of Professional Bull Riders (NFPB) has events in Eureka and Springfield, Missouri. The Professional Bull Riders (PBR) is the premiere level of bull riding. The circuit schedule includes stops in St. Louis; Springfield, Missouri; Amarillo, Texas; Tulsa, Oklahoma; and Albuquerque, New Mexico, with the November world finals in Las Vegas.

Before leaving Cuba, be sure to take in as many of the murals as you can, eat at **Missouri Hick Bar-B-Que**, and stop by the **Fanning Outpost** to see the world's largest rocking chair and get your Route 66 passport stamped.

ST. JAMES

On your way from Cuba to Rolla, you'll drive through St. James. The city of 4,200 elected Missouri's first female mayor in 1921 and is home to several Route 66 stops like **Finn's Motel**, the **Mule Trading Post**, and the **New Cardetti Store**.

St. James High School won a boys' basketball state championship in 1976, and both St. James Tigers basketball teams are still postseason regulars. St. James High is a few blocks south of Route 66, not far from the **Tiger Shark Waterpark** and **St. James Park on Lake Scioto**.

About 7 miles southeast of the city center is **Maramec Spring Park**, a popular trout fishing spot that claims to be "one of the most beautiful spots to be found in Missouri." The 200-acre park also has campsites, picnic tables and shelters, and playgrounds along the Meramec River. Getting there will take you by **St. James Golf Club**, a scenic nine-hole course 2 miles southeast of the Double Six along State Highway 68.

ROLLA

Although the St. James football program has been inconsistent, it has had a few players go on to compete collegiately. Two of those from the 2000s were Chad Shockley and Jake Harlan, who both played at the Division II level for the **Missouri University of Science and Technology (Missouri S&T)** Miners in Rolla.

Founded as the Missouri School of Mines and Metallurgy in 1870, it became the University of Missouri-Rolla in 1964 and switched to Missouri S&T in 2008. The Miners are members of the Great Lakes Valley Conference, which includes Lewis University in Romeoville, Illinois; the University of Illinois at Springfield; the University of Missouri-St. Louis; and Drury University in Springfield, Missouri. The Missouri S&T campus is right along Route 66 (Highway 63) in Rolla, 10 miles west of St. James. A half-sized replica of England's famous Stonehenge is on the northwestern edge of the school grounds.

With a green and gold pickax as its logo, the Miners baseball team chopped its way to division titles in 2011, 2012, and 2016 and a conference championship in 2019. Baseball is one of 15 varsity sports at Missouri S&T. One of the early alumni of the baseball team was pitcher Marv Breuer, who helped the New York Yankees win a World Series in 1941. Other sports alumni from Missouri S&T include multiple NFL players, 2004 World Series of Poker champion Greg "Fossilman" Raymer, and Olympic long-jumper Tyrone Smith.

The Miners football team, which has nine conference championships as of 2020, plays at the 8,000-seat **Allgood-Bailey Stadium**. Originally called Jackling Field when it opened in 1967, the stadium was renamed in 2000 to honor former football and basketball coach Dewey Allgood and benefactor Keith Bailey. The venue is also home to the Missouri S&T track teams and hosts the Dewey Allgood Invitational for small colleges every April. The Miners basketball and volleyball teams call **Gibson Arena** home.

A few blocks east of the S&T athletic complex is **Rolla High School**, which opened in 1921. Rolla is solid across the board in sports and produced Olympic athlete Chantae McMillan, who had the third-best jump in MSHSAA history in 2005 and competed for the United States at the 2012 London Games in the heptathlon.

Zeno's Motel and Steak House may have closed, but Rolla does offer several places to stay and eat for those wanting to spend the night and maybe see a game or two.

ST. ROBERT

Right after the Devil's Elbow curve of Route 66 between Rolla and Waynesville is one of the goofier spots along Route 66—the **Uranus Fudge Factory and General Store**. With the tagline "The best fudge comes from Uranus," the tiny "town" right off Interstate 44 is about as kitschy as it gets, with the world's largest belt buckle and apparel and knickknacks that include just about every butt or poop pun you can think of.

The attraction's site is also home to a gun and archery range because you have to shoot straight in Uranus. The archery range has distances of 20 and 40 yards and also includes a 3-D virtual range. The ranges were renovated in 2019 to open in 2020. Uranus hosts archery leagues, but the range is open to the public for those who want to practice.

The Uranus Fudge Factory is a punderful place.

Bows can also be tested at the range prior to purchase to ensure the customer gets one he or she is comfortable with.

The area around St. Robert and Waynesville is popular with hunters, and the Uranus range offers a place for hunters to hone their skills with both bows and arrows and rifles. Bow season for deer is from September 15 to January 15, with rifle season between November 16 and November 26. Bows can still be used during rifle season. Turkey hunting for bows and guns is available in October and each spring. You can also go bow fishing at nearby Boone Creek or the Big Piney River, which forms the aforementioned Devil's Elbow. Local fisherman Bryan Wilson provides full bow fishing and gigging guide services. Hunting permits can be purchased at the Missouri Department of Conservation website.

Uranus has its own newspaper—the *Uranus Examiner*—and offers an email newsletter for those who'd like to "probe Uranus deeper." If you're traveling through the area in June, after you've gotten some Uranus fudge and maybe purchased a bottle of wine from Uranus Liquors, you can see more bull riding at the Pulaski County Regional Fair in St. Robert. Held at **St. Robert City Park**, the fair has free admission and parking—though tickets for the bull-riding event are $15. There is also an ATV rodeo event, for which tickets are just $5. The park has also hosted the "Hangin' For 8 Xtreme Bull Riding" event with professional bull riders.

WAYNESVILLE

The town of Waynesville is a bedroom community for Fort Leonard Wood, an Army training facility with about 15,000 troops and a population of just 4,800. The high school has a larger-than-normal enrollment of 1,500 because of Fort Leonard Wood.

Waynesville High School sits atop a hill overlooking Interstate 44 and has a sprawling campus with the athletic facilities behind the school buildings.

With six classes for football in the Missouri State High School Activities Association, Waynesville competes as a 5A school and won a state championship in 2007. C. J. Mosley was an all-state defensive lineman for Waynesville prior to a decade-long NFL career from 2005 to 2015.

The football stadium, which is also home to the soccer and track-and-field teams, is a 23,000-square-foot venue that includes two field houses, a concessions building, synthetic turf field, and seating for 3,000 spectators.

Like most of Waynesville's teams, the basketball clubs are usually competitive, with each winning four district titles between 2009 and 2019. Dan Pippin, who captained the gold medal-winning U.S. Olympic basketball team in 1952, played at Waynesville before continuing as a Tiger at the University of Missouri.

As with much of Pulaski County, Waynesville is rich with Route 66 history. Waynesville was designated as the "Birthplace of the Route 66 Byway" in 1990 by Missouri Governor John Ashcroft. Missouri was the first state to award Route 66 historic status. A guide for three historic driving tours of Route 66 in Pulaski County can be picked up at the county tourism bureau and visitor center.

LEBANON

From Waynesville, Route 66 runs parallel to I-44 for 27 miles before reaching Lebanon. Before you get to Lebanon's famous **Munger Moss Motel**, you'll go past **Lebanon I-44 Speedway**. The track isn't actually along Interstate 44; it's on Old Route 66. The speedway has been "kickin' asphalt and taking names" on its three-eighths-mile oval track since 1982. From April to September, I-44 Speedway hosts races the first and third Saturdays of each month. Travelers heading west will drive on a hill overlooking the speedway, which has grandstand seating on the opposite side. Inside the high-banked oval track is a flat one-fifth-mile flat track used primarily for four-cylinder cars.

I-44 Speedway has been the training grounds for several professional race car drivers from Missouri. The Wallace family—brothers Kenny, Rusty, and Mike, and Mike's daughter Chrissy—all raced at Lebanon prior to advancing up the circuits. Rusty Wallace holds a "Race With Rusty" summer ride-along

Stay at the Munger Moss Motel while in Lebanon and go bowling across the street.

at the track. NASCAR drivers Carl Edwards, Jamie McMurray, Kevin Donahue, and Justin Jennings also honed their driving skills at Lebanon I-44 Speedway. The track is an approved NASCAR and ASA speedway and hosted ARTGO late model short-track racing series races four times and an ARCA Menards Series West event in 2013.

The Munger Moss Motel is 4 miles down Route 66 with the **Starlite Lanes** bowling alley directly across the street. Turning north onto Washington Avenue a mile farther will take you in the direction of **Lebanon High School**. If you're doing Route 66 in the spring or fall, you may want to check out one of the Yellowjackets teams that are consistently competitive in most sports.

The football team had just one losing season between 2010 and 2019, claiming district titles in 2017 and 2018. Justin Britt, a second-round pick of the Seattle Seahawks in the 2014 NFL Draft, was a standout at Lebanon before playing at the University of Missouri. Britt, who was an immediate starter on the Seahawks' offensive line, won a state wrestling championship at Lebanon in 2009 at the 285-pound class.

Lebanon also has the distinction of winning the first-ever Missouri State High School Activities Association girls' wrestling tournament. Quincy Glendenning led the group with an individual championship at 131 pounds.

The **Lebanon Route 66 Museum**, located at the **Lebanon-Laclede County Library**, doesn't include much in terms of sports memorabilia but is worth a visit before moving along.

MARSHFIELD

As you continue to travel west, the Double Six will take you through Marshfield on Hubble Street. A left turn on Jackson Street, or County Highway DD, will lead you to **Marshfield High School**.

The Marshfield Blue Jays have not been traditionally strong in most sports, with one exception. The Blue Jays girls' basketball program has been a powerhouse for more than 30 years.

After coach Scott Ballard led the Lady Jays to three straight state titles from 1988 to 1990, Gary Murphy took over, and the championship streak was extended to four seasons. Murphy led the Jays to three more state championships between 1996 and 1999 and had a record of 595–198 during his 22 years as the girls' basketball coach. Murphy also led the softball team to a state title in 1999.

After snapping a photo of the quarter-scale model of the Hubble Space Telescope at the **Webster County Courthouse**, you might want to check out a basketball game at Marshfield High.

STRAFFORD

Strafford is known as the "only town with two Main Streets and no back alley," thanks to a description in *Ripley's Believe It or Not!*. The statement captures how Route 66 bypassed Main Street in the town of 2,400 residents and ran behind businesses with a railroad on the other side. Instead of losing business to Route 66 travelers, those stores simply added new entrances to give their shops two storefronts.

That is Strafford's primary claim to fame. Another would be the female athletes at **Strafford High School**. The Strafford girls gave the school its first-ever state championship with a basketball title in 2016. The Steve Frank-coached Indians followed that 3A title with three more in 2017, 2018, and 2019. The Indians won 115 consecutive games over those four seasons, and when Frank stepped down, the streak continued with another state title in 2020. Frank was inducted into the Missouri Sports Hall of Fame in 2019.

The female dominance isn't limited to basketball. Dale Bean led the softball team to consecutive state titles in 2017 and 2018 as well.

There is no indication that Strafford's dominance in girls' basketball, or other girls' sports, will end any time soon, so you may want to spend a few hours at Strafford High to witness excellence, especially if the Indians are playing rival Marshfield.

SPRINGFIELD

If you're only going to make one sports stop in Missouri while traveling Route 66, make it the **Missouri Sports Hall of Fame**. The Hall itself is on the south side of Springfield, about 15 miles off the Route 66 path, but is worth the short detour. Located on Stan Musial Drive just off U.S. Highway 60, the Missouri Sports Hall of Fame opened in 1994 and is overflowing with sports memorabilia from some of the best athletes and teams to ever play in the Show-Me State.

Statues and busts of greats like Musial, Payne Stewart, Jackie Stiles, Lou Brock, Norm Stewart, and Bill Virdon line a path around the building.

A nominal fee of $5 is all it takes to see the hall's exhibits. Banners of each professional and NCAA Division I team from Missouri hang from the ceiling as you enter from the lobby. The St. Louis Cardinals are, of course, heavily prevalent in the Hall with jerseys of Hall of Famers Red Schoendienst, Whitey Herzog, and Tony LaRussa encased behind glass with other jerseys and memorabilia. The Kansas City Royals, and their two World Series titles, are not forgotten. The St. Louis Rams and Kansas City Chiefs both have their own displays to showcase their respective Super Bowl titles and Hall of Fame players. The college section is lined with helmets of every collegiate

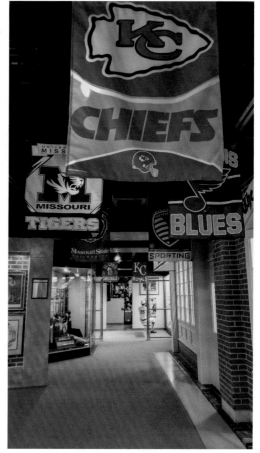

The Missouri Sports Hall of Fame has myriad memorabilia from across the Show-Me State.

program in the state. All-Americans in every sport at each Missouri school are honored annually during a January ceremony.

The Missouri Valley Conference Hall of Fame is included with plaques for greats like Larry Bird, Oscar Robertson, Doug Collins, Walt Frazier, Hersey Hawkins, Ed Macauley, and Stiles. Another section is dedicated to legendary broadcasters like Jack Buck, Harry Caray, Joe Garagiola, and Bob Costas. Top high school athletes, coaches, and programs are also recognized at the Hall.

"There are so many people across the state who have put in so much time and have had such great careers, from high school to pro," said the Hall's media relations director Kary Booher. "That's the beauty of this Hall of Fame. We not only honor the bigger names, but we capture the big names in a lot of communities."

The annual enshrinement ceremony typically draws more than 1,500 spectators. The 2019 Missouri Sports Hall of Fame class included former Missouri State basketball coach Charlie Spoonhour, while former Chiefs linebacker Derrick Johnson was among the 2020 class.

Missouri State and a multitude of teams

Downtown Springfield is home to **Missouri State University**, the next NCAA Division I school along the way. Spoonhour helped put the Bears basketball program on the map from 1983 to 1992. During his nine seasons at the helm of what was then Southwest Missouri State, Spoonhour compiled a record of 197–81 and took the Bears to the NCAA Tournament five times. He led MO State to its first-ever NCAA Division I Tournament victory in 1987 when the Bears upset Clemson in the first round. Steve Alford led Missouri State to a Sweet 16 berth in 1999 with upsets over Wisconsin and Tennessee before losing to No. 1 seed Duke.

The Bears play at **JQH Arena**, which replaced the Hammons Center in 2008. Both buildings are named after John Q. Hammons, a Springfield-based hotel developer whose name also festoons the baseball stadium used by the Springfield Cardinals—the Double-A affiliate of the MLB team in St. Louis. Spoonhour, who died in 2012, turned the Hammons Center into "Spoon's Temple of Doom" for opposing teams with a home record of 109–18.

JQH Arena has two sports venues: one for a volleyball program that regularly participates in the NCAA Tournament and another, larger space for men's and women's basketball. A giant banner for Jackie Stiles and her 2016 Women's Basketball Hall of Fame enshrinement hangs from the rafters above the basketball court. Stiles is Missouri State's all-time leading scorer and became the first NCAA Division I women's player with more than 1,000 points in a season when she scored 1,062 in the 2000–01 campaign. She led Missouri State to a Final Four appearance in St. Louis that season. Her 3,393 career points were an NCAA record until 2017. The Missouri State women also reached the Final Four in 1992.

The Missouri State football team plays its home games at **Robert Plaster Stadium**, which increased its seating capacity to 17,500 in 2014. It has more than doubled in size since it opened in 1941. Missouri State is a member of the Missouri Valley Conference, which is arguably the best football conference at the FCS level. The league includes powerhouse North Dakota State and perennially ranked Illinois State, Northern Iowa, Southern Illinois, and South Dakota State. Missouri State isn't quite at that level with just two playoff appearances in 1989 and '90. But the spacious Plaster Stadium can be raucous when marquee opponents come to town. The stadium has two grandstands along either sideline. The larger side holds the press box and some suites that offer a commanding view of the Springfield skyline.

Plaster Stadium also houses several handball courts, two with spectator seating; Missouri State's handball team won a national championship in 2018. Missouri State has won single national championships in golf, field hockey, and softball. Both soccer teams, which play at **Betty and Bobby Allison South Stadium**, are also nationally prominent programs.

The Bears baseball team, which reached the College World Series in 2003, is another strong program. The Bears regularly compete for conference championships, winning 10 regular-season and conference tournament titles through 2019. Missouri State made the NCAA Tournament 11 times from 1987 through 2018, winning three regionals. The most notable Missouri State baseball alum is Ryan Howard, but more than 20 former Bears have gone onto the big leagues since the program's first season in 1964.

Drury University's O'Reilly Center opened 2010 with a price tag of $13.5 million and has a capacity of 3,600.

Drury's Division II teams

Springfield is also home to **Drury University**, where the Panthers have won a total of 23 NCAA Division II national championships, including a 2013 men's basketball crown. The other 22 titles were in men's and women's swimming and diving. Drury is a swimming powerhouse, and coach Brian Reynolds was inducted into the Missouri Sports Hall of Fame in 2007. Twelve of those titles were won by the men, who earned 10 straight championships from 2005 through 2014. The 10 championships won by the women between 1997 and 2014 are an NCAA best.

Before competing at the NCAA Division II level, Drury won an NAIA men's basketball championship in 1979. The scoreboard inside the **O'Reilly Family Event Center**, which opened in 2010 with a capacity of 3,100, is flanked by banners representing national championships and NCAA Tournament appearances. The women's team reached the NCAA Division II Elite Eight

Springfield Central High School has been at the same location on Central Avenue since 1893.

in 2004, with the men getting there in 2014. Seven large jerseys of retired numbers hang above a sign for the Drury Sports Hall of Fame, which is essentially the main concourse with glass displays adorning the walls around the arena. The displays house various trophies and other memorabilia from some of Drury's athletic accomplishments.

The Drury soccer squads were started in 1992, and the Panthers play at **Harrison Stadium at the Curry Sports Complex**, which Drury shares with **Springfield Central High School**.

Visit "the Pit" at Springfield Central

The Springfield Central Bulldogs have had several team and individual state champions in golf, wrestling, track-and-field, swimming and diving, tennis, and cross-country. Although the football team hasn't had much success in recent years, including a 40-game losing streak from 2016 to 2019, the

Bulldogs are in the MSHSAA record books for scoring 105 points in a shutout victory over Greenfield in 1927.

The high school itself has been at the same location on Central Avenue since 1893 and is rumored to be haunted. The fourth-floor attic, Room 311 (which was renumbered when the school added a new building), and the old tunnels that were used for heat all have reports of the paranormal. The heating tunnels were originally connected to a series of caves that are the alleged source of the haunting and eerie noises. The school's history club began giving haunted tours in 2006. Game show host Bob Barker, a Drury graduate, is an alumnus of Springfield Central. So, too, is former NBA player Jack Israel, who played at Missouri State before getting drafted by the New York Knicks in 1959.

The basketball gym at Central is one of the oldest in the state. It is nicknamed "The Pit" because of its sunken floor and concrete bleachers that surround the court on three sides. Those sitting in the front rows are essentially on top of the court. It's intimate viewing for any basketball fan. Posters of senior athletes surround the floor, and centered on the wall without seating hangs a large banner for former coach Jim Ball, after whom the court is named. Ball won 603 games while at Central between 1951 and 1981 and was enshrined in the Missouri Sports Hall of Fame in 1993.

Where Cardinals find their wings

Springfield calls itself "The Birthplace of Route 66," and the downtown area offers plenty in terms of entertainment and Route 66 sites, including the **Route 66 Visitor Center**. The **History Museum on the Square** includes a "Birthplace of Route 66 Gallery." At the visitor center, you can pick up a pamphlet that identifies 50 "fun stops and photo ops along Route 66" between Devil's Elbow and Joplin.

Just around the corner from the visitor center is **Hammons Field**, which has been home to the Springfield Cardinals since 2005. The stadium is just a couple blocks from the **Steak 'n Shake** that opened in 1962 and is on the National Register of Historic Places.

Springfield isn't new to minor league baseball, hosting a variety of teams between 1905 and 1946. The current team competes at the Double-A level in

Hammons Field has been home to the Springfield Cardinals, the Double-A affiliate of the St. Louis Cardinals, since 2005.

the Texas League, which includes the Tulsa (Oklahoma) Drillers and Amarillo (Texas) Sod Poodles, both of whom can be found along Route 66.

The Cardinals have sent more than 100 players to the big leagues, and most of them made their MLB debut with the parent St. Louis team. The Cardinals' rich history is on display, even at the Double-A level, with the 11 World Series titles represented in the outfield. A Cardinals flag is among four—along with the U.S., state of Missouri, and Missouri State University flags—that wave in the wind between two towers over the main gates. The stadium once held 12,000 people, but now has a capacity of 8,000 after the addition of 28 luxury suites and a VIP lounge on the box suite level. The JumboTron is the "largest plasma screen television in Springfield" and shows highlights from the current game as well as that day's MLB contests. During the MLB All-Star Game in July, fans are invited to Hammons Field to watch the Summer Classic on the giant screen. Seeing future big-leaguers like Kolten Wong, Carlos Martinez, Trevor Rosenthal, Luke Voit, Matt Adams, Colby Rasmus, Lance Lynn, or Matt Carpenter is always a draw for minor league ball.

Hammons Field is the home turf of Missouri State and hosted the Missouri Valley Conference tournament four times between 2004 and 2017. The Bears won the Valley tourney in 1996, 1997, 2015, and 2018.

Next to Hammons Field is the **Jordan Valley Ice Park**, which is home to the MSU Ice Bears hockey team, as well as local youth clubs. Four different minor league hockey teams have called the Ice Park home since the 2,000-seat venue opened in 2001.

Both Jordan Valley Ice Park and Hammons Field are just blocks from the historic **Gillioz Theatre**, so see a show and then catch a game (or games) before leaving Springfield. There are plenty of options.

CARTHAGE

About an hour west of downtown Springfield on State Highway 96, or Route 66, is the city of Carthage. The castle-like **Jasper County Courthouse**, built in 1894 and listed on the National Register of Historic Places, dominates the Carthage skyline and is one of many architectural beauties in the city. The courthouse contains an interior mural depicting the history of Jasper County, which was founded in 1841. Carthage was chosen as the county seat, and a high school opened in 1860.

Carthage High School has remained in the same location ever since, though the buildings have changed. The current school building opened in 2009, and two of the three state championships won by Carthage have followed. The Tigers claimed their first state title in boys' golf in 1987, but the boys' track-and-field team earned a Missouri crown in 2018, and the football team won a Class 5 state championship in 2019. The football title was the culmination of 12 straight playoff appearances for the Tigers. Carthage has a strong football tradition, with brothers Charles and Felix Wright beginning their future NFL careers at Carthage High.

The Tigers are also strong in soccer, with the boys a regular state tournament qualifier. The football, soccer, and track teams all play at **David Haffner Stadium**. Haffner, a former executive for Carthage-based Leggett & Platt, purchased the naming rights before the blue stadium opened in 2016. Haffner Stadium can hold more than 4,000 spectators with a large grandstand topped with a spacious press box along the home sideline.

Across the street from Haffner Stadium is the **Fair Acres Sports Complex**, which contains the softball field and the Fair Acres YMCA. The Carthage swim teams use the indoor pool at the Y. A large water tower with the word "TIGERS" painted next to a tiger head stands along the road in front of Fair Acres. The Carthage baseball team plays at a nearby park owned by the city parks and recreation department.

The Tigers teams benefit from a community that supports them, which makes seeing a game at Haffner Stadium, Fair Acres, or the 2,400-seat gymnasium fun. The indoor teams, especially girls' volleyball, are consistently competitive, and championship banners bedizen the wall next to the scoreboard.

Carthage is worth a couple days of your time while traveling down Route 66. Not only does the high school provide excellent facilities for its teams and fans, the **Carthage Chamber of Commerce** has plenty of information about the area. The Chamber is just a block from the **Boots Court Motel**. Route 66 turns west at the Chamber onto Oak Street and goes past the **Powers Museum**, which has been open since 1987 and displays the history of Carthage. Across the street are the **Carthage Municipal Park**, which contains a roller rink; **Carthage Saddle Club Arena**; and the **Carthage Golf Course**. The latter is a challenging 18-hole course with 34 bunkers, 2 lakes, a driving range, an 8,000-square-foot area to practice your short game and putting, and concrete golf paths. Saddle Club Arena has hosted the **Carthage Stampede Rodeo** every June since 1977.

If you're traveling down Route 66 between April and September, be sure to see a movie at the historic **66 Drive-In Theatre**, just 2 miles west of the Powers Museum.

WEBB CITY

Route 66 is nicknamed "America's Main Street," and in Webb City, it literally is Main Street. Webb City is also home to one of the most successful high school football programs in Missouri.

After Jerry Kill led the **Webb City High School** Cardinals to their first state championship in 1989, Webb City added 13 more over the next 30 years. The Cardinals made their first playoff appearance in 1985 and have since been a perennial championship contender. John Roderique, who was an all-state linebacker on the 1985 team, took over as head coach in 1997 and won 10 of those 13 titles. Roderique, who played collegiately at Pittsburg State, has the best winning percentage of any high school football coach in Missouri. Despite annual turnover like at any school, Webb City seemingly doesn't have a down year and continues to reload instead of rebuild. It is one of the best programs in the Show-Me State and worth a visit for those curious to experience the unique appeal of high school football.

When a sports program does well, the facilities usually improve, and that has happened at Webb City. **Cardinal Stadium**, which is home to the football, soccer, and track teams, has an all-turf field with a permanent Cardinals logo similar to the University of Louisville's at midfield. Temporary bleachers are erected inside the track at the end zones to raise the capacity to more than 5,200.

While the football team has had a ridiculous amount of success, Webb City's other teams are no slouches with state championships in baseball (2005, 2006), softball (2004, 2007), girls' basketball (2010), and boys' basketball (1997). The basketball and volleyball teams play inside the 1,900-seat **Cardinal Dome**, which is more like a college arena.

Pullout bleachers are topped with permanent chairback seating around the court, above which hangs a four-sided scoreboard. The same Cardinals logo that is on the football field adorns the bottom of the scoreboard directly above the midcourt logo. Analog scoreboards are on the baselines, attached to the front of the curved seating sections. A concourse encircles the gym, and championship banners are affixed to the wall opposite the main entrance.

JOPLIN

From Webb City, Route 66 turns south on Madison Street, or Highway 49, toward Joplin. The Mother Road merges with the I-44 business loop and turns west into downtown Joplin.

A baseball bonanza at Becker Stadium

A young Mickey Mantle, who grew up along Route 66 in Commerce, Oklahoma, played at Joplin's **Joe Becker Stadium**. The ballpark, which opened in 1913, used to be the home to Missouri Southern State baseball until the school built its own facility in 2015. Becker Stadium has hosted several minor league baseball teams over the last 100-plus years. It has been the home venue for the Joplin Outlaws—a college wood-bat summer team in the MINK (Missouri, Iowa, Nebraska, Kansas) League—since 2009. The stadium also hosts several youth tournaments, most notably the Premier League from Texas, a high school summer travel league.

Joe Becker Stadium underwent a $4.7 million renovation in 2014. The project included improvements for the restrooms, team clubhouses, dugouts,

An intersection in downtown Joplin recognizes both Route 66 and Missouri Southern State University.

the addition of modern ticket booths, a merchandise store, and additional concessions stands. Outfield seating is restricted to a set of left-field bleachers, but just beyond the right-field wall is a small hill perfect for berm lawn viewing. The playing surface has a grass outfield, but the infield is all artificial turf painted green and brown to simulate grass and dirt.

Missouri Southern competes in MIAA

Missouri Southern State University is an NCAA Division II school that competes in the Mid-America Intercollegiate Athletics Association (MIAA). Other schools in the MIAA include Pittsburg State in Kansas, the University of Central Oklahoma in Edmond, and Rogers State University in Claremore, Oklahoma. The MIAA has produced multiple national championships in basketball and football, with MSSU capturing an NAIA football crown in 1972. Scrawled across the press box facade at **Fred Hughes Stadium** is a tribute to that 1972 national championship team.

"We play in probably the most competitive Division II conference in the country," said Missouri Southern sports information director Justin Maskus. "If you are competitive in this league, like top three or four, you're probably in the top 25 in the country. It's pretty tough."

Missouri Southern has produced multiple NFL players, most notably wide receivers Rod Smith and James Thrash, offensive lineman Allen Barbre, and defensive tackle Brandon Williams.

"You're going to see great football in this league. You're going to see great basketball in this league, and some pretty good baseball," added Maskus, who has served on the NCAA baseball tournament selection committee.

Missouri Southern's baseball

Take a side trip to Pitt State

One of Missouri Southern's biggest rivals is nearby **Pittsburg State University** in Pittsburg, Kansas. Pitt State is the only NCAA school with Gorillas as their mascot, and they play their home games at **Carnie Smith Stadium**, which is more commonly referred to as "The Jungle." Pitt State has won four football national championships as of 2020, and the program produced NFL players John Brown, Ronald Moore, and Brian Moorman. The stadium, formerly known as Brandenburg Field, opened in 1924 and has seating for 8,300, though standing-room-only crowds—common for games against Missouri Southern and Northwest Missouri State—can push the capacity over 11,000.

stadium, **Warren Turner Field**, is an all-turf venue that seats 600 and opened in 2015. The baseball team has been competitive, as has the softball team, which won a national championship in 1992. The softball field sits behind Fred Hughes Stadium, which is also home to MSSU's outdoor track teams.

Track-and-field is where the Lions really roar. The Missouri Southern women won a "Triple Crown" in the 2007–08 school year with national championships in indoor and outdoor track-and-field as well as cross-country. The MSSU indoor track facility at the **Leggett & Platt Athletic Center** has hosted several conference national championship meets and is one of the best track facilities you'll see anywhere in the country.

Adjacent to the track is **Robert Corn Court**, home to the men's and women's basketball teams since 1989. The court is named after former men's basketball coach Robert Corn, who is the school's all-time winningest coach with a record of 413–305 over 25 years at MSSU. Corn won 20 or more games nine times, leading the Lions to the NCAA Tournament five times—including a Final Four appearance in 2000 when the Lions were 30–3. Corn was named the MIAA Coach of the Year four times and inducted into the Missouri Sports Hall of Fame in 2016.

Before Corn's arrival in 1989, the basketball teams played at **Robert Ellis Young Gymnasium**, which is still used by the volleyball team. The Young gym is more of what you'd find at a high school with wooden bleachers pushed against sideline walls when not in use. The Young gymnasium building is also home to the women's athletics offices, racquetball courts, and a swimming pool that is used for community swim lessons and by the Joplin High School swim teams.

Joplin High: Rising from tornado destruction

While the Young gym at Missouri Southern is an older venue, **Joplin High School** has a brand-new arena, but because of horrible circumstances. Joplin High was completely rebuilt after being destroyed by an EF5-rated tornado that killed 161 people in 2011. The new school, which opened in 2014 with then-Vice President Joe Biden in attendance, looks more like an apartment complex than a school with a ton of green space and skywalks between buildings that feature huge windows to let in natural light. While the new school was being built, the athletics teams used the facilities at MSSU, and classes were held inside a former Shopko at the Northpark Mall.

The new school has three gymnasiums, two used for practices and physical education classes, and the primary gym is one of the best in the state. A walking track encircles the gym with a large red and white eagle head on the far wall. A small observation area overlooks an athletic field used for soccer and junior varsity football. The seating area in the primary gym consists of permanent blue and white bleachers on the upper level by the track and pull-out bleachers on three sides of the court below. Opposite the eagle wall are athletics offices, a first-class fitness center with exercise machines and free weights, and the entrance to the school's academic wings.

"We're very proud and blessed to have these facilities," Joplin athletics director Matt Hiatt said. "Unfortunately, we had to rebuild, but when the community was forced to, they did it right."

The court is named after legendary basketball coach Russ Kaminsky, who led the Eagles from the 1950s through the '70s and won a trio of state championships.

The varsity football team plays at **Junge Field**, a 4,000-seat stadium that opened in 1934. It was renamed the **Dewey Combs Athletic Complex** in 2014 to honor longtime Joplin football coach Dewey Combs, who won more than 200 games and four state championships over a 29-year career. The Eagles are consistently solid in football, winning 10 games in 2018 and reaching the Class 6 state semifinals. They were the state runner-up a year later under coach Curtis Jasper, who took over the program in 2015 and went 43–14 over his first five seasons. The 2019 season included a win over rival Webb City.

"Anytime you beat those guys, you know you're going to have a good season," Hiatt said.

Former NASCAR driver Jamie McMurray and former MLB player Steve Luebber are both Joplin graduates. Luebber was drafted out of high school by the Minnesota Twins in 1967 and contributed to a baseball program that has won three state championships, most recently in 2001, and remains competitive today.

The boys' golf team also has a trio of state titles and uses both the **Twin Hills Country Club** and **Schifferdecker Golf Course** as its home courses. Schifferdecker is located right along Route 66 in **Schifferdecker Park**, which also includes an athletic complex, an aquatic center, and the **Joplin Museum Complex**. The athletic facilities include basketball courts, horseshoe pits, sand volleyball courts, a skate park, and playgrounds. Schifferdecker is also the only public 18-hole golf course in Joplin. It has a state-of-the-art golf simulator added in 2017 for those rainy days, but a day on the course itself in 2019 cost just $33 for 18 holes and a cart.

When leaving Joplin, you'll see a sign for the old **Joplin 66 Speedway**, but the clay oval track closed in 2004 and only the sign remains.

Just 6 miles away is the Kansas state line, where you can stop by a handful of high schools.

Schifferdecker Park has an eighteen-hole golf course to go with an aquatics center, basketball and volleyball courts, a skate park, horseshoe pits, and playgrounds.

Missouri Route 66 Points of Interest

GATEWAY ARCH NATIONAL PARK – 11 N. 4th St., St. Louis, MO 63102

BUSCH STADIUM – 700 Clark Ave., St. Louis, MO 63102

BALLPARK VILLAGE – 601 Clark Ave., St. Louis, MO 63102

1401 CLARK AVE., ST. LOUIS, MO 63103

SAINT LOUIS UNIVERSITY – 1 N. Grand Blvd., St. Louis, MO 63103

CHAIFETZ ARENA – 1 S. Compton Ave., St. Louis, MO 63103

HERMANN STADIUM – 3330 Laclede Ave., St. Louis, MO 63103

PAPPY'S SMOKEHOUSE – 3106 Olive St., St. Louis, MO 63103

URBAN CHESTNUT BREWERY AND BIERHALL – 4465 Manchester Ave., St. Louis, MO 63110

WORLD CHESS HALL OF FAME – 4652 Maryland Ave., St. Louis, MO 63108

TED DREWES FROZEN CUSTARD – 6726 Chippewa St., St. Louis, MO 63109

SPENCER'S GRILL – 223 S Kirkwood Road, Kirkwood, MO 63122

KIRKWOOD HIGH SCHOOL – 801 W. Essex Ave., Kirkwood, MO 63122

SCHLAFLY BOTTLEWORKS – 7260 Southwest Ave., Maplewood, MO 63143

THE POST SPORTS BAR & GRILL – 7372 Manchester Road, Maplewood, MO 63143

MAPLEWOOD RICHMOND HEIGHTS HIGH SCHOOL – 7539 Manchester Road, Maplewood, MO 63143

LAFAYETTE HIGH SCHOOL – 17050 Clayton Road, Wildwood, MO 63011

ROUTE 66 STATE PARK – 97 N Outer Road, Eureka, MO 63025

MERAMEC CAVERNS – 1135 Hwy. W., Sullivan, MO 63080

SULLIVAN GOLF CLUB – 11 Country Club Drive, Sullivan, MO 63080

BOURBON WATER TOWER – 2-62 Paramount Drive, Bourbon, MO 65441

BOURBON HIGH SCHOOL – 1500 Historic US 66, Bourbon, MO 65441

CRAWFORD COUNTY HISTORICAL SOCIETY MUSEUM – 308 N. Smith St., Cuba, MO 65453

CUBA HIGH SCHOOL – 1 Wildcat Pride Drive, Cuba, MO 65453

CRAWFORD COUNTY FAIR – 1 Hood Park Drive, Cuba, MO 65453

CUBA SADDLE CLUB ARENA – 810 Saddle Club Road, Cuba, MO 65453

MISSOURI HICK BAR-B-QUE – 913 East Washington St., Cuba, MO 65453

FANNING 66 OUTPOST – 5957 State Hwy. ZZ, Cuba, MO 65453

FINN'S MOTEL – 777 Grover St., St. James, MO 65559

NEW CARDETTI STORE – 210 N. Jefferson St., St. James, MO 65559

ST. JAMES HIGH SCHOOL – 101 East Scioto St., St. James, MO 65559

TIGER SHARK WATERPARK – 500 S. Bourbeuse St., St. James, MO 65559

MARAMEC SPRING PARK – 21880 Maramec Spring Drive, St. James, MO 65559

ST. JAMES GOLF CLUB – 11780 MO 68, St. James, MO 65559

MULE TRADING POST – 11160 Dillon Outer Road, Rolla, MO 65401

MISSOURI S&T UNIVERSITY ATHLETICS – 705 W. 10th St., Rolla, MO 65401

ROLLA HIGH SCHOOL – 900 Bulldog Run, Rolla, MO 65401

URANUS FUDGE FACTORY AND GENERAL STORE – 14400 State Hwy. Z, St. Robert, MO 65584

ST. ROBERT CITY PARK – 132 J. H. Williamson Drive, St. Robert, MO 65584

WAYNESVILLE HIGH SCHOOL – 200 G. W. Lane, Waynesville, MO 65583

LEBANON I-44 SPEEDWAY – 24069 U.S. Rte. 66, Lebanon, MO 65536

MUNGER MOSS MOTEL – 1336 U.S. Rte. 66, Lebanon, MO 65536

STARLITE LANES – 1331 E, U.S. Rte. 66, Lebanon, MO 65536

LEBANON HIGH SCHOOL – 777 Brice St., Lebanon, MO 65536

LEBANON-LACLEDE COUNTY LIBRARY – 915 S. Jefferson Ave., Lebanon, MO 65536

MARSHFIELD HIGH SCHOOL – 370 State Hwy. DD, Marshfield, MO 65706

WEBSTER COUNTY COURTHOUSE – 101 S. Crittenden St., Marshfield, MO 65706

STRAFFORD HIGH SCHOOL – 201 W. McCabe St., Strafford, MO 65757

MISSOURI STATE UNIVERSITY – 901 S. National Ave., Springfield, MO 65897

JQH ARENA – 685 S. John Q Hammons Pkwy., Springfield, MO 65807

ROBERT PLASTER STADIUM – 1015 E. Grand St., Springfield, MO 65897

BETTY AND BOBBY ALLISON SOUTH STADIUM – 830 Bear Blvd., Springfield, MO 65807

DRURY UNIVERSITY – 900 N. Benton Ave., Springfield, MO 65802

O'REILLY FAMILY EVENT CENTER – 935 N. Summit Ave., Springfield, MO 65802

HARRISON STADIUM AT CURRY SPORTS COMPLEX – 900 N. Summit Ave., Springfield, MO 65802

SPRINGFIELD CENTRAL HIGH SCHOOL – 423 E. Central St., Springfield, MO 65802

ROUTE 66 VISITOR CENTER – 815 E. St. Louis St., Springfield, MO 65806

HISTORY MUSEUM ON THE SQUARE – 154 Park Central Square, Springfield, MO 65806

HAMMONS FIELD – 955 E. Trafficway St., Springfield, MO 65802

STEAK 'N SHAKE – 1158 E. St. Louis St., Springfield, MO 65806

JORDAN VALLEY ICE PARK – 635 E. Trafficway St., Springfield, MO 65806

GILLIOZ THEATRE – 325 Park Central E., Springfield, MO 65806

MISSOURI SPORTS HALL OF FAME – 3861 E. Stan Musial Drive, Springfield, MO 65809

JASPER COUNTY COURTHOUSE – 301 Grant St., Carthage, MO 64836

CARTHAGE HIGH SCHOOL – 2600 S. River St., Carthage, MO 64836

FAIR ACRES SPORTS COMPLEX – 770 E. George E. Phelps Blvd., Carthage, MO 64836

CARTHAGE CHAMBER OF COMMERCE – 402 S. Garrison Ave., Carthage, MO 64836

BOOTS COURT MOTEL – 107 S. Garrison Ave., Carthage, MO 64836

POWERS MUSEUM – 1617 Oak St., Carthage, MO 64836

CARTHAGE MUNICIPAL PARK – 521 Robert Ellis Young Drive, Carthage, MO 64836

CARTHAGE GOLF COURSE – 2000 Richard Webster Drive, Carthage, MO 64836

66 DRIVE-IN THEATRE – 17231 Old 66 Blvd., Carthage, MO 64836

WEBB CITY HIGH SCHOOL – 621 N. Madison St., Webb City, MO 64870

JOE BECKER MEMORIAL STADIUM – 300 S. High St., Joplin, MO 64801

MISSOURI SOUTHERN STATE UNIVERSITY – 3950 Newman Road, Joplin, MO 64801

LEGGETT & PLATT ATHLETIC CENTER – 3 Lion Pride Lane, Joplin, MO 64801

JOPLIN HIGH SCHOOL – 2104 S. Indiana Ave., Joplin, MO 64804

DEWEY COMBS ATHLETIC COMPLEX AT JUNGE FIELD – 800 Junge Blvd., Joplin, MO 64801

TWIN HILLS GOLF & COUNTRY CLUB – 2019 S. Country Club Drive, Joplin, MO 64804

SCHIFFERDECKER PARK – W. 4th St., Joplin, MO 64801

KANSAS

The Kansas portion of Route 66 consists of a 13-mile stretch off the interstate and through the small towns of Galena, Riverton, and Baxter Springs. All three Kansas towns were instrumental in the development of characters for the 2006 Disney Pixar film Cars and have high schools with competitive teams—especially on the diamond.

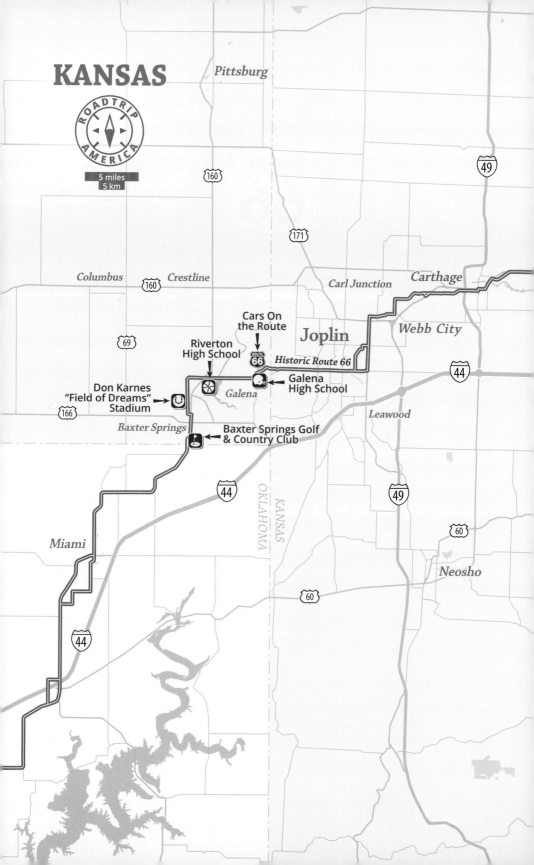

KANSAS

ROADTRIP AMERICA

5 miles
5 km

Pittsburg

49

160

171

Columbus   160   *Crestline*

Carl Junction   **Carthage**

69

Cars On
the Route

Joplin   *Webb City*

Riverton
High School

ROUTE 66   *Historic Route 66*   44

Galena
High School

Don Karnes
"Field of Dreams"
Stadium   *Galena*

166

Leawood

Baxter Springs   Baxter Springs Golf
& Country Club

44   OKLAHOMA   KANSAS   49

Miami   60

Neosho

44   60

GALENA

Galena, Riverton, and Baxter Springs have mid-sized Kansas high schools that usually compete in 3A with six classifications in Kansas and are obvious geographic rivals.

The first of these towns from east to west is Galena, which claims to be the oldest mining town in Kansas. The town of Galena was founded in 1877, and **Galena High School** was established some years later. Galena is famous for its "**Cars on the Route**," located at the historic Kan-O-Tex service station and home to the 1951 International tow truck which purportedly inspired the character "Tow Mater" in the Pixar film *Cars*.

The Galena Bulldogs fielded their first football team in 1906 and have had mixed results on the gridiron. They had yet to win a state championship in

The 1951 International tow truck, which is part of the "Cars on the Route" attraction is thought to be the inspiration behind "Tow Mater" in the Disney Pixar animated film, Cars.

football as of 2020 but did qualify for the Kansas state playoffs 10 times between 2005 and 2019 and reached the state semifinals in 2018.

A sign as you enter town lists all of Galena High's state qualifying teams, including the baseball team's state championships in 1979 and 2010. Baseball is probably the strongest sport at Galena, which has modest facilities and includes a nice display of the athletics history in the hall outside of the gymnasium. Galena's track program is solid, consistently sending male and female athletes to the state meet.

Former MLB player George Grantham grew up in Galena, but attended Flagstaff High School—a little farther down Route 66 in Arizona—and died in Kingman, another town on the Mother Road. Grantham helped the Pittsburgh Pirates win the World Series in 1925.

RIVERTON

Riverton is the smallest of the three Kansas communities along the Mother Road, with only about 900 people. While it may be the smallest, **Riverton High School** probably has the strongest athletics department and is right next to the **Old Riverton Store**.

The Rams have won several state championships across several sports. The school's first state championship came in 1990 with a 3A football crown. They were the 4A runners-up a year later and won another 3A championship in 1993. After competing for a state title for a couple of decades, the girls' softball team finally broke through in 2009 with the first of consecutive state championships. Another softball repeat followed in 2016 and 2017.

The diamond has been kind to the Rams with a perennial contender in softball and a strong baseball program that won a state championship in 2015. The baseball field has two sets of covered bleachers down either baseline and a small press box directly behind home plate. Several large trees stand behind the press box, and a white water tower with "RIVERTON RAMS" in blue letters towers above them.

As you head west from Riverton, you'll come to a roundabout with an interesting piece of art. A group of Riverton High students created a steel

Like Galena, Riverton has a sign near the high school honoring the Rams' state championship teams.

Kansas Route 66 sculpture in 2018. The piece stands 20 feet high and is located next to an informational Route 66 kiosk. It cost about $1,000 to make, and the FFA students used scrap metal donated by the Kansas Department of Transportation.

BAXTER SPRINGS

Between Riverton and Baxter Springs is the **Rainbow Bridge**, which is a single-span arch bridge over Brush Creek. It's the only surviving bridge of its type along Route 66 and can still be traveled with one-way traffic from east to west.

Baxter Springs is the most populous Kansas town along the Double Six with more than 4,200 people. Like other small towns on Route 66, Baxter

The Baxter Springs Rainbow Bridge is a one-way drive, and the only remaining Marsh Arch Bridge on Route 66.

Springs takes pride in its place along the Mother Road. The **Baxter Springs Heritage Museum**, **Route 66 Visitors Center**, and **Decade of Wheels** museum are downtown must-sees. But before you get to downtown, you'll drive right by **Baxter Springs High School**.

A Field of Dreams for a coach, players, and the community

The Lions have the same logo design as the NFL's Detroit Lions, but in red instead of Honolulu blue. While the Baxter Springs football team reached the Kansas 4A state championship game in 1986, the Lions have had a playoff drought in recent years.

Baxter Springs has a strong baseball program and even has its own **"Field of Dreams"—Don Karnes Stadium**, which is privately owned by the stadium namesake. Located on the north end of the city and less than

2 miles south of the Rainbow Bridge, Karnes Stadium has been the home venue for Baxter Springs High since 2012.

The stadium opened in 2000 and was created out of necessity. Karnes, who coached girls' basketball and baseball before retiring in 2005 after 25 years at Baxter Springs, founded the baseball program in 1981. His teams won the first of five state championships in 1985 despite not having a home

The Baxter Springs Lions play at John Hughes Stadium, where maybe a kid named Ferris watched a game with his Uncle Buck. (It's not THAT John Hughes.)

Baxter Springs has its very own Field of Dreams in Don Karnes Stadium, named for and built by the former baseball coach at Baxter Springs High School.

field. That 1985 team began a 28-game winning streak that extended into 1986. The Karnes-led Lions added four state titles between 1991 and 2003. Karnes laid a foundation for a strong baseball tradition, and the Lions continued winning state championships after he retired, with titles in 2006, 2007, and 2016.

But in the early days of the program, Karnes waited for the school to build an on-campus stadium. From 1981 to 1999, he kept waiting. Karnes, who also coached the local American Legion baseball team during the summer, decided after the 1999 season that he was done waiting.

"We had a basketball gym and had a football stadium, but didn't have a baseball field," said Karnes, who lives next door to the stadium that bears his

name. "I told my wife, 'Let's either do something or don't ever talk about it again.'"

Karnes set up a nonprofit he called Field of Dreams and donated 12 acres to the organization. He held fundraisers and asked the community for donations, which began pouring in. As in the movie, "If you build it, they will come," and they did.

Don Karnes Stadium is an active place during the summer with youth baseball tournaments and American Legion games. Today the stadium, with its brick facade, looks nothing like it did in 2000. The statues of young players that greet visitors at the outer gate weren't there. Neither were the two large baseball sculptures flanking the entrance tunnel. New fencing was added, along with a scoreboard and covered dugouts. Each year brought with it something new.

"It's kind of like Johnny Cash's Cadillac," Karnes said. "We built it in pieces."

Baxter Springs has a rich baseball history, dating back to the Junior League Whiz Kids teams of the 1940s. From 1947 to 1949, future New York Yankees Hall of Famer Mickey Mantle played for the Whiz Kids, and one of Mantle's jerseys from his Whiz Kids days is on display at the **Little League Museum** on 14th Street.

Hit where Hale got his start

The biggest sports celebrity to come out of Baxter Springs is not a baseball player, however. PGA golfer Hale Irwin was born in Joplin but raised in Baxter Springs before his family moved to Denver during his high school years. It was in Kansas where Irwin honed his skills when he started playing golf at the age of 4. Pay tribute to Irwin by playing a round at the **Baxter Springs Golf and Country Club**, on Hale Irwin Drive, before crossing into Oklahoma. The nine-hole golf course doesn't require a tee time, and the club has a kid-friendly pool and bar. Across U.S. Highway 69 from the golf course is the **66 Sports Complex**, a grouping of youth softball and baseball fields.

As you leave the short stretch of Route 66 in Kansas, know that the home of a baseball icon is just a few miles away.

Kansas Route 66 Points of Interest

CARS ON THE ROUTE – 119 N. Main St., Galena, KS 66739

GALENA HIGH SCHOOL – 702 E. 7th St., Galena, KS 66739

RIVERTON HIGH SCHOOL – 7120 S.E. 70th St., Riverton, KS 66770

NELSON'S OLD RIVERTON STORE – 7109 KS 66, Riverton, KS 66770

DON KARNES "FIELD OF DREAMS" STADIUM – 8933 S.E. 50th St., Baxter Springs, KS 66713

RAINBOW BRIDGE – S.E. Beasley Road, Baxter Springs, KS 66713

BAXTER SPRINGS HERITAGE MUSEUM – 740 East Ave., Baxter Springs, KS 66713

BAXTER SPRINGS HIGH SCHOOL – 100 N. Military Ave., Baxter Springs, KS 66713

ROUTE 66 VISITORS CENTER – 940 Military Ave., Baxter Springs, KS 66713

DECADE OF WHEELS – 1111 Military Ave., Baxter Springs, KS 66713

LITTLE LEAGUE BASEBALL MUSEUM – 1408 Lincoln Ave., Baxter Springs, KS 66713

BAXTER SPRINGS GOLF AND COUNTRY CLUB – 501 Hale Irwin Drive, Baxter Springs, KS 66713

66 SPORTS COMPLEX – 650 W. 30th St., Baxter Springs, KS 66713

OKLAHOMA

Oklahoma has been home to many sports legends, several of whom have their roots on Route 66. Towns along the Mother Road boast baseball hall of famers, football stars, Olympic medalists, and one athlete who won the most enduring foot race of all time. Oklahoma is also home to an NBA team, a Triple-A baseball club, and surprisingly thriving rugby and rowing scenes.

COMMERCE

After driving through the small town of Quapaw, which has numerous Route 66 murals, continue south on Highway 69 to reach the city of Commerce. Just a block off Route 66 in Commerce is a small white house nestled in a quiet neighborhood. No one lives in the home, but a plaque on the exterior wall near the door explains the home's significance. It is the house in which Yankees Hall of Famer Mickey Mantle was raised. The **Mantle boyhood home**, with a cracked foundation and peeling paint on its wood siding, isn't much to look at, but it's where Mantle spent his formative years and fell in love with baseball. The Commerce portion of Route 66 is named Mickey Mantle Boulevard.

In the backyard of the Quincy Street home is where Mantle, who lived there for 10 years, learned how to switch-hit from his father and grandfather. Behind the home is a tin garage that Mantle used during his after-school hitting lessons. Dents from balls hit by Mantle against the now-rusted structure remain today. Some of the baseballs struck by the young Mantle would carom off the family home or other houses, but Mantle later joked that he "was the only kid in town that didn't get in trouble for breaking a window."

Mantle's boyhood home is one of Commerce's best-known Route 66 stops, along with the **Dairy King** and **Allen's "Hole in the Wall" Conoco Station** on Main Street. Just a five-minute walk from the Mantle house is **Commerce High School**, where a statue of Mantle stands beyond the outfield fence at the baseball stadium.

The 9-foot statue, atop a 5-foot pedestal, is easily accessible with its own small parking lot and a walking path to its diamond-shaped plot. Inscribed on either side of the pedestal are Mantle's full name—Mickey Charles Mantle—with "Great teammate" beneath it and what would become his nickname, "The Commerce Comet," and "CHS class of '49." Mantle's number 7 is outlined in white on the concrete pad.

Despite Mantle's nickname, the Commerce High sports teams are not called the Comets; they are the Tigers. The baseball stadium is, of course, **Mickey Mantle Field**, and his number 7 is next to the venue name atop the digital outfield scoreboard. The stadium was named after Mantle in 2001 and has hosted the **Mickey Mantle Classic Wooden Bat Tournament** nearly every April since. High school teams from Oklahoma, Kansas, and Missouri participate, and the batters use only wooden bats, just as Mantle did when he was in high school. The tournament has drawn celebrity guests like Baseball Hall of Famers: Goose Gossage, Ferguson Jenkins, Juan Marichal, Rollie Fingers, Gaylord Perry, Andre Dawson, and Brett Saberhagen.

New York Yankees legend Mickey Mantle learned how to become a switch-hitter while in Commerce. Below: Mickey Mantle's boyhood home isn't much to look at, but its back yard is where he honed his baseball skills.

Commerce's own baseball program has had just one state playoff appearance, as of 2020, and that was in 1973. The April baseball tournament is the draw, with an opportunity to see the Mantle statue and maybe get an autograph from that year's big-league visitor.

Mantle also played football for the Tigers, and the pigskin program is strong at Commerce. Although Commerce has never won a state championship game, it made the state playoffs every year from 2001 to 2020 and reached the state championship game in 1978. **Tiger Field** is also home to the track-and-field teams that have claimed multiple individual boys' and girls' championships since 1974.

Like Mantle, former PGA golfer Bo Wininger played football and baseball at Commerce. He then attended Oklahoma State University before turning pro in 1952. Wininger even played himself in a 1964 episode of *I Love Lucy* titled "Lucy Takes Up Golf."

MIAMI

The small municipality of North Miami bridges Commerce with Miami, but the two Ottawa County towns sort of run together along this Route 66 stretch of U.S. Highway 69. Miami (pronounced my-AM-uh) is the seat of Ottawa County and the tribal capital of the namesake Miami Indians, as well as the Modoc, Ottawa, Peoria, and Shawnee tribes.

Miami has several Route 66 attractions with the historic **Coleman Theatre**, the **George Coleman House**, **the Dobson Museum**, and the ever-popular **Waylan's Ku-Ku Burger**. Miami is also home to one of the more unique high school nicknames in the country.

Miami High Wardogs

Like the Joliet Central Steelmen in Illinois, **Miami High School** has a mascot no other school in the country has adopted—the Wardog. Miami's first graduating class was in 1900, and the Wardogs have had a storied sports tradition. They won state championships in boys' basketball (1972) and baseball (1987) and multiple golf titles. Both the boys' and girls' basketball teams have qualified for the state playoffs several times since 1917, and the baseball program has been a regular playoff participant since its first appearance in 1959. The 1971–72 boys' basketball team, led by coach Don Overton, was one of the most dominant squads the Sooner State has ever seen on the court. The Wardogs were a perfect 27–0 with an average margin of victory of 27 points.

Even though the school has experienced a playoff drought from 2009 to 2020, Miami had been a postseason regular. And just as Commerce has Mickey Mantle, Miami has its own homegrown star with former Wardogs football player Steve Owens.

Owens was the 1969 Heisman Trophy winner at the University of Oklahoma before spending five seasons in the NFL with the Detroit Lions. His brother, Charles—nicknamed "Tinker"—was a two-time All-American at Oklahoma before a five-year NFL career with the New Orleans Saints. Tinker was also a member of that undefeated basketball team.

Football pros begin careers at Northeast Oklahoma

The Wardogs play their home football games at **Red Robertson Field**, an 8,500-seat stadium they share with **Northeast Oklahoma (NEO) A&M College**. NEO is a two-year school but has an excellent football program that has sent multiple alumni to four-year schools and eventually the NFL.

The most notable former NEO player is tight end Jeremy Shockey, an Ada, Oklahoma, native who was a junior college (JuCo) All-American before starring for the University of Miami (Fla.) Hurricanes. The 'Canes won the 2001 national championship, and Shockey was a first-team All-American. He was then selected in the first round of the 2002 NFL Draft by the New York Giants. Shockey was a four-time Pro Bowler and helped the Giants win Super Bowl XLII following the 2007 season. He won another Super Bowl two years later with the New Orleans Saints. A Saints teammate of Shockey's in 2009 was Remi Ayodele, who also played at NEO. Other NEO alumni who played in the NFL are six-time Pro Bowl linebacker Matt Blair, two-time Pro Bowl running back Marion Butts, three-time Pro Bowl defensive tackle Pat Williams, and two-time Pro Bowl receiver Ernest Givins.

Norsemen baseball is also strong and has produced multiple MLB players, most notably 1997 All-Star Jason Dickson.

Depending on the time of year you're traveling down Route 66, you may want to see at game at NEO. You never know which future star you may be watching.

AFTON

Afton High School is about a half mile south from the closed Afton Station and less than a mile from the **Nowhere on Route 66** restaurant.

Home to the orange-and-white Eagles, Afton's sports teams are usually competitive among Oklahoma's small schools. The football team has been the most consistent, but a state championship eluded the Eagles until 2017.

After going 12–1 and reaching the state semifinals in 2016, the 2017 Eagles won a Class A state championship with a perfect 14–0 campaign. It was the first state title in any sport for Afton, and when the team returned home, they were greeted at the school by 150 fans—15 percent of Afton's population.

The thing about sports at small-town schools is that they have outstanding support from the community, so basically the entire population of 1,000 comes out to watch their Eagles play. When the student sections get going with chants or choreographed antics, it really is a lot of fun to watch a high school game. That's true at Afton, as well as many of the other small-town schools along Route 66. If you want to discover things about the communities on Route 66 that you may not read in a book, attend a high school game and talk to your fellow spectators.

VINITA AND CHELSEA

Route 66 merges with U.S. Highways 60 and 69 on the west side of Vinita, the hometown of 1972 Olympian Jeff Bennett. The highways split just east of White Oak as Oklahoma Highway 66 begins and carries travelers to the town of Chelsea. Originally a stop on the Atlantic and Pacific Railroad line, Chelsea is mildly famous for being home to Gene Autry while he was a railroad telegraph operator. It was first incorporated as a Cherokee Nation town in 1889, the same year an oil field was discovered nearby. The oil field ran dry by 1916, and Chelsea never got the economic or population boom that was expected. Today, Chelsea is a town of 1,900 people and a literal turning point for Route 66.

The Mother Road turns south at the **Chelsea Motor Inn**, one of three Chelsea structures listed on the National Register of Historic Places. **Chelsea High School** is a few blocks west of the motel at the corner of Sixth and Park Streets. Chelsea's athletic fields are located north of the school along Park.

Chelsea's Green Dragons have been consistently strong in football and are regulars in Oklahoma's 2A state playoffs.

The best athlete to come out of Chelsea High is Ralph Terry, who was the MVP of the 1962 World Series for the Yankees. Terry graduated from Chelsea High before going on to play baseball at Missouri State. Chelsea's baseball team was solid between 1949 and 1963—a span that included Terry's time at the school. The Dragons haven't been as good in recent years but are still competitive against other small-school teams.

Less than 9 miles down the road, you'll find yourself in the hometown of a running legend.

FOYIL

The 1928 International Transcontinental Foot Race was a grueling 3,400-mile run from Los Angeles to New York, traversing Route 66 to Chicago before heading east to the Empire State. As author Andrew Speno noted in his book *The Great American Foot Race*, event organizer Charles Cassius (C. C.) Pyle said the runners would take part in "the greatest, most stupendous athletic accomplishment in all history."

The ballyhooed race was the brainchild of Pyle, who worked with Cyrus Avery, the father of Route 66, to make it happen. Pyle, who was the agent for early NFL star Red Grange, was a master sports promoter and wanted his own NFL team. When the fledgling league rejected his application in 1926, Pyle formed the first American Football League, but that folded after one season. Pyle, whose nickname was "Cash and Carry," took on a couple of professional tennis clients, but was always in search of "the next big thing." That next big thing was the transcontinental foot race.

The race attracted 199 runners from 20 countries and 30 states and averaged 40 miles a day for nearly three months in what became known as the Bunion Derby. The entry fee was $125, and the racers competed for a total prize purse of $48,500 with $25,000 to the winner. Foyil's very own Andy Payne outlasted veteran marathon champions and international stars to go home with the top prize.

Payne is honored in his hometown with a street and statue. **Andy Payne Boulevard** breaks off from Highway 66 just past **Annie's Diner**. The short loop reconnects with the highway near a small park that features the statue of Payne, who is captured in a running motion atop a small pedestal with a plaque that describes his achievements.

Payne was just 20 years old when the race began on March 4. As the derby went through Foyil, Payne picked up his pace and was greeted by large crowds cheering on their favorite son. He ran at an average pace of 6 miles per hour for 84 days to finish the run in

A statue of Andy Payne, a Foyil native who won the inaugural 1928 "Bunion Derby" is on the west side of Foyil.

573 hours, 4 minutes, and 34 seconds. Payne used the cash prize of $25,000 to pay off the mortgage on his father's farm. Payne never achieved any more fame as an athlete. Instead, he served in the U.S. Army and then was the clerk of the Oklahoma Supreme Court for 56 years.

Payne was a graduate of **Foyil High School**, which is a couple of miles south of the statue. The Panthers have had a few individual state champions in track, and the baseball and both boys' and girls' basketball teams have made state playoff appearances. The football team is also a regular playoff participant. Foyil missed the playoffs just three times between 1989 and 2011. They were back in the postseason hunt in 2018.

CLAREMORE

One of Route 66's nicknames is the Will Rogers Highway, and Claremore is the hometown of the famous vaudeville cowboy. Rogers, a friend of Andy Payne's father, was also supportive and proud of Payne's victorious run across the country. Claremore has often been associated with show business. The Rodgers and Hammerstein musical *Oklahoma!* is set in the Claremore area. *Where The Heart Is,* a 2000 movie starring Natalie Portman and Ashley Judd, takes place in Rogers County. Even a 1991 episode of the television show *Quantum Leap* takes place in Claremore. There is also plenty going on for sports fans.

Claremore is home to a pair of high schools 5 miles apart along Route 66, an NCAA Division II university, a lake perfect for bass fishing, and a pair of golf courses a stone's throw from the Mother Road.

Lakeside attractions

As you venture south toward Claremore, you'll pass **Sequoyah High School**, which has been in the same location since 1908 and has state championships in girls' basketball (1999) and football (2006). The route also takes you by **Claremore Soccer Club**, a youth soccer complex located just west of **Claremore Lake**. The lake covers 470 acres and is a popular fishing hole. A daily fishing permit at the manmade reservoir is just $3, and annual permits are only 10 bucks. Swimming is not allowed in the lake, but there is a pool at one of the nearby parks. Those parks also house a nine-hole disc golf course, a bike trail, and various hiking trails. If you want to make a day of it, grab one of the many picnic tables and grills, and cook the bass you just caught for that evening's dinner.

The **Will Rogers Stampede Arena** is also next to the lake. The arena is home to the Will Rogers Stampede Rodeo, which was first held in 1942 and has been recognized as the top rodeo in the nation five times by the Professional Rodeo Cowboys Association. Held every May, the Will Rogers rodeo features four nights of entertainment before some of the country's best rodeo cowboys and cowgirls compete in bronco riding, barrel racing, and bull riding.

Claremore High's cool turf

A different sort of equid is down the road at **Claremore High School**, where the sports teams are called the Zebras.

Claremore has won 23 state championships (through 2020) across various sports. The majority of those have been on the diamond. The baseball team won four titles from 1993 to 2005, and the fast-pitch softball team won another five from 1994 to 2003. Zebras baseball, which produced former MLB player Dave Rader, continues to be one of Claremore's most consistent programs, along with the girls' basketball and football teams. All three teams compete at the 5A level and are usually a playoff contender in any given season.

Claremore's gym is a college-like arena with 360-degree seating. A small section of balcony bleachers are above the baselines, while stadium seats run the sidelines. A four-sided scoreboard hangs above the court.

While the Claremore gym is nice, what everyone should see is the football field—not necessarily the 5,300-seat stadium, but the field itself. When Claremore installed AstroTurf in 2019, administrators wanted to make sure it stood out. At midfield, the word "Zebras" is scrawled in bright red letters across 26 yards. Claremore's colors aren't black and white like a zebra's, but red and white, and the end zones at **Lantow Field** sport bright red and white zebra stripes. MaxPreps recognized Lantow Field in 2019 as one of the top 10 turf fields in the United States.

Recognizing a hometown star

Claremore is also home to **Rogers State University**, a D-II school located on the west side of town next to the **Will Rogers Memorial Museum**. The RSU Hillcats didn't start their athletics program until 2005 and have built nationally ranked softball and men's basketball programs. RSU added both a men's and women's golf team in 2009, and those teams use nearby **Heritage Hills Golf Course** to practice but travel 16 miles west to host the Hillcat Classic in mid-March at the Bailey Ranch Gold Club in Owasso.

Will Rogers was and still is a big deal in Claremore, and there also is a horse track named for him. The Cherokee Nation-run **Will Rogers Downs** has a 2,700-seat grandstand for spectators to watch Thoroughbreds in the spring and Quarter Horses in the fall in addition to Appaloosa and Paint Horse races on the mile-long track. The attached casino has 250 electronic gaming machines, and the complex includes Oklahoma's largest RV park.

Another golf course lies 2.5 miles east of Route 66 between Claremore and Catoosa. The **Gordon Golf Course** is a quiet but challenging 1,581-yard nine-hole course that opened in 1993. Bermuda grass greens added in 2018 give Gordon some of the best putting surfaces in the state.

CATOOSA

Come for the whale, stay for the Indians. You can't miss the **Blue Whale of Catoosa** on Route 66. It's been one of the most popular Route 66 attractions ever since it was built in 1972 by Hugh Davis, who constructed it as an anniversary gift for his wife, Zelta. The smiling 80-foot sperm whale is in the middle of a spring-fed pond and was the centerpiece of a small zoo

The Catoosa Blue Whale has been a popular Route 66 stop since 1972.

called Nature's Acres, which included the Animal Reptile Kingdom—or ARK. The attraction fell into disrepair as the Davises aged, and it closed in 1988. A community fundraiser was held in 2011 to fund a fresh paint job for the whale, patch its holes, and reopen a small gift shop. Although swimming is no longer allowed at the pond, visitors can walk through the whale's open mouth and imagine sliding down its side into the water. The nearby Verdigris River is popular with fishermen, who cast their lines from **Rogers Point Park**.

Three miles down the road from the Blue Whale is **Catoosa High School**. The school building sports a banner that reads, "Importing potential, exporting excellence." The Catoosa Indians have an excellent wrestling program with team state championships in 1982 and consecutively from 2006 to 2008.

Catoosa also has state championships in soccer, with the girls claiming the 4A crown in 1996 and the boys taking the title in 2004. There have also been several individual state champs in track-and-field events. Catoosa's football program has been consistently solid, especially since dropping from 5A to 4A in 2008. The Indians made the playoffs every season from 2009 to 2018. **Frank McNabb Field** is modest by Oklahoma high school football standards but still has a capacity of 5,200.

On the other side of Route 66, just before the Mother Road merges with Interstate 44, is **Cherokee Hills Golf Club at the Hard Rock Hotel and Casino Tulsa**. Cherokee Hills, which opened in 1924, is one of the oldest and best golf courses in Oklahoma. With tree-lined fairways, varied elevation, several streams, and natural rock outcroppings, the course is "a true challenge for the most accomplished golfer, while inviting enough for the weekend player," according to the Cherokee Hills website.

TULSA

After Illinois State, Saint Louis, and Missouri State, the next NCAA Division I university on Route 66 is the **University of Tulsa**, which is one of just three D-I schools on the Double Six that compete at the top Football Bowl Subdivision (FBS) level. The Golden Hurricane (yes, that's correct; it's not plural) play in one of the oldest college football venues in the country. The facade of **Skelly Field at H. A. Chapman Stadium** faces 11th Street, also known as Route 66, and is 1 mile west of **Tally's Cafe**.

"We identify ourselves as the city's team, and obviously Route 66 has a lot to do with that," said Derrick Gragg, Tulsa's athletics director. "We want to endear ourselves to the city … There are a lot of Oklahoma and Oklahoma

The Tulsa Golden Hurricane have a Division I FBS program that is a member of the American Athletic Conference. Below: No matter the result on the field, the Tulsa students are always energetic.

State fans here, but we're the only one with Tulsa in our name. For us, it's important to identify with the city and Route 66. It's a historical thing and a big deal."

The first game played at Chapman Stadium was a 26–6 Tulsa victory over Arkansas on Oct. 4, 1930. That game drew 13,000 fans into a stadium that then had a capacity of 14,500. Chapman Stadium has since been expanded to seat more than 45,000 and held a record crowd of 47,350 on Sept. 26, 1987, when top-ranked Oklahoma rolled to a 65–0 victory.

Tulsa's football program has been up-and-down. After going 10–3 and beating Central Michigan in the 2016 Miami Beach Bowl, the Golden Hurricane had three consecutive losing seasons. The result has been poor fan attendance, but the student section above the visitors' sideline is always energetic.

Over the years, Tulsa has sent several players to the NFL—including Hall of Famers Bob St. Clair and Steve Largent. They are among the NFL players recognized in a display inside the **Case Athletic Complex** at the north end zone.

"We go up to several games every year, and my boys are old enough now to notice that kind of stuff," said former Tulsa and NFL player Chris

Chapman Stadium at the University of Tulsa is one of the oldest football stadiums in the country.

Chamberlain, who grew up in Bethany. "There's a stairwell with a big mural on the wall. It's got myself and some other players who have made it to the NFL. It's fun to show my boys that and enjoy it with them."

The Case building houses the football offices, home locker room and weight room. The third floor has a large banquet hall with huge windows to provide alumni and their guests an end zone view of the field. The grandstand houses the press box, 13 suites, and a club level with buffets and full bars. You can watch a Tulsa game in the luxury of a suite or the club, or snag a cheap seat near the student section.

Regulars at the Dance

The Golden Hurricane also have a proud basketball tradition, and the program has produced several NBA players. The 2019–20 men's team was co-champion of the American Athletic Conference but could not compete for a national championship because of the cancellation of the NCAA Tournament. But Tulsa has done plenty of dancing during March Madness. Tulsa punched its ticket to the Big Dance 16 times before the 2019–20 season. Tulsa has advanced to the Sweet Sixteen four times, and reached the Elite Eight in 2000. Tulsa won the National Invitation Tournament (NIT) in 1981 and 2001. The Golden Hurricane also won the 2008 College Basketball Invitational.

The Golden Hurricane basketball and volleyball teams play at the **Reynolds Center**, which is adjacent to Chapman Stadium. The quaint 8,355-seat arena opened in 1998, and Tulsa's basketball team regularly drew more than 8,200 fans for the next five years. Tulsa had just two losing seasons between 2005 and 2020, and you will almost always find a near-sellout crowd for a Tulsa basketball game because of its strong tradition. The Tulsa women have twice qualified for the NCAA tourney, in 2006 and 2013.

Golf for pros and amateurs

Tulsa has one national championship, and that came in 1982 when the women's golf team won it all. Tulsa eliminated men's golf in 2016, but the women continue with a solid program that practices and plays on several Tulsa-area courses—including the **Tulsa Country Club** and **Southern Hills Country Club**. World Golf Hall of Famer Nancy Lopez was an All-American at Tulsa in 1976 and 1977 before turning pro. Lopez is one of several former Tulsa golfers who went on to compete on the LPGA tour.

Before or after Tulsa football or basketball games, a visit to the **Mother Road Market** is a must. In addition to the wide variety of eating and drinking options, Mother Road has a nine-hole mini-golf course on its back patio. The small course features Route 66 attractions like the Gateway Arch, Chicago's Willis (Sears) Tower, Ed Galloway's Totem Pole Park, the Round Barn of Arcadia, and the Santa Monica Pier.

Ropers from Will Rogers High

Will Rogers High School abuts the east side of the University of Tulsa campus. The beautiful three-story Art Deco building is home to the Ropers, a perfect homage to the late cowboy. The school was built in 1939 and added to the National Register of Historic Places in 2007 with the National Park Service citing it as one of the best examples of Art Deco architecture in the country.

Mother Road Market has a plethora of eating and shopping establishments, plus a large bar at which to hang out and watch a game.

The Ropers have sporadically made the state playoffs over the years and produced multiple professional athletes. Baseball and boys' basketball have been the school's most consistent programs. The baseball team won five state championships between 1954 and 1979, and boys' basketball had four state titles between 1941 and 1988. Rogers High's boys' track and cross-country teams also had early success with five state titles apiece in the 1940s and '50s.

The Ropers football team played for a state title in both 1945 and 1964. Should they play in the championship game again, they wouldn't have to go far. Chapman Stadium hosts the Oklahoma Secondary School Activities Association (OSSAA) football state championships, and two teams that have played for the large-school championship most often are right in Tulsa.

Competition on and off the fields, stadiums, and arenas

Jenks High School and **Union High School** are two of the biggest high schools in Oklahoma, along with Owasso and Broken Arrow. "The Big Four" are consistently competing with one another for the best facilities in the state. When one school adds a Jumbotron, the others add one as well. When one school builds a new basketball arena, the others respond in kind. Teams have designated rooms for film study, and schools keep doctors on staff to treat injuries. Each of "The Big Four" is a public school with overwhelming community support. It's a sense of pride for each school district to have the biggest and best facilities in the state.

"You usually want to be the last one when it comes to video boards because everyone wants to make sure theirs is a little bit bigger," Jenks athletics director Tony Dillingham quipped. "It's like a brotherhood. It's OK if we beat up on each other, but we really don't want anyone else beating us."

The Jenks and Union football rivalry, known as the Backyard Bowl, is one of the best in the country. The two schools have won a combined 25 state titles (Jenks 17, Union 8) and played each other in the championship game 10 times through 2020. From 1996 through 2016, either Jenks or Union won the 6A-I state championship. When Jenks and Union face off during the regular season, the game is usually at Chapman Stadium and draws between 25,000 and 40,000 fans.

"I don't know of a greater high school football rivalry," said Union athletics director Emily Barkley, a Union High and University of Tulsa graduate. "We shared the football championship for 21 years. When I was in school, they were beating us and we could never get over the hump, but once we did, the rivalry evolved from a hated rivalry to a mutual respect. If we don't win, we want them to."

Seeing a game at either Jenks or Union is like attending a game at a Division I university. Some of their football games are nationally televised, and NFL Films featured the rivalry in a 2007 documentary.

The schools' facilities are usually accompanied by equally superb teams. Jenks sports teams won a total of 182 OSSAA state championships from 1972, when the school opened, through 2020. Union "only" has 72 total state championships, with baseball right behind the football program at seven titles. Both schools have sent several players to Division I schools and a few to the NFL.

Aside from football, the most successful Jenks programs have been cross-country, with the boys and girls claiming 15 titles apiece; golf, as the girls have 14 championships to 8 for the boys; swimming (boys, 18; girls, 12), and tennis (girls, 19; boys, 14). No matter the sport, Jenks has managed to build dynasties that span decades. Should Jenks ever run out of room on the walls of the athletics offices for the large photos of their state championship teams, assistant AD Jason Culler joked the school would just "build a new building."

"It's not just football. If we were playing jacks, if it's Jenks-Union, I could make money at the gate," said Dillingham, whose office overlooks the field at **Allan Trimble Stadium**. The 9,000-seat stadium is named for the longtime football coach who won 13 state titles over 22 years and died in 2019 after a battle with ALS. Trimble's tenure included four undefeated seasons, a 39-game win streak from 1999 to 2002, and six straight state championships from 1996 to 2001.

Like Jenks, the Union athletics offices are housed in a three-story building at one end of the football stadium. Union began renovations at its stadium in 2019. Those included an elevator to carry game-day workers, media members, and assistant coaches to a press box that was expanded to include a suite at one end and a covered camera deck above it.

The stadium already included a high-definition scoreboard to show replays—yes, replays at a high school football game. Timeouts and replays are sponsored by Route 66 Chevrolet.

Union's 6,000-seat basketball arena isn't just for Redskins home games. It regularly hosts dance competitions, various basketball and volleyball tournaments, and the Mid-America Intercollegiate Athletics Association (MIAA) basketball tournament. Jenks and Union also co-host an annual December basketball tournament, with games split between the two arenas.

Each athletics team, including the dance and cheerleading squads, at Union and Jenks has its own space. And the facilities are all top of the line. The indoor golf facilities boast cameras to review swings and virtual courses on which to play. The aquatics center at Jenks has hosted sectional Olympic swim trials.

While the Jenks gym isn't quite as large, **Frank Herald Field House** still seats more than 3,700. A digital scoreboard is affixed to wood paneling between cursive lettering that spells out "Jenks Trojans" above the entrance to an open gathering space. And, of course, the gym walls are lined with

The Tulsa Rising sculpture at the traffic circle at Mingo Road and Admiral Place was completed in 2018.

state championship banners.

If you're unfamiliar with the fanaticism of high school football in the United States, attending a Jenks or Union game—ideally when they're playing each other—would be an enlightening experience. Jenks coach Keith Riggs described the atmosphere as amazing with a "wow" factor. Both Riggs and Union coach Kirk Fridrich said the games are so much fun because every play is celebrated.

Roundball excellence at Tulsa Memorial High

On the way to Union, you may pass **LaFortune Park**, which holds the **Case Tennis Center** and three golf courses. LaFortune Park has a par-3 course as well as two 18-hole championship-level courses. The latter courses are affordable yet challenging with numerous water hazards and sand bunkers and bent grass greens. The tennis center has three indoor and 21 outdoor courts used for a variety of tournaments and recreational play. The park also includes **LaFortune Stadium**, home to the **Tulsa Memorial High School** Chargers.

While the football team that uses LaFortune Stadium is regularly competitive and won a 4A state championship in 1980, basketball is THE sport at Memorial. Of Memorial's 16 state championships through 2020, nine of them were won by the boys' basketball team—including three straight from 2017 to 2019. Those championship added to the consecutive titles won by the Chargers in 2013 and '14. Between 2000 and 2020, Memorial's seven state titles were the most by any school at the 5A or 6A level.

One of Tulsa's many Mother Road attractions is the **Route 66 Historical Village** on Southwest Boulevard. The village complex includes a short passenger train with a caboose next to an oil derrick and the Route 66 Village Station, a small building modeled after a cottage-style Phillips 66 gas station.

Directly across the street from the village is **Daniel Webster High School**, a Depression-era Art Deco beauty on a picturesque campus that skirts Southwest Boulevard.

Baseball's the game at Bishop Kelly High

Years before Dallas Keuchel won the 2015 American League Cy Young Award, he was a standout athlete at **Bishop Kelley High School** on Skelly Drive right off of I-44. Not surprisingly, baseball is one of the strongest sports at Bishop Kelley. The Comets won six state championships between 1976 and 2020, the last of which came in 2018. Keuchel led the Comets to a state championship in 2006. Keuchel also played football at Kelley and had his team in the playoffs every year. Kelley won its lone football championship in 1981. The Comets have won multiple state championships in several sports, and Keuchel is just one of many professional athletes groomed at Kelley.

Everything's grand at ONEOK Field

While the Tulsa Driller statue is located at the **Tulsa State Fair** on 21st Street, 10 blocks south of Route 66, the Tulsa Drillers baseball team plays 6 miles from the statue at **ONEOK Field**.

The Drillers are the Double-A affiliate of the Los Angeles Dodgers, an organization that has each level of its system along Route 66. The Dodgers' Single-A team is in Rancho Cucamonga, California; Double-A in Tulsa; Triple-A in Oklahoma City; and then Dodger Stadium in Los Angeles.

ONEOK Field is in the historic Greenwood District, an area chock-full of bars and restaurants. A large sports bar called **Elgin Park** is directly across the street from the main entrance to ONEOK Field. The Greenwood District abuts the famed **Blue Dome District** that also has several eating and drinking establishments as well as the very cool **"Center of the Universe"**—an acoustic

Tulsa's iconic "Golden Driller" is located at the Tulsa State Fair on 21st Street.

anomaly that acts as a sort of amplified echo chamber.

The 7,800-seat ONEOK Field is easily navigable with wide concourses and an outstanding view of downtown Tulsa. FC Tulsa, founded in 2013 as the Tulsa Roughnecks Football Club, is the other resident of ONEOK Field. The team competes in the United Soccer League Championship, a second-tier league under the Major League Soccer hierarchy.

Rugby finds fans in Tulsa

Tulsa also has a surprisingly robust rugby scene with **Tulsa Rugby FC**. Established in 1974, the men's and women's teams are part of the Mid-America Geographical Rugby Football Union and compete in the Frontier Conference of USA Rugby Division II. The men were crowned Western champions in 2007, '08, '11, and '13. The club's home pitch since 1982 is at 37th Street and Riverside Drive on the east side of the Arkansas River near the **Gathering Place**. Matches draw up to 500 fans in the spring.

Club president Luke Turner, who is also a Tulsa firefighter, said the popularity of rugby in the area coincided with the rise of the sport in the United States. When high schools started to add rugby clubs in the 1990s, it grew even more. But the players are still amateurs—or semi-pro if you're being kind—though a few professional players have come out of the program. Chance Wenglewski is on the U.S. National Team, and Tulsa Rugby alum Malon Al-Jiboori is on the Olympic 7s team. Former Tulsa player Neariah Persinger competes for the U.S. women's club.

Racing along Route 66

Another big draw in Tulsa is the **Route 66 Marathon** that has taken place every November since 2005. The race begins on First Street and ends in downtown Tulsa with various sections of Route 66 in between. Tulsa's Route 66 Marathon is also the world's shortest "ultra-marathon." An ultra-marathon is any run more than 26.2 miles. A detour to the "Center of the Universe" makes the run 26.5 miles. Taking the detour gets the runner a coin and a beer. Tulsa's Route 66 Marathon is mostly fun, but it is competitive as a Boston Marathon qualifier and draws more than 11,000 participants annually, including those who just do the 5K run.

Spectators can enjoy adult beverages, food, and ubiquitous jello shots while watching the runners, who also get to experience live music at various stages set up along the route.

"We're known for really good crowd support and lots of alcohol," marathon director Tim Drieling said. "The party during the race is almost as good as the party at the end."

Honoring the Route 66 visionary

Tulsa takes a lot of pride in its historical significance along Route 66. Another must-see for travelers is the **Cyrus Avery Centennial Plaza** on Southwest Boulevard. Avery was a farmer, real estate agent, oil businessman and insurance agent who also served as Oklahoma's highway commissioner. Avery was the first to suggest a paved highway from Chicago to Los Angeles through Illinois, Missouri, Oklahoma, Texas, New Mexico, Arizona, and California. The southern route avoided the highest peaks of the Rocky Mountains.

Waist-high monoliths and flags for every state surround large statues depicting travelers in a horse-drawn carriage and car to show the evolution of travel down the historic byway. A pedestrian bridge that features the Route 66 shield on either side connects the plaza with a parking lot across the boulevard.

SAPULPA

There are several "world's largest" items along the Mother Road, and the world's tallest fuel pump is in Sapulpa. The 66-foot-tall structure stands in front of the **Heart of Route 66 Auto Museum**. Directly across the street from the museum and fuel pump is the 18-hole **Sapulpa Golf Course**, a 6,675-yard course that opened in 1981. The complex also has a driving range; a weekend round of golf, with a cart, can be played for under $40.

Two miles up the road from the museum and golf course is **Sapulpa High School**. The school is right off the Mother Road and 1 mile east of the **"Crossroads of America"** sign at the corner of Main Street and Hobson Avenue.

The city of Sapulpa is named for a Lower Creek Indian Chief, and its high school teams are the Chieftains, whose sports programs have won eight state titles across four sports. The basketball, wrestling, and volleyball teams use the **Chieftain Center** as their home venue.

The football team, which won a state title in 1921, qualified for the 6A playoffs seven times between 2000 and 2019. The

Sapulpa brands itself as the "Crossroads of America. Right: The world's largest fuel pump is in Sapulpa, at the Heart of Route 66 Auto Museum.

Chieftains play their home games at **George F. Collins Stadium**, named for the founder of Liberty Glass, which was once a prominent Sapulpa company. Details of Liberty Glass can be found at the **Sapulpa Historical Museum**,

Bridge #18, or the Rock Creek Bridge, can still be driven on the west side of Sapulpa.

which offers information about several of the city's buildings that are on the National Register of Historic Places.

Collins Stadium accommodate more than 4,300 spectators. A small field house is on the home side of the field, which is surrounded by a six-lane track. The blue end zones are filled with white letters that spell out "SAPULPA" on one end and "CHIEFTAINS" at the other.

Sapulpa is worth a stop, and nearby **Sahoma Lake** provides wonderful fishing opportunities. The 340-acre lake is full of bass, catfish, crappie, perch, and blue gill and has a waterfowl hunting season in autumn. Before leaving Sapulpa, be sure to drive across the historic **Rock Creek Bridge**.

KELLYVILLE TO STROUD

Once you leave Sapulpa, you're out of the Tulsa metropolitan area. The stretch between Tulsa and Oklahoma City is bucolic, with ranches and pastures interrupted by the occasional small town. The first of these is Kellyville, population 1,150.

There are a couple of sporting points of interest around Kellyville. The first is **Creek County Speedway**, a quarter-mile dirt track that opened in 1985. The track is on Route 66 between Sapulpa and Kellyville. The oval track hosts races every Saturday night from March to September, and admission is $10. While weekly events include Champ 360 Sprints, A-Modifieds, Dwarf Cars, Mini-Stocks, and Factory Stocks, the speedway also hosts The American Bank of Oklahoma American Sprint Car Series (ASCS) Red River Region, the NOW600 Micros, and the Lucas Oil ASCS National Tour.

Route 66 skirts the western edge of the town, and **Kellyville High School** is a half mile south of the highway on Maple Drive. Route 66 passes over I-44 a few miles southwest of Kellyville, going from the south side of the highway to the north before merging with Highway 48. The route then turns south toward Bristow, which claims to have more miles of brick streets than any other city in Oklahoma. While exploring those streets where Olympic wrestler Josiah Henson grew up, you'll also see several structures on the National Register of Historic Places. Founded in 1898, Bristow was originally the seat of Creek County before Sapulpa won a 1912 election to hold the county government. Once a railroad town, Bristow transitioned to the auto industry and five car-related buildings—the **Bristow Motor Company Building**, **Bristow Tire Shop**, **Beard Motor Company**, **Bristow Chrysler Plymouth**, and **Texaco Service Station**—are among those on the National Register.

Bristow High School is right between Route 66 and Interstate 44. The purple-clad Pirates have won state championships in football, girls' and boys' basketball, and boys' track. But Bristow has been a wrestling power since winning its first state championship in 1994. That year was the first of nine titles for the Pirates, who have had a slew of individual champions. The Pirates won individual titles in 7 of the 13 weight classes in 2000.

Besides wrestling, football has been Bristow's most consistent sport. Bristow missed the playoffs just once (2014) between 2010 and 2019. Aside from their three state titles, the Pirates have played in the championship game three other times and have a total of 38 postseason appearances. The team entrance is a spectacle as the players emerge from an inflatable pirate ship, complete with a purple skull-and-crossbones flag. High school football games can be a lot of fun, and the folks at Bristow High make sure they are.

The 18 miles between Bristow and Stroud will take you by the small town of Depew as Route 66 runs parallel to I-44 on its south side.

STROUD

The **Stroud High School** basketball teams play at **Route 66 Coliseum**, a 2,800-seat arena on Old U.S. 66 that opened in 2011 and uses the Route 66 shield in its sign. The blue facade with huge windows facing Route 66 is not the coliseum, though; it's the school library. The entire school complex occupies a triangular space between Old Route 66, Seventh Street, and N3570 Road. Stroud takes pride in its spot along Route 66, and the high school exemplifies that with hallways marked at "66 East" and "66 West."

The Stroud coliseum hosts the Route 66 Classic basketball tournament every January. Stroud's boys' basketball program is no slouch, with state championships in 1962 and 2002. The coliseum is on the back side of the school and is truly a gorgeous high school gym. A wide lobby leads spectators into the arena with a four-sided scoreboard above the court and stadium seating on three sides. A sign recognizing the Sac & Fox Native American Nations is atop the scoreboard. The sign includes an image of Pro Football Hall of Famer Jim Thorpe, who grew up in Stroud and is arguably the greatest athlete to ever live. Thorpe won gold medals in the pentathlon and decathlon at the 1912 Olympics, was a founding member of the National Football League, played Major League Baseball, and founded a professional basketball league for Native Americans after his baseball and football careers were over.

While the collegiate-style basketball court with its sparkling floor and

Route 66 Coliseum at Stroud High School is a 2,900-seat facility that opened in 2011.

free-standing goals is the centerpiece of the Route 66 Coliseum, like at most Oklahoma high schools, football is king at Stroud. The Tigers play at **Jack Poskey Field** and have been a postseason regular since 1945. Stroud had four state championships as of 2020 and reached the Class A quarterfinals in 2018. Poskey Field is also home to the track-and-field programs, which have produced multiple individual champions and two boys' team titles in 1993 and 1995.

After you've visited the historic **Joseph Carpenter House** and eaten at the **Rock Cafe**, stick around Stroud to see a game at the high school. You'll be glad you did. And be sure to visit one of the many wineries around Stroud before moving on toward Davenport and Chandler. You could also get in some fishing or swimming at **Stroud Lake**, 3 miles north of town.

CHANDLER

With 20 sites on the National Register of Historic Places and the very cool **Route 66 Interpretive Center**, the city of Chandler is worth some time for Route 66 travelers. The Interpretive Center has a variety of videos taken along the Double Six to watch while reclining in seats from classic cars or lying in a replica bed from one of the historic motels, all while in a former National Guard armory.

After leaving the armory, you'll see **Chandler High School** less than 2 miles down the road. The school is right off of Highway 66 and is home to the Lions, who have won multiple state championships across several sports. The Chandler Lions and Stroud Tigers are geographic rivals, and both are members of the 66 Conference.

Chandler has championships in multiple sports, but the most noteworthy is baseball. The Lions had three state titles between 1997 and 2005 and boast a former player who reached the big leagues. A standout pitcher at Chandler, Jon Gray played minor-league ball in Tulsa and Albuquerque before the Colorado Rockies called him up in 2013.

A motel dating from the glory days, beautifuly restored.

ARCADIA

Highway 66 heads west from Chandler, breaking from the I-44 corridor that takes a more southern route. You'll drive through Luther before arriving in Arcadia. While the small town no longer has a high school, Arcadia does have two must-sees along Route 66. The **Round Barn** and **Pops** are popular stops. The barn was added to the National Register of Historic Places in 1977 and has a gift shop on the first floor. The upper level, with exposed oak rafters supporting the 60-foot diameter roof, is used as an event space. The building that once housed **Tuton's Drugstore** on Main Street is also listed in the National Historic Register.

Pops opened in 2007 and was an instant hit. There are gas pumps covered by a cantilevered truss for those needing fuel. Inside is a short-order restaurant with a small seating area and more than 700 varieties of soda. Pops also offers one of the better photo opportunities along the Mother Road with the world's largest soda bottle. The bottle is composed of LED tubes made

The Round Barn is Arcadia is one of the most popular Route 66 stops.

to resemble neon lights, and the best time to visit Pops is after dark when the illumination is at full effect.

Arcadia, with a population around 250, is part of the Edmond school district. There are three public high schools, a private high school, and two universities in Edmond.

EDMOND

You can bypass Edmond and head directly to Oklahoma City by taking I-44 to I-35, but that's not recommended. Not only does Edmond have several historic sites along Route 66, like **Oklahoma's first public schoolhouse**, the **Edmond Armory**, and the **Old North Tower**, but there is a wealth of quality sports in the OKC suburb of 94,000.

University of Central Oklahoma

As you enter Edmond, State Highway 66 merges with U.S. Highway 77, on the north side of which is the **University of Central Oklahoma**. Founded in 1890, UCO is the oldest public university in Oklahoma.

The UCO Bronchos have several sports programs that are among the nation's best at the NCAA Division II level. The strongest of these is the UCO wrestling program.

Former UCO coach Eddie Griffin built the Bronchos into a wrestling powerhouse and has been the athletics director since 2017. The Oklahoma City native and UCO graduate coached 26 All-Americans and 11 individual national champions while winning three NAIA team titles between 1978 and 1982. The three national championships were the first of eight at the NAIA level, and another seven came at the NCAA Division II level. There aren't many wrestling programs with a better tradition than UCO, and wrestling fans should definitely plan to see a meet in Edmond. Mixed martial arts fighters Jared Hess, Tim Elliott, and Muhammed Lawal all came out of the UCO wrestling program.

The Bronchos also have a very good football program, which currently ranks among the winningest Division II programs in the country and has produced several NFL players, including three-time Super Bowl champion Keith Traylor.

The Bronchos play at **Wantland Stadium**, a 10,000-seat venue on North Chowning Avenue. Built in 1965 and renovated in 2005, Wantland Stadium is one of the biggest Division II stadiums in the country. The football stadium is surrounded by the UCO soccer, softball, and baseball fields, as well as **Hamilton Field House**, home to the volleyball, wrestling, and basketball teams. The UCO softball team is also solid, with a national championship won in 2013. The men's basketball, baseball, women's tennis, volleyball, soccer, and both cross-country and golf programs annually compete for conference championships. Women's rowing is also strong at UCO, with back-to-back NCAA D-II rowing championships in 2018 and '19.

A block east of Wantland Stadium is **Kickingbird Golf Club**, an 18-hole championship course that opened in 1971 and is Edmond's only municipal golf course. Kickingbird is not the home course of the Bronchos, however. The UCO golf teams use **Oak Tree Country Club** on the north side of Edmond. The club has two 18-hole PGA courses, a driving range, and a practice facility for members and their guests. Oak Tree Country Club is adjacent to **Oak Tree National**, which hosted the 1988 PGA Championship, 2000 PGA Club Pro Championship, 2006 Senior PGA Championship, and 2014 U.S. Senior Open.

Edmond high schools

Edmond's three public high schools are all within 2 miles of Route 66. Each is highly competitive across the board and won state championships in 2019. Closest to the UCO campus is **Edmond North High School** on West Danforth Street. Of the three Edmond high schools, North has the most state championships with a total of 72 through 2020.

North has a very strong wrestling program that won a state team title in 2013 and touts Teyon Ware, who won four straight state championships from 1999 to 2002. Ware never lost in 132 high school matches, and then won a pair of NCAA national championships for the University of Oklahoma. Kelly Gregg was a three-time state wrestling champion at North and two-time all-state football selection before playing college football at the University of

Oklahoma. He then had a 13-year NFL career, most of it with the Baltimore Ravens.

Other notable North alumni include Olympic gymnastics gold medalist Shannon Miller, Olympic sprinter Mookie Salaam, PGA golfer Kevin Tway, and professional soccer player Chinedu "Bright" Dike, and his sister, Courtney, who plays on the Nigerian national team.

No matter the season, if you check out a game at Edmond North, you'll see a competitive team in every sport. The same is true at **Edmond Memorial High School**, which has a total of 47 state championships, including softball and girls' track titles in 2019. The latter was the fourth straight, and seventh overall, championship for the girls' track team. Memorial is a few blocks east of Highway 77 and is Edmond's oldest high school.

Two miles west of Memorial High School is **Edmond Santa Fe High School**, where the Wolves have won a total of 17 state athletics championships through 2020. Santa Fe's baseball team won its first-ever 6A title in 2019, a year after the volleyball program won its seventh title.

Santa Fe's 6,000-seat football stadium, colloquially known as the "**Wolf Den**," has nine concessions windows and NFL-quality field lighting, and cost just over $9 million. The school's interlocked S-F logo is centered on the two-level press box and sits atop the large video board at the south end. The football team missed the playoffs just once between 2011 and 2019, losing to either Union or Jenks four of those eight years. Although the football team has never won a state championship, the other squads that play at the Wolf Den have. The boys' soccer team won state championships in 1996 and 2009, the boys' track team won it all in 1997 and 2011, and the girls' track team earned a 6A state crown in 2012. The girls' basketball team won consecutive state championships in 2011–12, and the boys won the 6A title in 2005.

The fourth Edmond high school is **Oklahoma Christian School** (OCS), a private institution right at the Highway 66 and Interstate 35 junction. The Saints had 19 state sports championships through 2020. Nine of those were won by the boys' golf team, which won consecutive titles in 2017–18.

Basketball is the best sport at OCS with seven state championships, including four straight from 2004 to 2007 when NBA player Blake Griffin was the star of the team. The boys' basketball program is still the primary draw at OCS, but halftime shows at basketball or football games are also entertaining. The cheerleading squads at OCS have 11 state championships through 2020 and always put on a good show.

Oklahoma Christian University

Whether you take I-35 or Highway 77 south toward Oklahoma City, you'll be going by the other college in Edmond, **Oklahoma Christian University**. The NCAA Division II school is 5 miles southwest of OCS, but the two are not affiliated.

The college campus is between Smiling Hill Boulevard and Memorial Road. Next to the Payne Athletics Center is the **Dave Smith Athletic Center**, known as **The Barn** because of its design and home to the OCU basketball teams. The athletics facilities are centrally located on campus with **Dobson Field** for baseball, **Tom Heath Field** for softball, the **Ray Vaughn Track, Eagle Soccer Field**, and tennis courts surrounding the buildings at **Lawson Plaza**.

Before moving up to the NCAA Division II level in 2019, the OCU Eagles won a handful of NAIA national championships. The men's cross-country team won a 2011 championship, and the men's tennis team claimed national titles in 2003 and 2012. The men's golf program, for which Australian pro Rhein Gibson played, won NAIA championships in 2009 and 2011 and a National Christian College Athletic Association (NCCAA) title in 2012.

Disc golf fans can play the 12-hole **Oklahoma Christian University Disc Golf Course**, which is a fairly flat course with a few trees to navigate and entirely on the campus.

Edmond also has a pair of rugby clubs with the **Edmond Rugby Club Storm** and the **UCO Rugby Football Club**. The Storm play at **Mitch Park**, which is on the northwest side of Edmond and 5 miles west of the **Visit Edmond** tourist center.

OKLAHOMA CITY

When the Seattle SuperSonics were moved to Oklahoma City in 2008, it brought major professional sports to the Sooner State for the first time. The team was renamed the Oklahoma City Thunder and has played at the downtown **Chesapeake Energy Arena** ever since.

Following a dismal inaugural season in Oklahoma's capital, the Thunder were a playoff team in 2010. NBA superstars Kevin Durant, Russell Westbrook, and James Harden were all part of that 2009–10 team that won 50 games. Those three, along with Serge Ibaka, had the Thunder in the NBA Finals in 2012. The Big Three was broken up the next season when Harden was traded. Durant and Westbrook eventually left, but the Thunder remain a competitive NBA team, and Chesapeake Energy Arena is rocking for every game. They don't call it "Loud City" for nothing. Signs that read, "OKC Loud, OKC Proud" hang above almost every tunnel entrance from the concourses, and Thunder fans embody the phrase.

The 18,000-seat arena on Reno Avenue has plenty of amenities, including a large commons with a couple of eateries and an oval bar on the second

Club level seating for Thunder games can be pricey, but the view is spectacular.

A statue of Oklahoma native and Baseball Hall of Famer Johnny Bench greets fans at the home plate entrance of Chickasaw Bricktown Park.

level. Just outside of the commons is another gathering place that includes an outside patio overlooking downtown. The main concourse has a small basketball display from the Oklahoma Sports Hall of Fame to pay tribute to the team's brief history in the city. Other bars and eateries dot the concourses on every level. It is possible to attend a Thunder game and not watch a minute of live basketball on the court.

Chesapeake Energy Arena is nestled between the **Myriad Botanical Gardens** and **Chickasaw Bricktown Ballpark**. The Bricktown neighborhood is loaded with hotels, theaters, bars, restaurants, and a baseball stadium that is home to the Oklahoma City Dodgers, the Triple-A affiliate of the Los Angeles MLB team.

Busts of Hall of Famers who have called Oklahoma home line the sidewalk between the home plate and third base entrances at Chickasaw Bricktown Park.

Oklahoma City's baseball history

Oklahoma City had its first minor league baseball team in 1904 with the Metropolitans. They lasted five seasons before changing to the Indians. The name was changed to the Senators and Boosters, and back to the Indians through 1957. Following a five-year span without a team, baseball returned to OKC for good in 1962 with the 89ers, a minor league affiliate of the Houston Astros that recognized the Oklahoma Land Run of 1889. The parent club changed from the Astros to the Cleveland Indians to the Philadelphia Phillies to the Texas Rangers and then back to the Astros in 2010. The Dodgers became the parent club in 2015. OKC has played at Chickasaw Bricktown Park since 1998, when the 89ers name was ditched for the RedHawks, a name the franchise held until 2015.

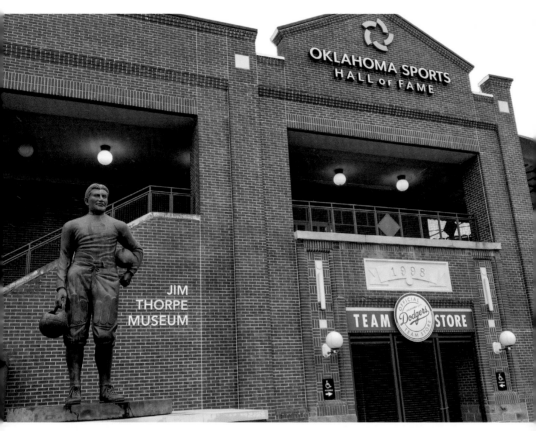

A statue of the legendary Jim Thorpe stands outside the entrance to the Oklahoma Sports Hall of Fame.

MLB All-Stars like Dallas Keuchel, George Springer, Nelson Cruz, R. A. Dickey, J. D. Martinez, Max Muncy, Cody Bellinger, Ian Kinsler, Carl Crawford, and Walker Buehler have all come through Bricktown. There are three statues of MLB greats outside of the ballpark, but none represents any of the aforementioned All-Stars. Instead the statues depict Oklahomans Warren Spahn, Johnny Bench, and Mickey Mantle. Neither Spahn, Bench, nor Mantle ever played for the Dodgers, Astros, or Rangers, but each is a Hall of Famer who had a legendary career.

Each statue is in a plaza named for the former player. Spahn, with a high leg kick as part of his delivery, greets visitors at the right-field gate. Mantle, frozen in what we assume is the follow-through on a home-run swing, is outside the third-base gate. The nine-foot likeness of Bench stands in front of the home plate entrance that is flanked by murals. Seven busts of other Hall of Famers who have called Oklahoma home line the sidewalk between Bench and Mantle. Chickasaw Bricktown Park is annually ranked as one of the best minor league stadiums in the country because of its atmosphere and amenities.

Connected to the stadium in left field is the **Oklahoma Sports Hall of Fame**. A statue of the great Jim Thorpe stands outside the entrance to the museum that bears his name. The hall of fame is above the Dodgers team store and includes a plethora of sports memorabilia from the Sooner State. Oklahoma isn't lacking in its number of sports legends, and the hall is definitely worth a visit. If you time it right, you can take in a baseball game, too.

Softball in the spotlight

While Route 66 has had a few alignments through Oklahoma City over the years, the most preferred path for travelers is the one that goes down Kelley Avenue to Northwest 23rd Street. Driving south on Kelley will take you by the **National Cowboy & Western Heritage Museum**. Within walking distance of the cowboy museum is the **National Softball Hall of Fame**, which is operated by USA Softball and has free admission.

The inaugural hall class was in 1976 with players Pat Harrison, Pat Walker, Bobby Spell, and Alberta Kohls Sims among the first to be enshrined. Notable inductees since have been USA Softball pitcher and Olympic gold medalist Jennie Finch in 2016 and Finch's Olympic teammate, Jessica Mendoza, who worked as an ESPN baseball analyst and was part of the 2019 hall class.

The softball hall recognizes umpires, commissioners, managers, and sponsors and has a large area dedicated to women's college softball teams. The softball hall complex includes **OGE Energy Field**. The ballpark has hosted the Women's College World Series every year since 1997. The Women's College World Series provides a huge boost for the Oklahoma City economy, with hotels and RV parks selling out months in advance. The NCAA-sanctioned tournament began in 1982 and three schools—Florida, Texas A&M, and Arizona State—have each won two titles. The University of Oklahoma has four national championships, and the University of Arizona has won eight. But the most decorated softball program in the nation is UCLA

The National Softball Hall of Fame and Museum has free admission. The Play at Home statue outside the National Softball Hall of Fame and Museum features three men and a woman as a base runner, catcher, umpire, and batter.

with 12 national championships and 7 runner-up finishes as of 2020. The Bruins advanced to the eight-team event 29 times through 2020, easily more than any other college.

OGE Energy Field, which opened in 1987, also holds the Big 12 Conference softball tournament and hosted the World Cup of Softball 10 times between 2005 and 2017. The stadium underwent multiple renovation projects between 2013 and 2019 that raised the capacity from 4,000 to 7,300.

Watch the Quarter Horses race

Just down the hill on the north side of the softball complex is Oklahoma City's own premier horse track. **Remington Park** opened on September 1, 1988, and Matt Vance has been around the track from the start. His father, David, was the first track president, and Matt is now the vice president of racing operations. Remington Park, which had the first-ever gambling license in Oklahoma, is best known for its spring American Quarter Horse season.

"Oklahoma is really the Kentucky of Quarter Horse racing and breeding," Vance said. "We're kind of the Churchill Downs of Quarter Horses."

The season's main event is the Heritage Place Futurity & Derby, held the first weekend in June for 2-year-olds. With a $1 million purse, the race attracts horses from across the nation, especially Kentucky, New York, and California. Another prestigious event on the calendar that brings horses from all corners is the Oklahoma Derby, a Thoroughbred race annually held the final Sunday in September.

One of the most famous horses to compete at Remington Park was Clever Trevor, who has been memorialized with a statue in the track paddock. Clever Trevor was an Oklahoma-bred horse and won the first Oklahoma Derby in 1989.

"It was kind of a Cinderella story," Vance said. "Little Clever Trevor, the Local Yokel, if you will, stayed here and defeated the royally bred horses that came in to win the big money, which was $250,000 at the time."

With 117 races held year-round, the Class 1 track also hosts the Springboard Mile—a Kentucky Derby-qualifying event—in December. The attached casino at Remington Park helps fill the large purses for the premier events, as well as the other cards throughout the year.

"We would not have survived without (the casino)," Vance said of state legislation passed in 2005 to allow casino gambling. "It turned our fortunes around and saved our business for sure. It was a huge shot in the arm to Oklahoma horse racing and breeding and everything that stems from that.

"We've put a lot of resources back into Remington Park ... and it's really a great place to come on a Saturday night."

Lincoln Park Golf Course and **Twin Hills Golf & Country Club** are to the south of the softball hall. The golf courses flank I-35, with Lincoln

Park to the west and Twin Hills on the east. Twin Hills opened in 1923 and features a 6,857-yard, par-72 course for its members and guests. Lincoln Park has a pair of public 18-hole courses, dubbed East and West. The West course is the better and more challenging of the two. It's a scenic 6,600-yard, par-71 course with tree-lined fairways and plenty of water to lose a few balls.

See the Stars at Oklahoma City University

Getting back on the Route 66 alignment from the softball complex, horse track, or golf courses is simple. Take either Northeast 50th Street or Northeast 36th Street and go west 2 miles to get back to Kelley Avenue. Continue south and turn onto 23rd Street to go past the **Oklahoma History Center**, **Oklahoma State Capitol**, historic **Tower Theatre**, and the vacant **Gold Dome**. You'll turn onto North Classen Boulevard at the Gold Dome and immediately see the **Milk Bottle Grocery** sign. Opposite Milk Bottle Grocery is the campus of **Oklahoma City University**.

OCU is a private Methodist university with an outstanding theater department that produced Tony Award-winning actresses Kelli O'Hara and Kristin Chenoweth. But the school also has elite sports teams that compete at the NAIA level.

Eight of OCU's 17 varsity sports teams have won a total of 49 national championships across 7 programs. The best sport at OCU is golf, with the men winning 10 national championships and the women adding another 7 between 2005 and 2014. Before the formation of a women's team at OCU,

---

Check a visit to OU off your bucket list

If you want to see college sports at the highest level, drive 30 miles south of OKC to Norman, home to the **University of Oklahoma**. The Sooners have a sports tradition incomparable to most with multiple national championships in baseball, football, golf, gymnastics, wrestling, and softball. The basketball team is essentially a lock to make the NCAA Tournament every year and has five Final Four appearances. The school has put out countless professional athletes, and **Gaylord Family Oklahoma Memorial Stadium**, also known as Owens Field, is a bucket-list item for most college football fans. The 80,000-seat stadium opened in 1925 with a capacity of 16,000. Fair warning: the "Boomer Sooner" fight song may be stuck in your head for hours after a game.

World Golf Hall of Famer Susie Maxwell Berning was a standout on the OCU men's squad before turning pro in 1964. The Stars teams use Lincoln Park as their home course.

The Stars are excellent on the diamond, with eight softball national championships through 2020 and an NAIA baseball title in 2005. The Stars have produced multiple MLB players, including three-time All-Star Freddy Sanchez. The softball team plays at **Ann Lacy Stadium** on the north side of campus, while the baseball team uses **Jim Wade Stadium** on the west side. Jim Wade Stadium shares a parking lot with the **Henry J. Freede Center**, which includes **Abe Lemons Arena** and is home to OCU's excellent basketball programs. The Stars men have six national championships, while the women won eight national titles between 1988 and 2015. The 3,360-seat Lemons arena opened in 2000 and is also used by the volleyball and wrestling teams.

Gaining momentum with Energy

Continuing on North Classen toward 39th Street will take you by one of Oklahoma City's oldest sports venues. **Taft Stadium** opened in 1934 and is the home venue for the Oklahoma City Energy Football Club and Northwest Classen High School football, track, and soccer teams. Taft's capacity has been reduced from more than 18,000 when it opened to around 7,500 seats today. The renovations took place between 2013 and 2015 and the only feature left unaltered was the stadium's iconic red-stone facade. The primary grandstand now has eight sections of green seats, though some seats in three sections are painted white to spell out "OKC."

The OKC Energy play in the USL Championship soccer league and made the first of two conference finals appearances in 2015, their second year of existence. Although the Energy averaged just 3,700 fans in their inaugural season, crowds swelled to nearly 6,700 by 2016. The crowds are much smaller for Northwest Classen football and soccer because the teams have not had a lot of success.

Oklahoma City high schools

Northwest Classen High School is kitty-corner from the stadium and is home to a statue that faces the stadium. It's not a sports figure, however. Country music star Vince Gill is depicted with a guitar outside the school. Gill is among Northwest Classen's alumni base that includes U.S. Senator Elizabeth Warren and sports personality Skip Bayless.

While Northwest Classen may not have top-tier athletics, another high school on Route 66 does. **Bishop McGuinness Catholic High School** at the intersection of Northwest 50th Street and North Western Avenue, along the Interstate 44 alignment, totaled 88 state championships through 2020. Athletics have been a big part of the culture at the school since it opened in 1950. Most of the titles won by the Irish have come on cross-country courses. The boys won 10 championships between 1984 and 2004, while the girls had a ridiculous 20 titles as of 2020. Naturally, the track-and-field teams are also superb. The boys have five team titles, while the girls have won eight.

The ladies rule at Bishop McGuinness. The girls' tennis team has 13 state championships to 5 won by the boys. The girls' volleyball team claimed a 5A crown in 2003. Irish girls also have a 2008 soccer title and three golf championships, though the boys have two titles in both golf and soccer.

While the girls have been dominant in nearly every sport, the boys have had their fair share of success. The football team won 4A state championships in 2006 and 2007, led by future NFL player Gabe Ikard. The Irish made the state playoffs every season from 1999 to 2019 and play at the 2,800-seat **Pribil Stadium**, which is shared by the prolific track and soccer teams.

The McGuinness basketball, volleyball, and wrestling teams use **McCarthy Gymnasium** as their home arena. McCarthy underwent significant renovations in 2008, the same year McGuinness added new weight training facilities and refurbished Pribil with a new facade and football offices. The Irish basketball teams have excelled on the court. The girls won a 5A title in 2005, and the boys had nine championships through 2020. The Irish won three straight boys' titles from 2006 to 2008 with future NBA player Daniel Orton at the helm. If you want to experience a riveting basketball atmosphere, attend a game at McCarthy when the Irish are playing their biggest rival—Bishop Kelley out of Tulsa. It's a battle between two Route 66 Catholic high schools.

The Oklahoma River runs through the capital city, and the USA Olympic Committee chose Oklahoma City as its site for the U.S. Olympic & Paralympic Training center. The **U.S. Rowing National High Performance Center** is located on the banks of the Oklahoma River, as is the **Oklahoma City Boathouse Foundation**. The sprawling complex is also used by the Oklahoma City University rowing squads. The facilities include a public water park with a towering slide that twists its way down to a pool. The river is a great place to drop in a kayak or watch the rowing teams practice.

Oklahoma City is worth all the time you can spend there because there is a lot to see and do along the Mother Road. Before leaving OKC, you'll definitely want to have a meal at **Cheever's Cafe** on 23rd Street near the Tower Theatre.

The U.S. Olympic Rowing facility is a unique structure along the banks of the Oklahoma River.

BETHANY

Bethany, a suburb of Oklahoma City, a town of 19,000 people has quaint storefronts along Route 66, as well as a high school, two universities, and an iconic bridge that John Steinbeck mentioned in *The Grapes of Wrath*.

Roots in Southern Nazarene University

Bethany was founded in 1909 by members of the Church of the Nazarene, so it only makes sense that **Southern Nazarene University** (SNU) is located there. The main campus is just north of Route 66 on the east side of town. Originally called Oklahoma Holiness College, SNU now has 2,100 students and 17 sports teams that compete at the NCAA Division II level. The school began its transition from the NAIA to the NCAA in 2011.

SNU was an NAIA basketball power with a men's national championship in 1981 and a runner-up finish in 1998. Both men's and women's basketball teams share the Sawyer Center with the SNU volleyball and indoor track teams.

The 5,000-seat **Sawyer Center** is right on the Mother Road and gained national recognition in 2005 when Hurricane Katrina forced the NBA's New Orleans Hornets to relocate. The team used the Sawyer Center as its practice facility for two seasons. The Hornets' temporary move was the beginning of bringing an NBA team to Oklahoma City permanently.

SNU's other athletics facilities are scattered around the city. The **Cypert Athletic softball and baseball complex** is west of the campus on Route 66. The **Wanda Rhodes Soccer Complex** is off 50th Street, a few blocks north of the Double Six. The football and track facilities are on the western edge of town, along the banks of the Canadian River. Making a right turn on Council Road gets you to the **SNU Football Stadium** at Riverside Park. The 10,000-seat venue with bleachers on either side and lawn seating at both ends is shared by Bethany High School. The college and high school have separate practice facilities that abut the stadium. While the football team hasn't had a lot of success since the program was established in 2000, the "Crimson Stix" drumline always puts forth an energetic performance.

Bethany High football works toward success

Basketball is a big deal in Bethany. The Sawyer Center used to host a basketball tournament for home-schooled children, and fans were turned away because the arena was at full capacity. The Bronchos of **Bethany High School** have a perennially solid basketball program and won a 3A state championship in 2001.

Chris Chamberlain was a freshman when the Bronchos basketball team won the state title. Chamberlain was a varsity member the next three years and also shined on the baseball field. But his primary sport was football. Chamberlain was the team's starting quarterback and safety, and led Bethany to its only state championship in 2003. Almost all of Chamberlain's football career was on Route 66. He played collegiately at the University of Tulsa before getting drafted in 2008 by the St. Louis Rams, for whom he was a standout special teams player for four seasons. When Chamberlain's playing career ended in 2013, he returned to Bethany and was an assistant football coach for a few years.

Bethany's football team remains a postseason regular, missing the play-offs just once between 2001 and 2019. Baseball is another strong sport at Bethany, with recent state tournament appearances in 2014 and 2016. The track-and-field teams, soccer, and softball teams were also state qualifiers during the 2010s.

"Bethany has turned into a school that, when I was coming up, was just starting to have success," said Chamberlain, who still lives in Bethany and works as an Oklahoma City firefighter. "They went from a school that was not very good every year to a school that expects to make the playoffs and make a deep run every year. The tradition and expectations have shifted over the years, and that's been cool to see.

"One cool thing about Bethany football games is that it's such a family atmosphere. Stands are packed. End zones are full of families with kids sitting on blankets and lawn chairs. The more serious fans are in the bleachers. It's an awesome atmosphere with a lot of community support.

"Bethany is in Oklahoma City, but still has that small-town feel."

As you head west from Bethany, you cross the Canadian River on the 748-foot-long **Lake Overholser Bridge**. The steel truss bridge opened in

1925 and is listed on the National Register of Historic Places. The river feeds **Lake Overholser**, a 1,500-acre reservoir that is a popular fishing spot. A covered pier on the southwest side of the lake is an ideal spot to hook bass, catfish, crappie, and bluegill.

YUKON

Yukon was founded in 1891 as a stop for cattle drovers on the Chisholm Trail. The town eventually drew a large number of immigrants from what is now the Czech Republic. That heritage is celebrated every October with the annual Czech Festival, which has free admission. Yukon also has a long history for milling, and **Yukon's Best Flour** mill is impossible to miss along Route 66.

Yukon High School pays homage to the city's primary industry by calling its sports teams the Millers. Although golfer Brad Dalke and NFL kicker Dan Bailey were born in Yukon, neither attended Yukon High. The school's most famous graduate is country music megastar Garth Brooks, who was a high school sports star before his music career began.

Brooks played football and baseball and ran track-and-field at Yukon. He was a good-enough athlete to earn a scholarship from Oklahoma State University and competed in the javelin.

Yukon's baseball team won a state championship in 1982, a couple of years after Brooks graduated. The Millers also earned boys' basketball championships in 1974 and 1979. Softball has been Yukon's most prolific sport, with five state titles between 1986 and 2010. Yukon has also enjoyed some success in golf and uses the **Greens Country Club** north of Oklahoma City as its home course. Yukon's Dax Johnston won an individual golf championship in 1990 before winning an NCAA Division II national title for the University of Central Oklahoma in 1996. He later led the Broncos golf team as its head coach for 10 years.

Yukon's baseball team is still highly competitive, as is the football team despite zero state championships through 2020. The 2009 season, which ended with a playoff loss to Jenks, was the first time since 1998 that Yukon had made the playoffs; that started a run of five straight postseason appearances. Attending a Millers game today, one can imagine Brooks on the field or how the school inspired a few of his songs. The notable Yukon-inspired song is "Unanswered Prayers," which is about Brooks seeing his high school flame while attending a football game with his wife.

Create your own Yukon memory by seeing a Millers game, and maybe write a song about it. If visiting Yukon in September, you can check out the free Rock the Route music festival over Labor Day weekend.

EL RENO

There isn't a lot in the 12 miles between Yukon and El Reno as the Double Six cuts through the bucolic terrain of the Oklahoma plains. El Reno is a classic Route 66 town, where it's easy to imagine the zeitgeist of the Mother Road. Residents of El Reno consider themselves traditional folks who are in tune with the town's history. The byway follows the I-40 Business Loop in El Reno, where the **Canadian County Historical Museum** on Grand is just one of several Route 66 attractions. Another "world's largest" item can be found in El Reno, with a giant fried onion burger cooked every May during the annual Fried Onion Burger Festival. **Sid's Diner** is one of several El Reno restaurants that serve up onion burgers year-round. Onion burgers are sometimes sold at **El Reno High School** football games.

The high school is two blocks south of Sid's, but the Indians sports teams play on the west side of town. The El Reno football, soccer, and track teams compete at **Memorial Stadium** at **Adams Park**, which spans either side of State Highway 66. El Reno teams enjoy outstanding community support, especially during winning seasons, something the Indians basketball teams have a lot of. The boys' basketball program has the fifth-most postseason victories in Oklahoma history and eight state championships. The hoops squads share **Jenks-Simmons Field House** at Adams Park with the wrestling and volleyball teams.

El Reno has one of the best wrestling programs in Oklahoma. The Indians won 12 consecutive state championships from 1996 to 2007. The Indians have had a pair of four-time individual champions with Cory Dauphin completing the feat in 2010 after Derrick Fleenor did it from 1999 to 2002.

Adams Park includes the **Route 66 Skate Park**, **Denny-Crump Rodeo Arena**, and the El Reno High School baseball and softball complex. The El Reno baseball team has a long history of excellence. The program has a trio of state championships between 1967 and 1992 and state semifinals in 2016 and 2018.

El Reno also has a state championship in golf, winning a 1987 team title while led by future PGA golfer Lance Posey. The El Reno golf teams use **Crimson Creek Golf Club** as their home course. Crimson Creek is a city-owned par-72 public course along **Lake El Reno**, just south of Adams Park. The lake provides a beautiful backdrop for the course, which has tree-lined fairways on its front nine and a links-style layout on the back nine with the final three holes wrapping around the lake.

Lake El Reno has an ATV course on the opposite side from the golf course. The lake is a popular swimming hole and has plenty of fish for those wanting to cast a line. Although no city permit is required to fish at Lake El Reno, a state license is required to fish in anywhere in Oklahoma.

Another huge Route 66 draw in El Reno is **Fort Reno**, a former United States Army post that operated from 1874 to 1949. After leaving Fort Reno, you'll want to get back on Interstate 40 because Route 66 is a very rough road and not recommended for travel. Take the business loop to I-40 and then exit at Calumet Road, or U.S. Highway 270, and head north.

GEARY

Eleven miles west of Calumet is Geary, a town of nearly 1,300 people where U.S. Highways 270 and 281 meet. **Geary High School** is just north of that intersection. The Geary Bison have a solid football program and an excellent wrestling team.

Even if you bypass the 270 alignment of Route 66 and stick to the I-40 corridor, you're going to want to take the Highway 281 Spur at Exit 108 toward Geary/Watonga. Shortly after taking the exit, take a left on Old Route 66 and then another left on 281 to reach the **William H. Murray Bridge**. Spanning the Canadian River, the nearly mile-long bridge is one of the oldest pony truss bridges in the nation. The 3,944-foot Pony Bridge completed in 1933 appears in the film version of *The Grapes of Wrath* in the scene when Grandpa dies and is buried on the west end of the bridge. If coming from Geary, head south on 281 and go west when it forks at the 281 Business Spur. After you cross the bridge, the recommendation is to get back on I-40 because Old Route 66 is rough and narrow, and you won't miss anything noteworthy on the way to Hydro.

HYDRO

Hydro had one of the best diners on Route 66 with **Lucille's Roadhouse**, a popular eatery that you wouldn't leave hungry. A new location with the same name awaits you in Weatherford, but the original building still stands on Route 66 in Hyrdo. The diner named after Lucille Hamons, "The Mother of the Mother Road," has had several monikers over the years. It opened in 1941 as the Provine Service Station but has been called Hamons Court, Hamons Service Station, and Lucille's Place. Hamons died in 2000, but not before seeing the business she operated for six decades added to the National Register of Historic Places in 1997.

Hydro, named for the abundance of well water in the area, has fewer than 1,000 residents. There is one high school in Hydro, which co-ops with nearby Eakly to the south to form Hyrdo-Eakly High School on 7th Street. The HEHS Bobcats girls' basketball team has five state championships, including a Class A title in 2020.

WEATHERFORD

Just west of the **Stafford Air & Space Museum** and north of Route 66 is **Weatherford High School**. The Eagles had 19 state championships through 2020. Those championships are spread across eight programs, but the baseball team owns six of them between 1973 and 2010.

The best athlete to come out of the school is probably Wes Sims, who led the Eagles football team to its third state championship in 1999. Sims then played at the University of Oklahoma before having a brief NFL career with the San Diego Chargers and Carolina Panthers. Sims was also a four-time high school state champion in the shot put.

The Eagles track and football teams play at a stadium between the high school and elementary school on Burcham Drive. The baseball and softball teams have their home fields at **Rader Park** on the north side of the air museum and airport.

Rader Park also houses a skate park and **Prairie West Golf Club**, which boasts that it's one of Oklahoma's "must-play" courses with pristine greens. It's an affordable public course; a round of golf, including a cart, can be played for under $30. A small water park and disc golf course are just west of Rader Park.

Weatherford is also home to **Southwestern Oklahoma State University**, which has a second academic campus on Route 66 in Sayre. Southwestern Oklahoma has a rather impressive list of athletic alumni with NFL coaches Rob and Rex Ryan, NFL players Carl Birdsong and Arnie Shockley, MLB players Ray Burris and John "Red" Patterson, former NBA player Grady Lewis, and rodeo cowboys Shane Drury and Cord McCoy. Drury succumbed to cancer in 2006 at the age of 27, and a rodeo scholarship bearing his name is now given out annually.

The SWOSU baseball program is solid, and the football team won an NAIA national championship in 1996. The championship game was played at the 7,500-seat **ASAP Energy Field at Milam Stadium**, which is the home venue for the SWOSU football and women's track-and-field teams. The **Pioneer Cellular Event Center** is home to SWOSU's basketball and volleyball teams. The Lady Bulldogs won five NAIA basketball championships before 2014.

SWOSU also has several National Intercollegiate Rodeo Association (NIRA) national championships. The women won titles in 1994 and 1998, while the men won four championships between 1985 and 1999. The **Don Mitchell Rodeo Arena** is also inside Rader Park. NIRA allows collegiate cowboys and cowgirls to compete as professionals while in school, unlike NCAA- and NAIA-sanctioned sports. The NIRA includes colleges at all levels, including two-year schools.

Weatherford is a decent-sized town with around 11,000 people and worth an overnight stay. The **Heartland of America Museum** has a variety of Route 66-inspired exhibits.

CLINTON

Another museum awaits you in Clinton, home of the **Oklahoma Route 66 Museum**. Route 66 follows the I-40 Business Loop in Clinton, and the museum is just north of I-40. The lobby features a classic automobile parked in front of the huge window that faces the road. A yellow Ford Mustang adorned the lobby in 2017; it was swapped for a red Chevy Nova in 2018. The lobby has a few interesting items, in addition to a nice gift shop. After you pay the modest $7 admission, you can enter the museum and stroll through history with Route 66 images, quotes, old trucks, replica diners, and a few debunked myths.

Just a block up the street from the museum is **Clinton High School**, which has a unique nickname for its sports teams. The Clinton Red Tornadoes have won state championships in volleyball, girls' track, girls' soccer, boys' and girls' golf, baseball, and boys' basketball. Those 14 combined championships still don't equal the 16 won by the Red Tornadoes football program.

Clinton's first state title came in 1965 when future Canadian Football League star Roy Bell, along with brother Carlos, led them to the championship. Two years later, Bell led the Red Tornadoes to an undefeated season, and Clinton was cited as the best high school football team in the country. The Red Tornadoes have been blowing away their competition ever since. After missing the 4A state playoffs in 1988 and 1989, Clinton qualified for the postseason every year from 1990 to 2019 and won nine state championships during that span. They reached the championship game six other times. That's 15 title games in 30 seasons.

Clinton is a city obsessed with high school football, and the **Tornado Bowl** is the place to be on Friday nights. Young kids in Clinton who dream of playing football aren't necessarily thinking about the NFL— they want to don the Red Tornadoes uniform. You can't really go anywhere in Clinton without seeing

Right: Flags representing the eight states of Route 66 line the street in front of the Oklahoma Route 66 Museum. Below: Get your kicks at the Oklahoma Route 66 Museum in Clinton.

The Oklahoma Route 66 Museum is designed to resemble a diner.

people wearing the high school's maroon and gold colors. The 4,200-seat Tornado Bowl is packed for every home game. Given that the population of Clinton is around 9,000, that's nearly half the town cheering loudly for their Red Tornadoes while the band entertains at halftime.

Try to plan your trip to Clinton to coincide with a Friday. Visit the museum in the afternoon and then take in the wild atmosphere that is Clinton Red Tornadoes football.

ELK CITY

When leaving Clinton, Route 66 runs parallel to Interstate 40, and taking the interstate west provides a much better road with the same views. The highway skirts the south end of the small town of Foss before arriving in Canute, 21 miles southwest of Clinton, and then on to Elk City.

Elk City prides itself on "western hospitality," and that mantra is exemplified at the **National Route 66 Museum**. The highlight for Route 66

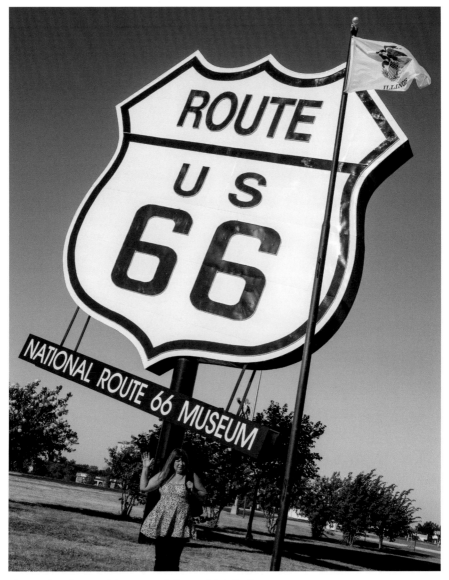

The National Route 66 Museum is located in Elk City.

travelers through Elk City, the museum is comprised of five buildings, each with a trove of Route 66 items and displays from Chicago to Santa Monica.

The National Route 66 Museum is on Route 66, which takes the form of the Interstate Business Loop in Elk City. The museum is adjacent to the sprawling Elk City school complex, with athletics fields separating the

Historical exhibit at the National Route 66 Museum is located in Elk City.

museum from two elementary schools along Pioneer Road, a middle school, and the high school.

Elk City High School is the largest school in southwest Oklahoma. Its sports teams are appropriately called the Elks, and they've claimed 22 state championships through 2020. The most successful programs have been boys' cross-country and boys' golf, each with six titles. The girls won a cross-country title in 1993 and a golf championship in 2005. The golf teams hold home meets at the **Elk City Golf & Country Club**, which has been in operation since 1955 and is the city's only course. The golf club is south of the city and features a 6,179-yard, par-71 course with Bermuda grass fairways and undulating bent grass greens.

Elk City's basketball, wrestling, and volleyball teams play inside the on-campus gymnasium. Each basketball program has won state championships and produced professional players. The Elk City Elks football team is also a playoff regular with four state championship game appearances, but just one title. That came in 1998 when the Elks upset Clinton. Elk City home games are held at **Big Elk Stadium**, a 2,700-seat venue on West A Avenue that also hosts the Elks track teams.

The stadium is next to **Ackley Park**, which has a softball complex among its amenities, and the **Elk City Rodeo**. The rodeo arena's biggest event is held every September over Labor Day weekend when spectators can get a brief taste of the Old West.

SAYRE AND ERICK

As you near the end of Route 66 through Oklahoma, you will pass through two towns that are worth a stop for their small-town charm. Both Sayre and Erick have small high schools with excellent girls' basketball programs that have won multiple state titles.

Sayre has a quaint downtown with several eateries and the palatial **Beckham County Courthouse** on Main Street. Visit Erick to see the **100th Meridian Museum** and the quirky **Sandhills Curiosity Shop**, where owner Harley Russell might treat you to an impromptu music show. The Sandhills shop is an ideal spot for photos because of the myriad road signs inside and outside the store. If it gets too late, spend the night at the historic **West Winds Motel**. Be sure to grab a bite at the **Tumbleweed Grill** in Texola before you leave the Sooner State and enter the Lone Star State.

Oklahoma Route 66 Points of Interest

MICKEY MANTLE CHILDHOOD HOME – 319 S. Quincy St., Commerce, OK 74339

DAIRY KING – 100 N. Main St., Commerce, OK 74339

ALLEN'S CONOCO FILLIN' STATION – 101 S. Main St., Commerce, OK 74339

COMMERCE HIGH SCHOOL – 420 Doug Furnas Blvd., Commerce, OK 74339

COLEMAN THEATRE – 103 N. Main St., Miami, OK 74354

GEORGE COLEMAN HOUSE – 1001 Rockdale Blvd. Miami, OK 74354

DOBSON MUSEUM – 110 A St. S.W., Miami, OK 74354

WAYLAN'S KU-KU BURGER – 915 N. Main St., Miami, OK 74354

MIAMI HIGH SCHOOL – 2000 E. Central Ave., Miami, OK 74354

NORTHEAST OKLAHOMA A&M COLLEGE – 200 I St. N.E., Miami, OK 74354

AFTON HIGH SCHOOL – 410 S. Main St., Afton, OK 74331

NOWHERE ON ROUTE 66 – 300 S. 1st St, Afton, OK 74331

CHELSEA MOTOR INN – 325 E. Layton St., Chelsea, OK 74016

CHELSEA HIGH SCHOOL – 401 Redbud, Chelsea, OK 74016

ANNIE'S DINER – 12015 Poplar St., Claremore, OK 74017

FOYIL HIGH SCHOOL – E. 4th & Pine, Foyil, OK 74031

ANDY PAYNE STATUE – 12901 OK 66, Claremore, OK 74017

SEQUOYAH HIGH SCHOOL – 16441 S. 4180 Road, Claremore, OK 74017

CLAREMORE SOCCER CLUB – 2556 N. Sioux Ave., Claremore, OK 74017

CLAREMORE LAKE PARK – E. Blue Starr Drive, Claremore, OK 74017

WILL ROGERS STAMPEDE ARENA – 13601 E. 480 Road, Claremore, OK 74017

CLAREMORE HIGH SCHOOL – 201 E Stuart Roosa, Claremore, OK 74017

ROGERS STATE UNIVERSITY – 1701 W. Will Rogers Blvd., Claremore, OK 74017

WILL ROGERS MEMORIAL MUSEUM – 1720 W. Will Rogers Blvd., Claremore, OK 74017

HERITAGE HILLS GOLF COURSE – 3140 Dave Wilber Lane, Claremore, OK 74019

WILL ROGERS DOWNS – 20900 S. 4200 Road, Claremore, OK 74019

GORDON GOLF COURSE – 800 S.W. Gordon Road, Claremore, OK 74017

ROGERS POINT PARK – 4000 N. U.S. Rte. 66, Claremore, OK 74019

THE BLUE WHALE OF CATOOSA – 2600 U.S. Rte. 66, Catoosa, OK 74015

CATOOSA HIGH SCHOOL – 2000 S. Cherokee St., Catoosa, OK 74015

CHEROKEE HILLS GOLF CLUB – 777 W. Cherokee St., Catoosa, OK 74015

UNIVERSITY OF TULSA – 800 S. Tucker Drive, Tulsa, OK 74104

H. A. CHAPMAN STADIUM – 3112 E. 8th St., Tulsa, OK 74104

TALLY'S GOOD FOOD CAFÉ – 1102 S. Yale Ave., Tulsa, OK 74112

TULSA COUNTRY CLUB – 701 N. Union Ave., Tulsa, OK 74127

SOUTHERN HILLS COUNTRY CLUB – 2636 E. 61st St., Tulsa, OK 74136

MOTHER ROAD MARKET – 1124 S. Lewis Ave., Tulsa, OK 74104

WILL ROGERS HIGH SCHOOL – 3909 E. 5th Place, Tulsa, OK 74112

UNION HIGH SCHOOL – 6636 S. Mingo Road, Tulsa, OK 74133

JENKS HIGH SCHOOL – 205 E. B St., Jenks, OK 74037

LAFORTUNE PARK – 5202 S. Hudson Ave., Tulsa, OK 74135

CASE TENNIS CENTER – 5302 S. Hudson Ave., Tulsa, OK 74135

MEMORIAL HIGH SCHOOL – 5840 S. Hudson Ave., Tulsa, OK 74135

ROUTE 66 HISTORICAL VILLAGE – 3770 Southwest Blvd., Tulsa, OK 74107

DANIEL WEBSTER HIGH SCHOOL – 1919 W. 40th St., Tulsa, OK 74107

BISHOP KELLEY HIGH SCHOOL – 3905 S. Hudson Ave., Tulsa, OK 74135

TULSA STATE FAIR – 4145 E. 21st St., Tulsa, OK 74114

ONEOK FIELD – 201 N. Elgin Ave., Tulsa, OK 74120

ELGIN PARK – 325 E. Reconciliation Way, Tulsa, OK 74120

CENTER OF THE UNIVERSE – 1 S. Boston Ave., Tulsa, OK 74103

GATHERING PLACE – 2650 S. John Williams Way, Tulsa, OK 74114

CYRUS AVERY CENTENNIAL PLAZA – 1330 Southwest Blvd., Tulsa, OK 74127

HEART OF ROUTE 66 AUTO MUSEUM – 13 Sahoma Lake Road, Sapulpa, OK 74066

SAPULPA GOLF COURSE – 1200 W. Dewey Ave., Sapulpa, OK 74066

SAPULPA HIGH SCHOOL – 1201 E. Lincoln Ave., Sapulpa, OK 74066

SAPULPA HISTORICAL MUSEUM – 100 E. Lee Ave., Sapulpa, OK 74066

SAHOMA LAKE – 8853 Sahoma Lake Road, Sapulpa, OK 74066

ROCK CREEK BRIDGE – W. Ozark Trail, Sapulpa, OK 74066

CREEK COUNTY SPEEDWAY – 18450 U.S. Rte. 66, Kellyville, OK 74039

KELLYVILLE HIGH SCHOOL – 14903 Maple Drive, Kellyville, OK 74039

BRISTOW TIRE SHOP – 115 W. 4th Ave., Bristow, OK 74010

BEARD MOTOR COMPANY – 210 E. 9th St., Bristow, OK 74010

CROWN AUTO WORLD BRISTOW CHRYSLER PLYMOUTH – 901 S. Roland St., Bristow, OK 74010

BRISTOW HIGH SCHOOL – Highway 16 and Ash, Bristow, OK 74010

STROUD HIGH SCHOOL – 212 W. 7th St., Stroud, OK 74079

JACK POSKEY FIELD – 701 N. 2nd Ave., Stroud, OK 74079

JOSEPH CARPENTER HOUSE – 204 W. 6th St., Stroud, OK 74079

ROCK CAFE – 114 W. Main St., Stroud, OK 74079

STROUD LAKE – N. 3580 Road & E. 840 Road, Stroud, OK 74079

ROUTE 66 INTERPRETIVE CENTER – 400 E. 1st St., Chandler, OK 74834

CHANDLER HIGH SCHOOL – 901 S. CHS St., Chandler, OK 74834

THE ROUND BARN – 107 OK 66, Arcadia, OK 73007

POPS 66 – 660 OK 66, Arcadia, OK 73007

TULON'S DRUGSTORE – 201 N. Main St., Arcadia, OK US 73007

1889 TERRITORIAL SCHOOLHOUSE – 124 E. 2nd St., Edmond, OK 73034

EDMOND ARMORY – 600 S. Bryant Ave., Edmond, OK 73034

OLD NORTH TOWER – University of Central Oklahoma campus, Edmond, OK 73034

UNIVERSITY OF CENTRAL OKLAHOMA – 100 N. University Drive, Edmond, OK 73034

KICKINGBIRD GOLF CLUB – 1600 E. Danforth Road, Edmond, OK 73034

OAK TREE COUNTRY CLUB – 700 W. Country Club Drive, Edmond, OK 73025

OAK TREE NATIONAL – 1515 Oak Tree Drive, Edmond, OK 73025

EDMOND NORTH HIGH SCHOOL – 215 W. Danforth Road, Edmond, OK 73003

EDMOND MEMORIAL HIGH SCHOOL – 1000 E. 15th St., Edmond, OK 73013

EDMOND SANTA FE HIGH SCHOOL – 1901 W. 15th St., Edmond, OK 73013

OKLAHOMA CHRISTIAN SCHOOL – 4680 E. 2nd St., Edmond, OK 73034

OKLAHOMA CHRISTIAN UNIVERSITY – 2501 E. Memorial Road, Edmond, OK 73013

MITCH PARK – 1501 W. Covell Road, Edmond, OK 73003

VISIT EDMOND – 2901 Conference Drive, Edmond, OK 73034

CHESAPEAKE ENERGY ARENA – 100 W. Reno Ave., Oklahoma City, OK 73102

MYRIAD BOTANICAL GARDENS – 301 W. Reno Ave., Oklahoma City, OK 73102

CHICKASAW BRICKTOWN BALLPARK – 2 S. Mickey Mantle Drive, Oklahoma City, OK 73104

OKLAHOMA SPORTS HALL OF FAME – 20 S. Mickey Mantle Drive, Oklahoma City, OK 73104

NATIONAL COWBOY & WESTERN HERITAGE MUSEUM – 1700 N.E. 63rd St., Oklahoma City, OK 73111

NATIONAL SOFTBALL HALL OF FAME – 2801 N.E. 50th St., Oklahoma City, OK 73111

REMINGTON PARK – 1 Remington Place, Oklahoma City, OK 73111

LINCOLN PARK GOLF COURSE – 4001 N.E. Grand Blvd., Oklahoma City, OK 73111

TWIN HILLS GOLF & COUNTRY CLUB – 3401 N.E. 36th St., Oklahoma City, OK 73121

OKLAHOMA HISTORY CENTER – 800 Nazih Zuhdi Drive, Oklahoma City, OK 73105

OKLAHOMA STATE CAPITOL – 2300 N. Lincoln Blvd., Oklahoma City, OK 73105

TOWER THEATRE – 425 N.W. 23rd St., Oklahoma City, OK 73103

CHEEVER'S CAFE – 2409 N. Hudson Ave., Oklahoma City, OK 73103

OKLAHOMA CITY UNIVERSITY – 2501 N. Blackwelder Ave., Oklahoma City, OK 73106

TAFT STADIUM – 2501 N. May Ave., Oklahoma City, OK 73107

NORTHWEST CLASSEN HIGH SCHOOL – 2801 N.W. 27th St., Oklahoma City, OK 73107

BISHOP MCGUINNESS CATHOLIC HIGH SCHOOL – 801 N.W. 50th St., Oklahoma City, OK 73118

U.S. ROWING NATIONAL HIGH PERFORMANCE CENTER – 725 S. Lincoln Blvd, Oklahoma City, OK 73129

SOUTHERN NAZARENE UNIVERSITY – 6729 N.W. 39th Expy., Bethany, OK 73008

SAWYER CENTER – 6401 N.W. 39th Expy., Bethany, OK 73008

WANDA RHODES SOCCER COMPLEX – 5099 N. Thompkins Ave. #4301, Bethany, OK 73008

BETHANY HIGH SCHOOL – 4500 N. Mueller Ave., Bethany, OK 73008

LAKE OVERHOLSER BRIDGE – 8703 Overholser Drive, Bethany, OK 73008

YUKON'S BEST FLOUR – 45 S. 3rd St., Yukon, OK 73099

YUKON HIGH SCHOOL – 1777 S. Yukon Pkwy., Yukon, OK 73099

CANADIAN COUNTY HISTORICAL MUSEUM – 300 S. Grand Ave., El Reno, OK 73036

SID'S DINER – 300 S. Choctaw Ave., El Reno, OK 73036

EL RENO HIGH SCHOOL – 407 S. Choctaw Ave, El Reno, OK 73036

MEMORIAL STADIUM – 2001 Sunset Drive, El Reno, OK 73036

JENKS-SIMMONS FIELD HOUSE – 252 N. Country Club Road, El Reno, OK 73036

DENNY-CRUMP RODEO ARENA – 215 N. Country Club Road, El Reno, OK 73036

CRIMSON CREEK GOLF CLUB – 801 Babcock Drive, El Reno, OK 73036

FORT RENO – 7107 W. Cheyenne St., El Reno, OK 73036

GEARY HIGH SCHOOL – 300 S. Blaine Ave., Geary, OK 73040

WILLIAM H. MURRAY BRIDGE – U.S. Highway 281, Hinton, OK 73047

LUCILLE'S HISTORIC HIGHWAY GAS STATION – U.S. Route 66, Hydro, OK 73048

LUCILLE'S ROADHOUSE DINER – 1301 N. Airport Road, Weatherford, OK 73096

STAFFORD AIR & SPACE MUSEUM – 3000 Logan Road, Weatherford, OK 73096

WEATHERFORD HIGH SCHOOL – 1500 N. Washington Ave., Weatherford, OK 73096

RADER PARK – 3317 Lyle Road, Weatherford, OK 73096

PRAIRIE WEST GOLF CLUB – 3500 Lyle Road, Weatherford, OK 73096

SOUTHWESTERN OKLAHOMA STATE UNIVERSITY – 100 W. Campus Drive, Weatherford, OK 73096

DON MITCHELL RODEO ARENA – Lyle Road at Lawter Road, Weatherford, OK 73096

HEARTLAND OF AMERICA MUSEUM – 1600 S. Frontage Road, Weatherford, OK 73096

OKLAHOMA ROUTE 66 MUSEUM – 2229 W. Gary Blvd., Clinton, OK 73601

CLINTON HIGH SCHOOL – 2130 W. Gary Blvd., Clinton, OK 73601

NATIONAL ROUTE 66 MUSEUM – 2117 W. 3rd St., Elk City, OK 73644

ELK CITY HIGH SCHOOL – 1221 Pioneer Road, Elk City, OK 73644

ELK CITY GOLF & COUNTRY CLUB – 108 Lakeridge Road, Elk City, OK 73644

BIG ELK STADIUM – 2325 W. A Ave., Elk City, OK 73644

ACKLEY PARK – 417 Ackley Park Road, Elk City, OK 73644

ELK CITY RODEO – 2251 W. A Ave., Elk City, OK 73644

BECKHAM COUNTY COURTHOUSE – 104 S. 3rd St., Sayre, OK 73662

100TH MERIDIAN MUSEUM – 101 S. Sheb Wooley St., Erick, OK 73645

SANDHILLS CURIOSITY SHOP – 201 S. Sheb Wooley St., Erick, OK 73645

WEST WINDS MOTEL – 623 Roger Miller Blvd., Erick, OK 73645

TUMBLEWEED GRILL – U.S. Rte. 66, Texola, OK 73668

TEXAS

Welcome to Texas, where everything is bigger and football is king. Outside of the 13-mile portion in Kansas, Texas has the shortest stretch of Route 66 at 178 miles, but there's still plenty to see and do in the Lone Star State.

TEXAS

ROADTRIP AMERICA

25 miles
25 km

KANSAS
OKLAHOMA

Guymon

OKLAHOMA
TEXAS

270

83

54

287

Dumas

Borger

Pampa

83

60

Mid-Point Cafe

Hodgetown

Amarillo
Civic Center

U-Drop Inn

40

Historic Route 66

40

66

Shamrock

Adrian

Bushland
High School

Amarillo

Duncan Field
McLean High School

Canyon

385

27

Hereford

287

87

70

Plainview

62

83

84

84

Levelland

62

Lubbock

84

SHAMROCK

There are just a handful of towns along the Route 66 corridor through the Texas Panhandle. The first of these towns is Shamrock, which has the iconic **U-Drop Inn** and restored **Magnolia service station**.

Although there have been movies and television shows made about Texas high school football, none had the Shamrock Irish in mind. **Shamrock High School** has never played for a state championship in football, but it does have 15 playoff appearances through 2020. The Irish have won titles in other sports. The girls' track-and-field team won 1A state championships in 2002 and 2003. The Shamrock girls won a golf title in 2006, and the boys have links championships in 1958 and 1998.

Shamrock's U-Drop Inn provides a neon glow for Thursday's Under the Neon weekly music show from June to August.

Daylight reveals the beautifully restored, art deco designed Magnolia service station and the U-Drop Inn café.

The football and track teams compete at the 2,500-seat **El Paso Field** on Illinois Street, a mile south of the U-Drop Inn. The stadium sits behind the school complex, which occupies acreage at the east end of First and Second Streets. The stadium is painted green for obvious reasons, and October would be a great time to see a game there. The October Irish Craft Fest is a regional hit, and the U-Drop Inn provides a neon glow for Thursday's Under the Neon weekly music show from June to August. As expected, Shamrock also has a big St. Patrick's Day celebration.

If you need an incentive to spend the night in Shamrock, local hotels and motels offer a free round of golf at the **Shamrock Country Club** with any overnight stay. Both Shamrock golf teams use the semi-private country club

as their home course. The nine-hole course has rolling fairways and water hazards, but no sand bunkers along its 3,200 yards.

MCLEAN

McLean was named after William Pinkney McLean, a hero of the Texas war for independence, but it was founded in 1902 by Alfred Rowe, an Englishman who died 10 years later while coming back to the United States on the ill-fated *Titanic*. A *Titanic* exhibit is on display at the **Devil's Rope Museum**, which is much more interesting than you'd think a museum about barbed wire would be.

A sign that welcomes you to McLean informs you that the McLean High School Tigers football team won a Class 1A state championship in 2018. That sign indicates you are about to get your first taste of the craze that is Texas high school football.

McLean High School is a few blocks north of Route 66 and the Devil's Rope Museum. Because McLean has fewer than 800 people, it plays a different sort of football. The Tigers compete in six-man football, and the games can get wild. McLean's 2018 championship came as a result of 100–70 victory over Milford in the title game. One hundred points in a football game! McLean was defeated by Blum in the 2019 championship game by a 58–52 count. McLean has competed in the Texas University Interscholastic League (UIL) playoffs 14 times. Even though **Duncan Field** at Grove Street and Wood Avenue has a capacity of 1,000—more than the town's population—the stands are almost always packed.

Golfers can get in a quick, unique round at the **McLean Golf Course**, a short, pasture-like, nine-hole course that opened in 1950. The 2,802-yard course is one of the last Texas courses with sand greens, something on which most golfers have never putted.

After experiencing the course, or before a Tigers football game, you'd be remiss if you didn't have a meal at the famed **Red River Steakhouse**. The Route 66 mainstay has huge portions of excellent food at modest prices.

AMARILLO

Between McLean and Amarillo is a barren stretch of 74 miles along Interstate 40 that includes the desolate communities of Alanreed, Jericho, Groom, and Conway. Jericho is a ghost town best known for the treacherous Jericho Gap during the early alignment of Route 66 through the black gumbo known as Texas mud. Groom boasts the **Leaning Tower of Texas**—a tilted water tower with "Britten USA" painted on its side.

Route 66 in Amarillo essentially follows the I-40 Business Loop through downtown to Amarillo Street and then to Taylor and into the historic San Jacinto District of Sixth Avenue. A stretch of the original alignment awaits with a plethora of shops and restaurants, including the **Golden Light Cantina**, lining the street.

A Texas-sized collection of photos is on display at the Amarillo Travel Information Center off of I-40.

The "Leaning Tower of Texas" is a water tower in Groom.

The Amarillo Sod Poodles debuted in 2019 at the brand new Hodgetown in the heart of Amarillo.

Watch the Sod Poodles at Hodgetown

Before you get to Sixth Avenue, you'll drive past a couple of sports venues. The first is **Hodgetown**, a baseball stadium that opened in 2019 and is home to the Amarillo Sod Poodles, who were a Double-A affiliate of the San Diego Padres in 2019 but joined the Arizona Diamondbacks in 2021. What's a Sod Poodle? It's a little-used nickname for prairie dogs, which are prevalent in northwest Texas.

You can't miss Hodgetown with its bright yellow main entrance topped with bold red letters. Making their debut on April 4, 2019, the Sod Poodles won the Texas League in their inaugural season.

"It was awesome," said Sam Levitt, the play-by-play voice of the Sod Poodles. "It was a magical season in every way, shape, and form. The Padres had an extremely talented farm system. Heading into the year, they were ranked as the number one minor league system in baseball, so we got to see a lot of really highly touted prospects."

Hodgetown provides a great opportunity to watch future MLB stars before they reach the big leagues.

The Sod Poodles filled a void in Amarillo, a city that has a long history of minor league baseball. The Amarillo Gold Sox played their inaugural season in 1939 and had several MLB affiliations before the team was moved to Beaumont, Texas, in 1983. The Gold Sox had several players advance to the big leagues, but the greatest of all was Tony Gwynn. The late Gwynn played 23 games for the Gold Sox in 1981 and hit an astounding .462. He made his MLB debut the next summer and spent his entire Hall of Fame career with the Padres.

Another player who remains a legend in Amarillo baseball lore is Bob Crues. Although Crues, who died in 1986, never made it to the big leagues, he set a baseball record in 1948 with 254 runs batted in (RBI) in 140 games. To put that into perspective, the MLB single-season RBI record is 191, set by Chicago Cubs slugger Hack Wilson in 1930. Wilson played 155 games that year. Crues, nicknamed "Round Trip" because of his frequent home runs, hit .404 with 69 homers in 1948 for the greatest individual season in minor league history.

It didn't take long for the residents of Amarillo to get excited about their new baseball club. Hodgetown was filled well beyond its listed capacity of 6,631 for the 2019 opener. Nearly 7,200 people showed up to see that first game, and more sellout crowds followed. One concessions stand on the third-base side is called the Route 66 Grill.

"As far as this team being embraced by the city and region, it was beyond my expectations and anybody's expectation," said Levitt, a New York native who previously worked for the Gateway Grizzlies in Sauget, Illinois, and the Corpus Christi Hooks, the Double-A affiliate of the Houston Astros. "We averaged 6,300 people and sold out 40 of 68 home games. The place was rocking every night.

"No matter where I go throughout the course of my career, being a part of the first season in Amarillo will be one of if not the most special and rewarding experiences of my career.

"When I took the job, I wasn't sure what to expect—new team in a new city with a new stadium. I had never stepped foot in Amarillo before. It blew away my wildest expectations."

The Sod Poodles create a lot of fun during games, and Levitt frequently gets involved, whether it's tossing T-shirts from the broadcast booth, running "wacky games" or dancing between innings, or calling a game from the seats behind home plate.

"It's not really part of my job description, but my goal was to help create a special connection between the fans and the organization," Levitt said. "I want to bring energy, creativity, and fun to the ball park every night ... We want to create a family-friendly fun experience."

Wranglers, Rattlers, Gorillas, and Bulls

The Sod Poodles aren't the only professional sports team in Amarillo. The Amarillo Bulls play in the North American Hockey League (NAHL) and continue the city's long history with minor league hockey.

The Bulls play at the **Amarillo Civic Center**, which is a sprawling downtown complex with exhibit and banquet halls, meeting rooms, a concert venue, and the 4,900-seat **Cal Farley Coliseum**. The civic center, at the intersection of Buchanan and historic Sixth Avenue, has been a frequent host of pro hockey since the Amarillo Wranglers were founded in 1968.

Because of its relatively small size, Cal Farley Coliseum allows fans to sit close to the ice to watch minor league hockey.

That team folded in 1971, but a second edition of the Wranglers arrived in 1975 and won the Southwest Hockey League in its inaugural season. When the Wranglers again folded in 1977, Amarillo went nearly 20 years without hockey before the Amarillo Rattlers were launched in 1996. The team name changed to the Gorillas in 2002, but the franchise enjoyed some success in the now-defunct Western Professional Hockey League and Central Hockey League. The Gorillas were an affiliate of the Carolina Hurricanes but ceased operations in 2010. There would be no hockey hiatus this time. The Bulls moved to town later that year and had immediate success. Amarillo reached the NAHL semifinals in each of its first two seasons and then won a league title in season three.

The names and leagues may have changed, but Cal Farley Coliseum is a great place to watch hockey. Named in honor of a local philanthropist, Farley Coliseum offers a dazzling display of color on its walls and catwalks. While most arenas want the overhead walkways to blend in with the ceiling, the red, orange, green, and blue platforms stand out at the coliseum. Banners that illustrate Amarillo's hockey history dot the walls, interrupting colorful motifs.

Indoor football matches and rodeos

The arena also hosts the Amarillo Venom, an indoor football team established as the Dusters in 2003. The team changed its name to the Venom in 2010 when it was moved from AF2 (Arena Football 2) to the Indoor Football League. The Venom currently play in the Champions Indoor Football (CIF) league, which they joined in 2015. No matter the league, the Venom have been successful, with 11 playoff berths and three championships in their first 15 seasons. Former NFL quarterback Nate Davis led the 2013 championship team. Because of a smaller field and different rules from traditional American football played in large domes or open-air stadiums, indoor football games have a lot of action and scoring. It can be a fun and exciting way to spend an evening.

The civic center is also home to one of the country's biggest rodeo events. The Working Ranch Cowboys Association (WRCA) takes over the various spaces in the civic center every November for its championship event. The four-day event has daily trade shows, expos, and panel discussions before culminating with WRCA competitions each night. The WRCA, founded in 2001, holds events in Arizona, Oklahoma, New Mexico, Texas, Kansas, Colorado, Wyoming, and Nebraska before punctuating its season in Amarillo.

Amarillo has a big rodeo scene, and the **Tri-State Expo**, 2 miles east of the civic center, is another spot to see cowboys and cowgirls do their thing. The Expo hosts two primary events, both in September. The Nevada-based Exceptional Rodeo holds a one-day event in Amarillo in early September, while the Professional Rodeo Cowboys Association (PRCA) puts on a three-day show in the latter part of the month.

The PRCA event is held at the Expo's **Amarillo National Center** and has more traditional rodeo events with competitors from the United States, Canada, Mexico, and Brazil. The Amarillo rodeo is part of the PRCA championship Pro Rodeo tour and is a perfect event to see some of the world's top cowboys and cowgirls in action.

If you want a feel-good event to attend, Exceptional Rodeo offers children with special needs an opportunity to compete in events like mechanical bull riding or calf-roping at **Bill Cody Arena**.

A taste of Texas high school football

The Expo is adjacent to **Dick Bivins Stadium**, which is primarily used as the home stadium for Amarillo's high school football teams. There are four public high schools in the Amarillo Independent School District: Amarillo High, Caprock, Tascosa, and Palo Duro. Bivins Stadium holds the distinction of being the first stadium in the world to install the synthetic grass known as FieldTurf for its playing surface. The stadium is larger than some Division I college venues with 15,000 seats. Like the large Tulsa venues, Bivins Stadium shows replays on its JumboTron, has public Wi-Fi, and includes a multilevel press box with separate television and radio broadcast booths, coaches' rooms, a kitchen, private restrooms, and VIP luxury suites. This is high school football at the next level, and because it's a shared venue, Dick Bivins Stadium is packed nearly every Friday night.

All four public high schools are within 5 miles of the Mother Road. The closest school is **Tascosa High School**, 2 miles south of the Double Six on

Westlawn Avenue and just off of I-40. Tascosa produced former pro tennis player Alex O'Brien and Olympic wrestler Brandon Slay.

The Tascosa Rebels have a solid football program, and their primary rival is **Amarillo High School**, 4 miles south of Route 66 on Danbury Street. Amarillo's sports teams are called the Golden Sandstorm, or Sandies for short. The football rivalry with the Rebels dates back to 1958, when Tascosa first opened. Amarillo has largely dominated the series, but Tascosa's recent success started to turn the tide. No matter how good or bad the Rebels or Sandies are in any given season, their games are always emotionally charged and usually played in front of a full house.

Caprock High School is southeast of the city center and is a girls' wrestling powerhouse with 10 state championships between 2000 and 2020, including 9 straight between 2004 and 2012. The Longhorns boys' wrestling program is also very good and produced former pro wrestler Dick Murdoch and UFC fighter Evan Tanner. **Palo Duro High School** is on Amarillo's north side. The Dons have never won a Texas state football title but do have a solid program that has produced a few NFL players.

A small school, a stellar golf course, and a big steak meal

Although none of the four public high schools is directly on Route 66, one private school is. **San Jacinto Christian Academy** (San Jac) is located in the center of the historic district on Southwest Sixth Avenue. The Patriots compete in football, track, softball, baseball, volleyball, and basketball. Only the basketball and volleyball teams compete in the on-campus gym, which is just a long three-pointer off Sixth Avenue. The Patriots are not part of the UIL but are members of the Texas Association of Private and Parochial Schools (TAPPS). Because the school has an enrollment of fewer than 150 students, the Patriots play six-man football. San Jac started its football program in 2004, and the Patriots play at tiny **SANJAC Stadium**, 4 miles south of the school. While the Patriots teams have had some success in basketball, San Jac baseball is probably the school's strongest program, with deep runs in the TAPPS playoffs, including a 2019 Division IV state championship.

One mile west of SJCA on Route 66 is the **Amarillo Country Club**, which opened in 1919 and has a golf course recognized as one of the best in

Texas. The 18-hole course with tree-lined fairways, various water hazards and sand bunkers, and bent grass greens has hosted several PGA events over its history. The country club also has tennis courts for its members and guests.

If you're up for a challenge, try the 72-ounce steak at the **Big Texan Steak Ranch and Brewery**. The Big Texan may have moved from its original spot on Route 66, but the current location is conveniently located off of Interstate 40. The kitschy saloon will comp your meal if you can polish off a 72-ounce sirloin and its side items in under an hour. If you can't complete the challenge, you will be charged $72 for the meal, but you get to take the leftovers with you. The challenge has been featured on *Man vs. Food,* and the world record holder is a tiny woman named Molly Shuyler, a competitive eater who polished off three of the giant steak meals in less than 20 minutes.

If you're feeling gluttonous, try the 72-ounce steak challenge at The Big Texan Steak Ranch.

BUSHLAND

Just past **Cadillac Ranch** is another high school right on Route 66. If you want to see why Texas high school football is so revered, **Bushland High School** is a must-stop.

The Falcons have a really good football program with tremendous community support. **Falcon Stadium**, nestled in the middle of Texas farmland, is usually near its 3,000-seat capacity. Bushland is always in the playoff hunt and was 12–0 in 2019 before falling to Brock in a region semifinal to end its season.

NFL players Weston Richburg and Crockett Gillmore—both drafted in 2014 out of Colorado State—magnified the school's profile. With Richburg and Gillmore on the team, the Falcons were perennial playoff participants but lost to eventual state champion Muleshoe their senior year. The Falcons

Visitors can leave their mark at Amarillo's famous Cadillac Ranch on the west side of the city.

reached the state championship game the following season.

"It's a lot of fun," Bushland coach Jimmy Thomas said. "We've got great kids, great support from the community and our administration. This is the place to be on a Friday night."

Visit a breeding ground for NFL players

West Texas A&M University in Canyon, about 9 miles south of Route 66 in Amarillo, has one of the better NCAA Division II programs in the country. The Buffaloes have won five Lone Star Conference championships since dropping from the Division I-A level in 1986 and made the D-II playoffs five times between 2006 and 2013. The Buffs are 6–0 all-time in bowl games, and WTAMU has produced NFL players like Mercury Morris, Ethan Westbrooks, Eugene Sims, Khiry Robinson, and Keith Null. The late Dusty Rhodes played football in Canyon before his professional wrestling career began. Another WWE legend, Ted DiBiase, also played football for the Buffs.

"Texas high schools have Friday night lights, and Texas universities have Saturdays," said Texas Old Route 66 Association President Nick Gerlich. "The state comes to a halt for football, and nothing beats gridiron action between Division II teams. The talent is still high, but these kids are playing more for the love of the game. A few make it to the pros, but that's not the goal; education is. Excitement rules the night at WTAMU's new stadium on the north edge of campus, where the thin air and relentless wind make seemingly impossible punts and passes very possible indeed. Or not, depending on which end zone you're protecting."

VEGA

Vega may have fewer than 1,000 residents, but there is still plenty to see in the West Texas town. Among the highlights are the restored **1920s Magnolia service station** and the **Milburn-Price Culture Museum**, which is a treasure trove of nostalgic items. The "world's largest branding iron" is in front of a large mural on the museum's exterior wall. The 22-foot-long branding iron may appear to say TIX, but actually represents the old XIT Ranch. The former ranch, which operated from 1895 to 1912, once occupied 3 million acres across 10 counties for its 150,000 head of cattle.

The legacy of cattle ranches in the area is represented by the sports teams at **Vega High School**. The Vega Longhorns have strong athletics programs at

A mural depicting a cowboy and Native American shaking hands decorates an exterior wall at the Milburn-Price Culture Museum.

the UIL 2A level. The boys and girls each have a state championship, and the football team is in the playoffs more often than not, including a 2019 berth.

The high school is on the northeast part of Vega but very close to Route 66. Despite being a small school in a small town, Vega has excellent athletics facilities. The gymnasium has a four-sided scoreboard above its polished floor. **Longhorn Field** is a modest football stadium, but the well-maintained grass field is encircled by a state-of-the-art track. A large Longhorn statue greets spectators at the entrance to the stadium, which can seat 1,600 people. That is nearly double the size of the population, just in case you needed a reminder of how seriously they take high school football in Texas.

Vega is the last opportunity on Route 66 to see Texas high school football because the much smaller town of Adrian doesn't have a team.

ADRIAN

Adrian's claim to fame on Route 66 is that it's the midpoint between Chicago and Los Angeles. A sign across the street from the **Midpoint Cafe**, which opened in 1928 as Zella's, designates the official spot with Chicago 1,139 miles to the east and Los Angeles 1,139 miles to the west.

Fewer than 200 people live in Adrian, but **Adrian High School** draws from the surrounding area and has an enrollment of 120 students. Adrian High is the last Texas high school on Route 66, and its Matadors compete at the UIL IA level in cross-country, track-and-field, basketball, tennis, and golf. Both boys' and girls' basketball teams have had some success over the years and enjoy excellent community support.

Before crossing into New Mexico, be sure to visit the ghost town of **Glenrio**. The 17 remaining buildings of the once-vibrant border town were added to the National Register of Historic Places in 2007.

Adrian, Texas, is the halfway point of Route 66 with Chicago and Los Angeles equally 1,139 miles away.

Texas Route 66 Points of Interest

U-DROP INN – 111 U.S. Rte. 66, Shamrock, TX 79079

MAGNOLIA SERVICE STATION – 200 N. Madden St., Shamrock, TX 79079

SHAMROCK HIGH SCHOOL – 100 S. Illinois St., Shamrock, TX 79079

SHAMROCK COUNTRY CLUB – 900 N. Wall St., Shamrock, TX 79079

DEVIL'S ROPE MUSEUM – 100 Kingsley St., McLean, TX 79057

MCLEAN HIGH SCHOOL – 6th and Main, McLean, TX 79057

MCLEAN GOLF COURSE – Z Rd., McLean, TX 79057

RED RIVER STEAKHOUSE – 101 U.S. Rte. 66, McLean, TX 79057

GOLDEN LIGHT CANTINA – 2906 S.W. 6th Ave., Amarillo, TX 79106

HODGETOWN – 715 S. Buchanan St., Amarillo, TX 79101

AMARILLO CIVIC CENTER – 401 S. Buchanan St., Amarillo, TX 79101

TRI-STATE EXPO – 3301 S.E. 10th Ave., Amarillo, TX 79104

DICK BIVINS STADIUM – 801 S. Marrs St., Amarillo, TX 79104

TASCOSA HIGH SCHOOL – 3921 Westlawn Ave., Amarillo, TX 79102

AMARILLO HIGH SCHOOL – 4225 Danbury Drive, Amarillo, TX 79109

CAPROCK HIGH SCHOOL – 3001 E. 34th Ave., Amarillo, TX 79103

PALO DURO HIGH SCHOOL – 1400 N. Grant St., Amarillo, TX 79107

SAN JACINTO CHRISTIAN ACADEMY – 501 S. Carolina St., Amarillo, TX 79106

SANJAC STADIUM – 4100 Republic Ave., Amarillo, TX 79109

AMARILLO COUNTRY CLUB – 4800 Bushland Blvd., Amarillo, TX 79106

BIG TEXAN STEAK RANCH AND BREWERY – 7701 I-40 East, Amarillo, TX 79118

CADILLAC RANCH – 13651 I-40 Frontage Road, Amarillo, TX 79124

BUSHLAND HIGH SCHOOL – 1201 FM2381, Bushland, TX 79012

MAGNOLIA GAS STATION – 105 S. Main St., Vega, TX 79092

MILBURN-PRICE CULTURE MUSEUM – 1005 Coke St., Vega, TX 79092

VEGA HIGH SCHOOL – 200 Longhorn St., Vega, TX 79092

MIDPOINT CAFE – 305 W. Historic Rte. 66, Adrian, TX 79001

ADRIAN HIGH SCHOOL – 301 E. Matador Drive, Adrian, TX 79001

NEW MEXICO

Three sports truly define New Mexico athletics: rodeo, soccer, and basketball. The Land of Enchantment is home to an iconic college basketball venue, one of America's best sports bars, and some of the best balloon racing in the world.

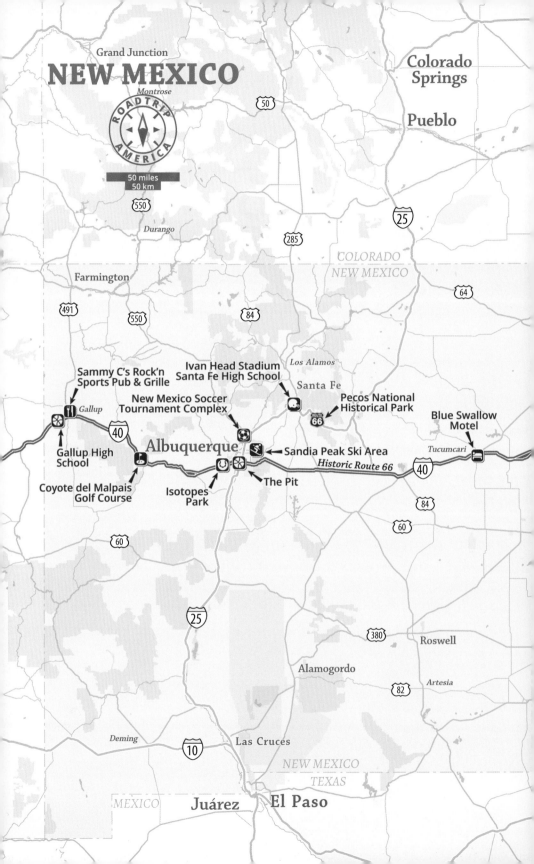

NEW MEXICO

Grand Junction

Montrose

50 miles
50 km

Colorado
Springs

Pueblo

550

Durango

25

COLORADO
NEW MEXICO

Farmington

64

491

550

84

Los Alamos

Sammy C's Rock'n
Sports Pub & Grille

Gallup

Ivan Head Stadium
Santa Fe High School

Santa Fe

Pecos National
Historical Park

New Mexico Soccer
Tournament Complex

Blue Swallow
Motel

40

Albuquerque

ROUTE
66

Tucumcari

Gallup High
School

Sandia Peak Ski Area

Historic Route 66

40

Coyote del Malpais
Golf Course

Isotopes
Park

The Pit

60

84

60

60

25

380

Roswell

Alamogordo

82

Artesia

Deming

10

Las Cruces

NEW MEXICO
TEXAS

MEXICO

Juárez

El Paso

285

TUCUMCARI

Tucumcari tonight? Yes. Tomorrow night, too.

The eastern New Mexico town is a Route 66 gem. Although it may not have quite the energy it did in the Mother Road's heyday, Tucumcari is a must-stop, and the above slogan still applies.

There is no shortage of places to stay along Route 66, which is the Interstate 40 Business Loop through town. The **Motel Safari** and **Blue Swallow Motel** are among the most popular places to lay your head. A suggestion is to grab a meal or an adult beverage at the **Pow Wow Restaurant and Lizard Lounge**. Say hi to Jerome the lizard while you're there. Larger lizards can be seen at the **Mesalands Community College Dinosaur Museum**.

Welcome to Tucumcari.

Mesalands is a rodeo standout

The two-year college is a block south of Route 66 just past the Pow Wow and is a rodeo hotbed. The college rodeo season runs the entire school year, from August to May, and **Mesalands Community College** has one of the best programs in the country. Some Mesalands rodeo alumni include Cody Heffernon, Jordan Spears, and Sydney Blanchard.

The program was built by former coach C. J. Aragon, who had Mesalands ranked number one in the country during his six-year tenure from 2007 to 2013. Matt Hughes was hired as the Mesalands coach in 2016 and has continued the program's success. Mesalands sent four rodeo cowboys, three of them bull riders, to the NIRA finals in Casper, Wyoming, in 2019.

Despite being a two-year school, Hughes said it's "not hard at all" to compete with four-year schools like Arizona State, University of Nevada, Las Vegas (UNLV), or New Mexico State.

"What makes it tough is that the recruiting part never ends for me," explained Hughes, who was the NIRA coach of the year for the 2018–19 season. "When a kid comes in, the year after, I'm looking to replace him already. There's good and bad with it. If you get a kid who's a pain in the ass, at a four-year school, you're kind of stuck with him. Often times, it works the other way."

The Mesalands Stampede have wonderful community support, especially when they host their annual October NIRA event at the **Quay County Fairgrounds**. The two-day competition coincides with the city's Fossil Day Festival.

"Every year, we've grown in every area. We've grown in numbers. We've

grown in ads. We've grown with people in the stands," added Hughes, a West Plains, Missouri, native who was an amateur calf-roper and professional bull rider before he got into coaching. "Every way you can grow as a program, we've grown.

"The cool part about college rodeo is we're the only collegiate sport that you can professionally do while in college at the same time ... College rodeo is pretty awesome."

Sports success at Tucumcari High

Many Mesalands students come from **Tucumcari High School**, where the Rattlers have celebrated multiple state championships. Those titles are listed on a hilltop water tower near Interstate 40. The Rattlers won football championships 1959, 2000, and 2002; boys' basketball titles in 1950 and 1951; boys' track in 1927, 1928, 1979, 1983, and 2008; girls' track in 2002 and 2003; and boys' cross-country in 1990. There are six classifications in New Mexico for high school sports. Cross-country has three classes with the lower three classes combined into one classification. Tucumcari currently competes at the 2A level.

The high school is on South Seventh Street, two blocks off Route 66. All of the athletics facilities are right on campus. **Rattler Stadium**, home to the football and track teams, is a 1,660-seat stadium with simple bleachers on either side of the grass field where former NFL player Stan David got his start. Rattlers games can be more of a social gathering for some, though plenty of fans follow every play.

A large Route 66 mural is on an exterior wall of a Tucumcari grocery store.

Beyond sports in Tucumcari

When Tucumcari had a larger population in the 1950s, the fairgrounds complex was almost always bustling with activity. It's not as busy today, but there are still many attractions at the fairgrounds, including the rodeo, the adjacent **New Mexico Route 66 Museum** (which features several classic cars), the convention center, and ball fields.

A Route 66 monument stands in front of the Route 66 Museum. The monument was created in 1997 by artist Thomas Coffin and resembles a tailfin on a classic 1950s car. The athletic complex behind the museum includes a varsity baseball field, three softball fields, and two Little League fields. Batters and spectators watching from behind home plate at the varsity field have a superb view of Tucumcari Mountain.

Hikers are no longer allowed on the mountain, but those looking for outdoor activities can head over to nearby **Tucumcari Lake** and **Ute Lake State Park**. Both lakes have plenty of walleye, bass, and perch.

Tucumcari's Route 66 monument was placed in front of the New Mexico Route 66 Museum in 1997 and resembles a tailfin on a classic 1950s car.

SANTA ROSA

A different watering hole awaits you in Santa Rosa. The **Blue Hole** is a natural artesian well world-renowned for SCUBA diving. Because the perfectly clear water is a constant 62 degrees, which can be refreshing during the hot desert summers, the Blue Hole is a destination for locals and tourists alike. The **Santa Rosa Visitor Center** is right next to the tiny rock-lined lake, which is a short detour off Route 66 with a couple of left turns onto Lake Drive and then Blue Hole Road.

Santa Rosa calls itself the City of Natural Lakes, and just around the bend from the Blue Hole is **Park Lake**. The recreational lake is wonderful for families because of its inflatable water slides during the summer months. The park has softball fields used for

The sign in front of the Blue Hole in Santa Rosa provides information on the famous swimming hole.

tournaments every Memorial Day, July 4, and Labor Day weekends. **Perch Lake** to the south has plenty of its namesake fish, and **Santa Rosa Lake State Park** to the north has bass, catfish, and walleye. The state park also has an RV park and several hiking and biking trails. Santa Rosa hosts the City of Lakes Triathlon, a USA Triathlon sanctioned event, in early June.

Less than a mile from the Blue Hole, and just south of Route 66 on Highway 91, is **Santa Rosa High School**. The Santa Rosa football program has a storied history of success. The Lions have played for a state championship 16 times through 2020, winning half of those games. The football stadium is on the south side of the school. The field is surrounded by a black track used by girls' and boys' teams that have a combined five state championships. The girls' cross-country team also won a state championship in 2001.

Three sections of bleachers with a small press box atop the middle section are on the home side with a small set of bleachers on the opposite side. A

The Blue Hole in Santa Rosa is a destination for many SCUBA divers.

baseball field with a row of trees behind the left-field fence is behind the football stadium. Santa Rosa's baseball team won a 2A state championship in 1981. Santa Rosa's gym is in the school itself and home to a boys' basketball program that has four state championships.

One quirky sport at Santa Rosa is lawnmower racing. Yep, lawnmower racing. The school was one of the first in the country to establish a lawnmower racing club. Lawnmower racing began in England in 1968 and migrated to the United States in the 1980s. It's a different spin on motorsports, and there are now more than 120 lawnmower races in New Mexico every year, most of them on the local level.

More traditional vehicles can be found at the **Route 66 Auto Museum** on the east side of town. The museum has a large collection of classic cars and street rods that you can peruse after paying a modest admission price. Directly across the street from the auto museum is the entrance to the **Santa Rosa Golf Course**, which is a 9-hole course that also has a 20-tee driving

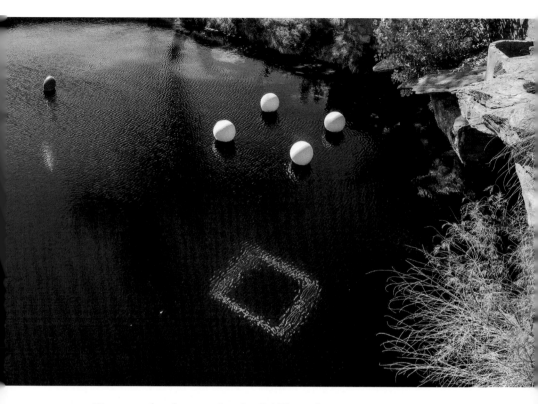

range. The grass bunkers make the 3,158-yard course a unique experience.

Route 66 resumes on the west side of Santa Rosa on I-40, where you have a decision to make 17 miles down the road.

ALBUQUERQUE CUT-OFF OR SANTA FE LOOP

Whether you take the I-40 corridor straight through to Albuquerque or decide to drive the pre-1937 route to Santa Fe, there is not much of anything between Santa Rosa and either city. But you will see vast plains and stupendous terrain no matter the path you take. The Santa Fe loop is the recommended route because it offers much better views, and you'll even pass by legendary Starvation Peak. There isn't much for sports along the I-40 corridor, but you can get your fix at **Moriarty High School**. The **MAGS Indoor Shooting Range** is also in Moriarty, a town of 1,900 41 miles east of Albuquerque.

Moriarty High is 24 miles west of the **Clines Corners** travel depot, and 2 miles south of Interstate 40 on Center Avenue. The Moriarty Pintos have several state championships across seven sports. The athletics facilities are what you'd expect at a smaller school. And although the facilities are modest, the energy from the student body is fantastic.

The mountains meet the plains in Edgewood, a small Route 66 community that is home to the **Wildlife West Nature Park**. The park is a 122-acre animal rescue habitat right along I-40. Edgewood is also where motocross racer Jason Anderson and UFC fighter Donald "The Cowboy" Cerrone reside. A different sort of cowboy is showcased every summer when Edgewood hosts its annual Cowboy Days. The three-week festival that ends July 4 weekend features live music, car shows, craft beers, cowboy shooting performances, and, of course, rodeo events. The **Greater Edgewood Chamber of Commerce** hosts Cowboy Days and has all the information you'd need about the year's schedule of events.

If you take the Santa Fe loop off I-40, you'll exit at Highway 84 and head north. Another option would be to take the Clines Corners exit and take Highway 285 north to Santa Fe. But Highway 84 is the original alignment through Dilia to what is now Interstate 25 at the old hamlet of Romeroville.

Clines Corners in New Mexico is a nice spot to fuel up and grab some Route 66 souvenirs.

Take a chance on Las Vegas, New Mexico

New Mexico has its own Las Vegas, and it's worth the 7-mile detour. The city of 13,000 is loaded with murals in its quaint downtown and several buildings on the National Register of Historic Places. One of those buildings is the **Plaza Hotel**, where Teddy Roosevelt hosted his first Rough Riders reunion.

Las Vegas is also home to **New Mexico Highlands University**. The NCAA Division II school has strong rugby, rodeo, football, and wrestling programs. NMHU is the alma mater of former WWE star Eddie Guerrero; NFL players Lionel Taylor, Charlie Cowan, Carl Garrett, Len Garrett, and Don Woods; and USA Rugby player Kevon Williams. For a D-II school, NMHU has excellent facilities with **Sanchez Family Stadium** for football and soccer, **Brandt Field** for baseball and softball, and the **John A. Wilson Complex** for basketball, wrestling, and volleyball.

PECOS

The first thing that comes to mind when people think of Pecos, New Mexico, is **Pecos National Historical Park**. The park features the Glorieta Pass, ancestral Native American dwellings, 200-year-old ranches, and an American Civil War battlefield. Pecos is an outdoorsman's paradise with pristine spots to camp, hike, hunt, and fish along the Pecos River. There's even the **Santa Fe Fly Fishing School** on the north end of town for those who want to learn that skill.

There are fun things to see indoors as well. Less than 2 miles from the park entrance is **Pecos High School**, where its Panthers have built a strong basketball legacy.

Pecos won its first boys' basketball championship in 1966, and the Panthers have been a New Mexico state playoff regular since. They were runners-up in 1967, 1983, 1987, and 2005 before finally winning another championship in 2017. That victory came at the expense of Santa Rosa High School and was the first of four consecutive titles. The first two were at the 3A level before Pecos dropped down to 2A because of declining enrollment. Pecos was coached by Ira Harge Jr.—the son of former professional basketball player Ira Harge, who played at the University of New Mexico—during its four-peat. The Panther girls completed a 2A sweep in 2019 with their first state championship. The recent success has resulted in the school's gym being packed for home games. Pecos also has a cheerleading squad that has won multiple state competitions, and the group adds to the entertainment and excitement of Panthers basketball games. Despite being a 2A school with fewer than 200 students, the Panthers aren't afraid to take on teams from 5A schools with enrollments 10 times their size.

There is no football at Pecos, but there is soccer. The small stadium has a grass pitch surrounded by a dark track used by the track-and-field teams. If you do attend a meet, try not be distracted by the scenic mountain backdrop. It won't be easy.

SANTA FE

Santa Fe has three public high schools and four institutions of higher learning. The colleges do not field athletics, and you won't see any stadiums or other sports venues along Route 66 through Santa Fe. You also won't find any towering buildings in New Mexico's capital city, founded in 1610. What you will see is a sprawling collection of adobe pueblo buildings that are the heart of the city of 84,000 people.

New Mexico's oldest bar and restaurant is in Santa Fe—**El Farol** on Canyon Road. El Farol has been in business since 1835 and is now an upscale tapas restaurant.

High school dedicated to Native American students

Santa Fe Indian School (SFIS) is the only high school along Route 66. The school was founded in 1890 and currently has an enrollment of around 700 Native American students. Though operated by the 19 Pueblos of New Mexico and not the state, the SFIS Braves still compete within the New Mexico Activities Association (NMAA). SFIS is known for its studio that has helped developed several prominent Native American artists, but the Braves athletics teams are pretty good.

The Braves have won multiple state titles in several events. The boys' cross-country team owned four state championships as of 2020, while the girls won a trio of titles. The Braves earned boys' basketball titles in 1989 and 2019, and the girls won five hoops titles between 1986 and 2019. The baseball program claimed state championships in 1957, 1987, and 1989.

A long history at Santa Fe High

Santa Fe High School isn't visible from Route 66, but it is less than 2 miles from the historic **El Rey Court** motel. Santa Fe High dates back to 1899 and is one of the oldest high schools in New Mexico. One of the best athletes to come out of Santa Fe High was 1992 Olympian Carla Garrett, a competitive weightlifter who was a standout on the Santa Fe soccer, basketball, and track teams. She threw the discus at the 1992 Olympic Games.

Santa Fe High is home to the Demons, who had a cross-country dynasty in the 1970s and '80s. The Santa Fe boys won six of seven 4A state championships from 1974 to 1980, and the girls overlapped with six of their own state titles from 1979 to 1986. The Demons volleyball team won four state championships between 1978 and 1996. The ladies won a trio of tennis titles between 1994 and '97. Golf titles were won by the boys in 1976 and girls in 1985, and a 4A baseball championship came in 1977.

The Demons basketball teams have had more recent success. The girls won their third overall championship in 2014. The boys' program has a storied history that dates back to 1940, when the Demons won their first state title. The program produced Toby Roybal, who went on to have a stellar career at the University of New Mexico in Albuquerque. Roybal's number 44 is the only number retired by the UMN program. Santa Fe won its second state title in 1941, and the Demons added their fifth championship in 2019.

The Demons football team won its only championship with a 4A title in 1979. Santa Fe competes at the 5A level today and is a regular playoff contender. The Demons play at the creatively built **Ivan Head Stadium**. The stadium seats 6,000 with a large grandstand on the home side and a smaller seating section for the visitors. The stadium is dug into a hill, and berms of sand and desert grass give the stadium a horseshoe effect. The press box atop the grandstand is part of a brick athletics building that abuts the stadium.

Capital High thrives on rivalries

Santa Fe's biggest rival is **Capital High School**, located a mile and a half west of Cerillos Road. The school was founded in 1988 as Santa Fe's second public school. The entrance has towering white columns that make the building resemble the old state capitol, which is now the **Bataan Memorial Building**. The sports rivalry with Santa Fe was natural, and the Capital Jaguars have developed strong rivalries with St. Michael's and Española Valley to the north. When Capital plays any of those three schools, expect the stands to be near capacity.

The Jaguars are competitive in most sports, but boys' basketball is easily Capital's best program. The Jaguars won a 4A championship in 2004, with second-place finishes in 2005 and 2007. Even after reclassification moved them up to 5A, the Jaguars still go deep in the playoffs. Capital was the state runner-up in 2016, 2017, and 2020 under longtime coach Ben Gomez.

The basketball, wrestling, and volleyball teams use Capital's in-house gymnasium. The outdoor teams play on adjacent fields separated by tennis courts used by the Capital boys' and girls' teams. **Jaguar Stadium**, used by the football, soccer, and track teams, takes up a substantial parcel of land. The 2,300-seat stadium has an artificial turf pitch adorned by a jaguar inside at wishbone "C"—a logo similar to the one used by the Chicago Bears and Cincinnati Reds—at midfield.

St. Michael's High fields strong teams

St. Michael's High School, which is 2.5 miles east of El Rey Court, has Santa Fe's most successful sports programs. The De La Salle Christian Brothers Catholic school has won more than 70 NMAA state championships. While the spirit and cheerleading teams have more than 20 of those titles, the most successful sports program at St. Michael's has been boys' basketball. The Horsemen played in the state championship game 19 times as of 2020, winning 11 titles. The girls played for a 3A title in 2008 but lost to Pojoaque in the championship game.

The St. Michael's wrestling and volleyball teams have enjoyed success over the years. The volleyball team won 3A titles in 2002 and 2018 and was the 2019 runner-up. The wrestling team won five straight team championships in the 1960s before falling off, but the Horsemen were back with consecutive championships in 2012 and '13.

Next to the school is **Brother Edward de Raina Park**, which is more of an athletic complex than a traditional park. Brother Edward de Raina houses the St. Michael's football and baseball stadiums. The colorful football stadium has a large bright blue section in one end zone. That area is used as the high-jump area for track-and-field meets. The word "Horsemen" bisects a large white "M" in the middle of the grass field, which is surrounded by a black track with blue trim.

The outdoor sports have been just as successful as the indoor ones. The football team is always in the mix for a state title. The Horsemen first played in the championship game in 1954 and has since played for a state championship 12 times with 5 victories.

After placing second in the state boys' soccer tournament four straight years from 2001 to 2004, the Horsemen finally claimed their first championship in 2019 with a win over the New Mexico Military Institute from Roswell. The St. Michael's ladies have had a little more success on the pitch. The Horsemen girls have played in the championship game 10 times since 2000, winning 3 titles.

The St. Michael's baseball team won consecutive 3A titles in 2003 and '04 and placed second in 2006 and 2010. Former professional baseball player Ron Porterfield, who has been a trainer for the Tampa Bay Rays since 2006, is a notable alumnus of the St. Michael's baseball program. The St. Michael's girls won four straight cross-country titles from 2005 to 2008, led by two-time champion Irene Ossola and three-time individual winner Kate Norskog. The two also helped lead the Horsemen to four straight girls' track championships from 2004 to 2007. Ossola went on to compete as a professional cyclist. The Horsemen boys were state track champions in 2019.

There really isn't a sport in which St. Michael's doesn't field a strong team, so no matter the season you'll see one of New Mexico's best high school programs should you decided to spend an evening getting to know the Horsemen.

A mix of other sports and cultural features

Santa Fe is home to an independent minor league baseball team. The Fuego play at **Fort Marcy Ballfield** about a mile and a half north of Old Town. The Fuego were founded in 2012 and play in the Pecos League, which has teams across Texas, Kansas, Colorado, New Mexico, Arizona, and California. The Fuego finished second to the Roswell Invaders in 2015.

When visiting Santa Fe, it's easy to forget about sports for a bit and just enjoy the centuries-old culture, wonderful food, and bountiful art galleries and museums. Santa Fe is known as a creative art city, and one of the places where that stands out is **Meow Wolf**, right along Route 66. The "interactive art gallery" is more like an art gallery on drugs and definitely a fun way to spend an evening. You'll even get some exercise climbing on Meow Wolf's exhibits or exploring its twisting tunnels. Even if you get lost among Santa Fe's dizzying web of one-way streets, you'll likely discover a site of historical significance in North America's oldest capital city. The city does offer a free shuttle through its historic and museum districts.

Golfers can take advantage of one of the best municipal courses in the country while in Santa Fe. **Marty Sanchez's Links de Santa Fe** has a perfectly manicured 18-hole course tucked between the Sangre Cristo, Jemez, Sandia, and Ortiz mountain ranges. If you want to get a quick game in, the Links has a par-28 course recognized by *Travel & Leisure* as one of the top five "big little courses" in the United States. There's also a driving range at the course, which is just past a sports complex comprised of rugby, softball, and soccer fields along Caja del Rio Road. The **Santa Fe Country Club** is another option for golfers. The semi-private club on Highway 284 has hosted various PGA events and pro-ams. Greens fees are pretty reasonable to play the course with treelined fairways, rolling mounds, and two small lakes.

Santa Fe is perfect for outdoor recreation with miles of trails for hiking, biking, or horseback riding. The **New Mexico Department of Game & Fish** near the Links issues certain hunting and fishing licenses, and has maps and information on various recreational activities.

Don't let the winter months scare you away from Route 66 in New Mexico. **Ski Santa Fe** has 83 trails on 660 acres in the Sangre De Cristo mountains. The resort is 16 miles northeast of the city center.

Meow Wolf in Santa Fe is a trippy "art gallery" unlike any other.

When heading south from Santa Fe, you will see a large stadium complex along Interstate 25. That was **The Downs**, a horse track that opened in 1971 but closed for good in 1997. It is used today primarily as a concert venue and hosts other outdoor events—just not horse racing. Before leaving Santa Fe, you may want to check out **La Bajada Hill**. La Bajada was part of the original Route 66 alignment but quickly abandoned because of its steep incline and dangerous switchbacks. It's a bit of an off-road trek, but the payoff is worth it.

BERNALILLO

Bypassing La Bajada Hill, the Santa Fe loop returns to the modern I-40 corridor in Albuquerque, via what is now Interstate 25. The 64-mile stretch includes a few small villages and the municipality of Bernalillo. The town of 8,300 is 17 miles north of downtown Albuquerque and has a high school right off I-25.

Bernalillo High School is home to the Spartans, who had 12 state championships to their credit as of 2020. While the Bernalillo cross-country team won four state titles between 1966 and 1971, the school's most prolific

The rough seven-mile dirt road out to La Bajada Hill, part of the original route, is rough but worth the detour. Info can be found at the Santa Fe BLM office.

program has been boys' basketball. The Spartans won their first of five state championships in 1977 but fell off in the 1990s. They were back with consecutive championships in 2004 and '05 under coach Terry Darnell, who led them to the 4A title game in 2018.

The Bernalillo gym, which is also used by the volleyball and wrestling teams, has two levels of bright red bleachers lining its glossy wood floor. When the upper bleachers are pushed in, one side reads BHS with a red Spartan logo, while the other spells out Spartans. Of course games are more fun when those bleachers are pulled out and full of fans.

Bernalillo is also home to the **New Mexico Soccer Tournament Complex**, which hosts the boys' and girls' state tournaments. The Spartan boys won the small-school soccer tournament in 1986. The complex is just west of the Rio Grande and **Santa Ana Star Casino**. Each of the complex's 22 pitches has lights for evening matches. Another sports complex is the **State Farm Soccer Complex** with 22 fields highlighted by a pair of championship-level pitches. The soccer complex has hosted the NAIA national championships in addition to a slew of local and regional tournaments.

September is a great time to visit Bernalillo. Not only can you attend a Spartans football game, but the New Mexico Wine Festival is held in Bernalillo every Labor Day weekend and draws thousands to the town where the first New Mexico wines were made some 400 years ago.

ALBUQUERQUE

Route 66 and sports are rarely linked, but there are plenty of sports to enjoy in New Mexico's largest city, and it's all along the Mother Road. If you come into Albuquerque from the east along Interstate 40, don't miss the **Musical Highway** near Tijeras. If you drive 45 miles per hour, you will hear "America the Beautiful" as you pass over the short stretch. If you arrive in Albuquerque from Santa Fe on the I-25 corridor, the Musical Highway is worth a detour.

Heading west from Tijeras, you'll pass the **Route 66 Open Space**, a popular hiking area in the Tijeras Hills. The public land occupies what was once the Little Beaver Town theme park. Route 66 becomes Central Avenue

Albuquerque's Route 66 arch spans Central Avenue.

at the Open Space and cuts through the heart of downtown Albuquerque. Central Avenue takes you by the **KiMo Theatre**, the neon lights of the **Nob Hill** neighborhood, historic **Old Town** that includes **San Felipe de Neri Church**, the Fourth Street Historic District, and the **Dog House Drive In** that had cameos in the television shows *Breaking Bad* and *Better Call Saul*. One fun sports bar in downtown Albuquerque is **The Library**, which has an amusing facade that includes altered book titles like *Tequila Mockingbird, Gone With the Gin, A Midsummer Night's Drink,* and *Lord of the Onion Rings.*

No other venue like The Pit at UNM

Before you get to downtown Albuquerque, the Mother Road bisects the **University of New Mexico** (UNM) campus. UNM was founded in 1889 and is the largest university in the Land of Enchantment. Its sports teams are called the Lobos, and the entire campus is dotted with small wolf statues. UNM is part of the Mountain West Conference, and each of the Lobos programs competes at the Division I level. New Mexico teams have won three national championships—skiing in 2004 and women's cross-country in 2015 and 2017.

The university is also home to one of the most revered college basketball venues in the country. **The Pit**, formally known as **University Arena**, is

Albquerque's famous Dog House has appeared in multiple television shows, most notably Breaking Bad and Better Call Saul.

rich with hoops history. It opened in 1966 and has been a regional host for NCAA Tournament games nine times between 1968 and 2012. Before UNM joined the Mountain West, The Pit held the Western Athletic Conference men's tournaments in 1987, 1995, and 1996. The Pit hosted NCAA women's tournament games six times between 2003 and 2011. The Pit was also the

The entrance to The Pit was renovated in 2009.

site of one of college basketball's biggest upsets. The arena hosted the 1983 Final Four when the North Carolina State men's team, coached by Jim Valvano, upset heavily favored Houston to win the national championship.

The Pit got its name because the floor is 37 feet below street level. If you're fortunate enough to have a seat near the court, you've got a pretty long—and steep—walk. But it's worth it because you really get the feel of being in The Pit. Signs around the arena read, "Welcome to The Pit, a mile high and louder than ..." The public address announcer says the same thing before games, but fans finish the sentence by yelling, "Hell."

Before a 2011 remodel eliminated 3,000 seats to add luxury suites and large video boards at either end of the arena, The Pit was one of the loudest college basketball venues in the country with crowd noise reaching 125 decibels. All 18,000 seats were regularly filled to create a home-court advantage few teams enjoy. *Sports Illustrated* ranked The Pit as the world's 13th best sports venue of the 20th century.

"It was the best. It seemed like during the national anthem, we were 10 points up," said Gary Colson, who was the Lobos men's basketball coach from 1980 to 1988. "What success we had here, we didn't do it alone."

Colson cleaned up a scandal-ridden program and led the Lobos to three 20-win seasons and five National Invitation Tournament (NIT) appearances. Despite a top-20 ranking in 1988, the Lobos were snubbed from the more prestigious NCAA Tournament. New Mexico has qualified for the NCAA tourney 15 times, including 3 straight automatic berths from 2012 to 2014 by virtue of winning the Mountain West Conference tournament. The women's team has been selected to the NCAA Tournament eight times and made a run to the Sweet 16 in 2003.

The concourse at The Pit is lined with posters and placards of the program's best teams and players. Images of Basketball Hall of Famer Mel Daniels; WNBA player Jordan Adams; and NBA players Michael Cooper, Luc Longley, Kenny Thomas, Charles Smith, Danny Granger, J. R. Giddens, Darington Hobson, and Tony Snell hang on the walls inside the Rudy Davalos Basketball Center.

"I've never gotten numb walking into The Pit, understanding what this place is about and what it means to so many people," said New Mexico basketball coach Paul Weir, who took over the Lobos program in 2017. "It's a blessing to coach here. To be the basketball coach here is the honor of a lifetime."

The Pit's luxury suites are often empty because of their price and distance from the court. Although the crowds aren't as rowdy today as they once were, The Pit still provides an outstanding atmosphere for a basketball game. Despite some sparse crowds for women's hoops in an arena that seats around 15,000, the Lobos faithful are loud.

"I love it," guard Ahlise Hurst, who came to New Mexico in 2018 as a true freshman, said of playing at The Pit. "It gives us something to play for—to play for the fans and to hear their energy. That drives us to play. It brings so much energy and confidence to us when we play."

The Pit is also home to the NMAA high school state basketball championships. And they're a huge draw for both the boys and girls.

"The teams that get to play in The Pit every March, that's a big thing—especially for some of the teams from the reservations like Shiprock or Gallup. They'll fill The Pit just to see their teams play there," said Rio Rancho sports editor Gary Herron, who is a member of the New Mexico Route 66 Association.

The Pit at the University of New Mexico prior to a women's basketball game in 2019.

UNM's other sports facilities

The Lobos football team plays across the street at the 39,000-seat **University Stadium**. But the program that produced Pro Football Hall of Famer Brian Urlacher won just seven total games in the three seasons following consecutive bowl appearances in 2015 and 2016. A sign outside the stadium reminds visitors to "Get Your Kicks." The stadium has held the New Mexico Bowl every December since 2006. The Lobos have played in their own bowl game four times, including the inaugural game when they lost to San Jose State. New Mexico won its bowl game twice, beating Nevada in 2007 and the University of Texas-San Antonio in 2016.

Adjacent to University Stadium are a pair of practice bubbles that one might assume are for the Lobos football team, but they are actually part of the UNM tennis complex, which has six outdoor courts in addition to the two practice bubbles. On the same side of Chavez Boulevard as The Pit is the UNM baseball and softball field, as well as the **McKinnon Family Tennis Stadium. Santa Ana Star Field** has been home to the baseball team since the 1960s, though it did play at Isotopes Park—home to the city's Triple-A baseball team—from 2003 to 2013. New Mexico has played in the NCAA baseball tournament five times, including four appearances between 2011 and 2016. The program was started in 1899 and has since produced multiple MLB players, including Minnesota Twins catcher Mitch Garver. The softball, tennis, and baseball fields all provide stunning sunset views of the city.

The UNM track teams compete during the indoor season at the **Albuquerque Convention Center**, which has a six-lane 200-meter Mondo oval track. The convention center facility hosted the USA Track & Field Indoor Championships seven times between 2010 and 2018. The downtown convention center is two blocks north of Central Avenue.

UNM has its own golf course, though it's 4 miles south of the campus, just off Interstate 25 next to the Albuquerque airport. The **University of New Mexico Golf Course** is rated as one of the top public courses in the country. The Championship Course opened in 1967 and has hosted NCAA championships five times in addition to a handful of conference meets. At 5,300 feet, the thin air allows golfers to launch significant drives down the blue and rye grass fairways. Because Albuquerque has clear, sunny skies for an average of 310 days per year, you almost always have a wonderful view of the downtown skyline from the course.

A must-see for *Simpsons* fans

Isotopes Park sits kitty-corner from The Pit and is a fun place to watch baseball. The Albuquerque Isotopes got their name from *The Simpsons*, specifically the episode "Homer at the Bat." Another episode, "Hungry, Hungry Homer," has a storyline of Homer going on a hunger strike when he finds out Springfield's team is moving to, of all places, New Mexico. When the Calgary Cannons moved to Albuquerque in 2003, a fan poll was held to pick a new name for the team. The name "Isotopes" garnered two-thirds of the vote. The Isotopes replaced the Dukes, who moved to Portland, Oregon, in 2000 after a 29-season stay in Albuquerque.

The Simpsons connection with the Isotopes is

Below: The Sandia Mountains provide the backdrop beyond the wall at Isotopes Park, where the grounds crew maintains the field year-round. Right: The elaborately decorated Isotopes Park is home to the Triple-A affiliate of the Colorado Rockies.

prevalent, and there are statues of Marge, Homer, Bart, Lisa, and Maggie scattered throughout the park. Homer is sitting on a bench directly behind home plate on the main concourse.

The team was met with much fanfare. After the team was introduced in 2002, Isotopes merchandise flew off the shelves. Before the team had played a single game, the Isotopes had sold more merch in three months than the Dukes did in an entire season. With a capacity of more than 13,000 at Isotopes Park, the team consistently has some of the best attendance numbers in the Pacific Coast League.

The Isotopes were originally an affiliate of the Florida Marlins and switched to the Los Angeles Dodgers in 2009. The 'Topes have been the Triple-A team of the Colorado Rockies since 2015. Several notable MLB players, including All-Stars Joc Pederson and Manny Ramirez, have donned an Isotopes jersey. Minor league baseball games are a ton of fun, and the Triple-A product—just one level below MLB—is very good.

Isotopes Park, nicknamed "The Lab," is also home to the New Mexico United of the United Soccer League. The club began play in 2018 and is the fourth minor league soccer team Albuquerque has had. The team's branding borrows from the Zia symbol used on the New Mexico state flag.

ABQ High's long history

As you'd expect in a city of more than half a million, Albuquerque has a multitude of high schools, and a few are along Route 66.

The city's oldest school is **Albuquerque High School**, which opened in 1879 and is just off of I-25 on Odelia Road and 2 miles north of Central Avenue. The old high school building, which still stands at the corner of Central Avenue and Broadway Boulevard, was added to the New Mexico State Register of Cultural Properties in 1977. The old school is now a luxury apartment building.

The Albuquerque Bulldogs were once the top dogs of New Mexico high school sports. ABQ High won 10 of the first 11 state baseball tournaments from 1940 to 1950, the first two state basketball tourneys in 1921 and '22, and the first boys' track championship in 1913. The track title was the first of 20 for the Bulldogs between 1913 and 1960. The wrestling program had six titles from the first championship tourney in 1957 through 1974. The basketball program has remained competitive with 12 total state titles, most recently in 1998. Kenny Thomas led the Bulldogs to a state championship in 1995 before attending the University of New Mexico and spending 11 seasons in the NBA. The Bulldogs played in the title game 10 other times during that eight-decade span. ABQ High is still a regular contender, qualifying for the state tournament four times between 2015 and 2020, advancing to the 6A state semifinals in 2015 before losing to Rio Rancho's Cleveland High.

The ABQ High football team plays at **Milne Stadium**, a 6,500-seat venue shared by four other schools. The Highland Hornets, Rio Grande Ravens, Valley Vikings, and Hope Christian Huskies also play at the stadium, which is owned and operated by Albuquerque Public Schools. The ABQ High football team has had some rough times, including the dubious state record of 43 consecutive losses over 2010–14. Despite the lack of football success, ABQ High produced NFL player Billy Jenkins, who had a six-year professional career from 1997 to 2002.

Milne Stadium may have modern amenities like a mondotrack around the artificial turf field and a glass-encased press box, but it is saturated with local history. Built in 1939 as a Works Progress Administration (WPA) project, Milne Stadium has been the site of many state playoff and championship football games, as well as numerous state track-and-field meets.

In a city that's a hotbed for high school soccer, ABQ High holds its own with the proverbial big dogs. The Bulldog boys won 6A state titles in 2015, '17, and '19, and were the state runners-up in 2014 and '16.

Sandia Prep shines

Several Albuquerque high schools have won multiple state soccer championships. The school with the most soccer titles is **Sandia Preparatory School**. Sandia Prep, which is on Osuna Road just west of I-25, has 17 boys' state championships, while the girls have won six titles, including four straight from 2016 to 2019. The girls have also placed second six times, while the boys are seven-time runners-up.

The Sandia Sundevils didn't win their first state title until 1985, when the boys' soccer team beat Hope Christian. That was 19 years after the school opened, but Sandia Prep easily made up for lost time—and not just in soccer. The baseball team won six state titles between 2001 and 2016. There were four volleyball championships from 2004 to 2017; 15 combined tennis titles; and consecutive girls' track championships in 1998–99.

The Sandia Prep campus occupies 30 acres with five athletics fields, four tennis courts, and a recently renovated track and soccer stadium. The school also has a pair of gymnasiums, a 600-seat arena with four courts on the west side, and an 800-seat field house used for varsity sports.

The Sundevils do not field a football team, but Sandia Prep is the only high school in the state with its own observatory. So catch a game and then look at the stars.

Sandia High strong in soccer

The private Sandia Prep is not to be confused with the public **Sandia High School**. The Sandia Matadors football program won a 4A state championship in 1976. The Matadors also played in the 4A title game in 1968 and 1977, and for a 5A championship in 2012. Sandia High is almost equidistant from both I-40 and I-25 on Candelaria Road. Its campus takes up about 17 city blocks with a pool on the north side and the baseball, football, and softball fields on the east side.

Sandia's soccer teams are among the perennial state championship contenders. The Sandia boys won state titles in 1982 and '92 and were state runners-up six times between 1995 and 2006. The 1999 team was undefeated before falling to city rival Manzano in the championship match. The Sandia girls claimed five state championships between 1985 and 2018.

Sandia's football team doesn't play its home varsity games on-campus but rather at the school district-owned **Wilson Stadium** on Lomas Boulevard. The 5,100-seat stadium is adjacent to **Manzano High School** and shared by Sandia, Manzano, Highland, La Cueva, and Eldorado for football and track.

Manzano Monarchs football has perfect season

The Manzano Monarchs won their first football crown in 2017 by beating La Cueva in the 6A title tilt to cap a perfect 13–0 season. The Monarchs previously played for a state title in 1996 and 2010. The Monarchs are not left out of the soccer championship list, with a pair of boys' titles in 1987 and 1999. The Manzano girls played in the championship game in 1990 and 1997. UFC fighter Holly Holm was a freshman in 1997 and was on the soccer, gymnastics, and swim teams while at Manzano.

Manzano has a strong boys' basketball program, with state championships in 1973 and '74 and again in 2006 before falling to Rio Rancho the following season. The gray-and-purple bleachers on either side of the small Manzano gym aren't often packed, but games against cross-town rivals usually bring bigger crowds.

Coaches Sanchez and Sanchez led Highland track to victory

Highland High School is a few blocks south of Central Avenue and east of downtown. The Hornets have played for a football championship 10 times, winning half. While the program remains competitive, Highland hasn't won a state championship since 1989. Highland won its first state championship in 1954, a few years after future Pro Football Hall of Famer Tommy McDonald graduated. McDonald was a star athlete for the Hornets as a football and basketball player and sprinter.

Nearly every other Highland program has multiple state championships to its credit. Of the more than 60 state championships, a third belong to the boys' track team. Hugh Hackett guided the Hornets to their first title in 1952 and won seven consecutive titles before giving way to Henry Sanchez, who pushed the streak to eight. Sanchez coached the team from 1959 to 1983, winning 10 state titles. Sanchez's son, Gary, took over following the elder's retirement and kept the proverbial ball rolling. Gary Sanchez led the Hornets to five championships with six second-place finishes over his 29-year tenure. Both father and son were inducted into the virtual New Mexico Sports Hall of Fame in 2013.

Although the girls' swim program has just one championship, it produced 1972 Olympic gold medalist Cathy Carr. The Highland softball team is 1–5 in state championship games, getting its lone victory in 1981 by beating Manzano. The baseball program that produced MLB players Tito Landrum and Rod Nichols won state championships in 1951, '59, and '87. The Highland softball and baseball fields face downtown, giving fans—and batters—a view of the downtown and mountain skylines.

Eldorado: Championship-game regulars

Another prolific Albuquerque high school is **Eldorado High School** at the base of South Sandia Peak. Eldorado has played in the state football championship game a total of eight times but has just one championship. The Golden Eagles won their lone football title in 1980. That team was led by quarterback Jim Everett, who went on to have an 11-year NFL career and was a Pro Bowler in 1990 for the Los Angeles Rams. Other NFL players who got their start at Eldorado are Vince Warren, who won a Super Bowl with the New York Giants in 1986, and Zach Gentry, who was a 2019 draft pick of the Pittsburgh Steelers. Before 2020, the Eagles last played in the state championship game in 2015, but they are a regular playoff participant.

Eldorado has multiple state championships in soccer, basketball, tennis, swimming, and wrestling. The Eagles played in the first-ever state championship soccer match in 1981 but fell to Highland. They earned their first of eight total championships in 1995 with a win over Sandia High. Devon Sandoval, who plays for the local New Mexico United after a four-year stint in Major League Soccer, led the Eagles to a pair of state championships while at Eldorado. The Eldorado girls have played for a state title 18 times with seven titles through 2020.

The Eldorado baseball team has eight state championships in 12 title game appearances. The Eagles were led by longtime coach Jim Johns in all but one of those 12 championship game berths. Johns, who retired in 2016 after 29 years at Eldorado, is one of just three high school baseball coaches in the state to win more than 500 games.

As good as soccer is in Albuquerque, basketball is the city's most popular sport. Heck, it's the state's most popular sport. It's no different at Eldorado, where both girls' and boys' programs consistently compete for state championships. After losing in the 1982 4A championship game, the Eagle boys won their first state title the following year. Eldorado won three more championships in 2004, '05, and '12. The 2004–05 teams were led by Daniel Faris, who went on to play at the University of New Mexico and then professionally in the Netherlands and Lebanon. Trying to find a season when the Eldorado girls haven't played for a state championship is a little difficult. The Lady Eagles were in the title game 21 times from 1975 through 2020.

The Eldorado gym has plenty of seating with two levels of gray pullout bleachers on either side of a court that was installed in 2016. As with the other Albuquerque high schools, attendance can be sporadic, but it's excellent when the teams are winning and especially when they're playing a cross-town rival. If you can catch a game between Eldorado and La Cueva, expect an electric atmosphere.

Swimming is *the* sport at Albuquerque Academy

There isn't an Albuquerque high school with a more dynastic legacy than **Albuquerque Academy** and swimming. The Chargers boys had 24 state titles, while the girls owned 21 as of 2020. Anika Apostalon, who became a member of the Czech Republic national team, set a trio of New Mexico state records in 2013.

Academy, a private co-ed school just east of I-25, also dominates in cross-country, with 15 boys' state championships and 6 girls' titles through 2020. The Chargers are also very good in track, with 17 titles for the boys and 8 for the girls.

Professional soccer player Kyle Altman, golfer Notah Begay III, Olympic gymnast Chainey Umphrey, NBA members Cody Toppert and James Borrego, and MLB All-Star Alex Bregman are among Academy's notable alumni. Bregman was a freshman starter on the 2009 championship team and was the national player of the year as a sophomore.

Unique experiences in Albuquerque

One could spend a week in Albuquerque and still not see everything. **Petroglyph National Monument** is wonderful for casual hikes among rocks filled with ancient symbols.

Albuquerque Downs is right along Central Avenue Southeast and has a storied history dating back to 1938. The first races were part of the New Mexico State Fair, and the fairgrounds are still adjacent to the track. The Downs features 34 races each year on its one-and-an-eighth-mile

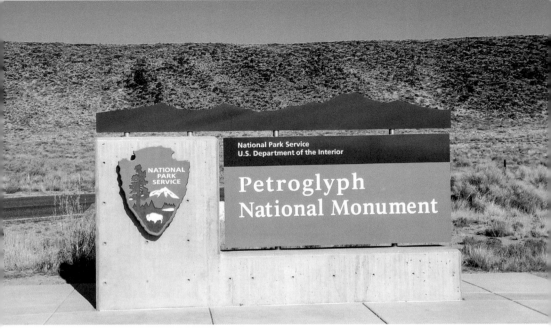

Petroglyph National Monument is a great place to enjoy a hike while checking out some ancient graffiti.

track. The race season begins in June and is highlighted by the $200,000 Downs at Albuquerque Handicap Thoroughbred race in early August and October's American Quarter Horse Association Bank of America Challenge Championships. The Downs is also an entertainment hub with a full casino, three restaurants, and live music every weekend.

One of the most popular things to do in Albuquerque is taking the **Sandia Peak Tramway** to the top. Whether there is snow or not, the 10,378-foot summit offers stupendous views of the valley below. The tramway is the third-longest aerial tram in the world and the longest in the United States. It takes you to the **Sandia Peak Ski Area**, which has some of New Mexico's best powder for winter sports. The **Snow Sports School** offers lessons for those unacquainted with skiing.

Even if you're not visiting the ABQ in winter, the mountaintop has several trailheads for hiking or biking. If you want to ride a bicycle at the top of the mountain, you need to drive to the ski resort. A suggestion is to take not the highway but the rocky dirt road on the backside of the mountain. It's a much more scenic drive through Cibola National Forest, though at a slower pace. The road can be accessed on the north side of the forest on Highway 165 at Placitas.

Duke City BMX is a mile south of the UNM campus and has events year-round. The bike track hosts the USA BMX Spring Nationals and USA BMX Gold Cup qualifiers.

Then there are the balloons. Albuquerque is the epicenter of hot-air ballooning and home to the **International Balloon Museum**. The museum opened in 2005 and details the history of hot-air ballooning from its early days of trial-and-error to weather balloons. There are several interactive exhibits, and you can virtually lift and land your own hot-air balloon. The museum also includes the **International Ballooning Hall of Fame**. The Hall recognizes balloon contributors in science and technology, math, and engineering, as well as legendary race pilots from around the globe.

The museum's featured event is October's Balloon Fiesta. The week-long celebration includes chainsaw carving demos, skydivers, fireworks, and of course, competitive balloon races. The real highlights of the Balloon Fiesta are the night-time balloon glows and early morning mass ascensions. Adjacent to the museum is **Balloon Fiesta Park**, which has 21 fields for football, soccer, softball, disc golf, or lacrosse.

The multiuse **Sandia Motor Speedway** west of the city includes two paved oval tracks of a quarter mile and half mile, a 1.7-mile road course with a 1.1-mile configuration capacity, a motocross track, a paved quarter-mile midget track, and a paved remote control track. The speedway, which is a stone's throw south of Route 66, hosts more than 40 road course events every year, so you can probably catch a race while you're in town.

October is a great time to head through Albuquerque in terms of sports. You can watch the balloon races, attend college and high school football games, hit the ski slopes, and get in a round of golf or two. The **Albuquerque Country Club** is right along Route 66 at West Park on the Rio Grande. The club traces its roots to 1914 but officially opened in 1928. The golf course feels more like a city park with its myriad trees, but those trees add to the challenges that include sand bunkers, water hazards, and contoured greens.

Albuquerque does have four public courses, including **Los Altos Golf Course** just north of Central Avenue. Los Altos has a 6,180-yard 18-hole course designed for the weekend golfer. There is also a nine-hole, par-3 course for quicker play. Both golf courses are mostly flat, but the layouts feature two lakes, numerous mature trees, and large sand traps. One can play a round of 18 for under $30.

If you just want to grab a beer and watch a professional game on television, Albuquerque has an excellent craft brewery scene. **Boxing Bear** is one downtown brewery directly on Central Avenue. The **Route 66 Casino Hotel** has an RV park and gas station and opened a huge sports bar called **Stadium 66** in 2019. The bar has a full menu and bar with 74 televisions and a sports book near the entrance to the casino floor. Across the highway from the casino at the old **Rio Puerco Bridge** is the **66 Pit Stop**, which claims to be the original home of the Laguna Burger, a delicious patty topped with lettuce, tomato, onions, and New Mexico's famous green chile.

The Rio Puerco Bridge is near the Route 66 Casino Hotel and Stadium 66 sports bar.

LAGUNA

Another stretch of desolate yet divine terrain awaits you as you drive the 28 miles west from the 66 Pit Stop to the pueblo of Laguna. Adobe ruins of bygone towns like Budville and Cubero dot the enchanting landscape with buttes and mesas serving as beautiful backdrops. New Mexico, rich with history, might be the most aesthetically pleasing state of Route 66. Laguna is home to the only high school between Albuquerque and Grants.

Laguna-Acoma High School is home to the Hawks, who field several competitive teams at the 2A level. The girls' cross-country team won four straight state championships from 1982 to 1985, and the boys have 23 cross-country titles and a few runners who have stood atop the podium multiple times. Oddly enough, Laguna-Acoma has just one boys' track championship, and that came in 1977.

The Hawks have been pretty good on the diamond as well. The girls won a pair of softball championships in 1984 and 2006. The baseball team had not won a state title as of 2020, but the Hawks played in the championship game seven times between 1962 and 1993.

The Laguna-Acoma girls' basketball team lost its only championship game appearance in 2013. But the Laguna-Acoma boys were able to win their lone title that same year. Laguna-Acoma High has a small gym with short sets of blue bleachers straddling the court. The goal at one end of the floor is flanked by the scoreboard and a large hawk painted on the wall. Because of the gym size and popularity of basketball among New Mexico Native Americans, the bleachers are almost always filled to capacity for a Hawks basketball game.

The Laguna-Acoma area is drenched in history. Acoma traces its roots to 1150, making it one of the oldest continuously inhabited communities in North America.

GRANTS

The scenic drive along the I-40 corridor leads you to Grants, which is the gateway to **El Malpais National Conservation Area**. El Malpais, which means the bad country—or badlands—is south of Grants and is one of the most popular hiking areas in the state. An RV park across the road from the **El Malpais Visitor Center** includes a craft brewery where one can enjoy a brew or two after a long hike.

Grants is on the north side of Interstate 40 and Route 66. Founded in the 1880s as a railroad camp by three brothers with the surname Grant, the town today has a population of about 9,100 residents served by one high school.

Grants High School is a mile north of the Mother Road on Second Street. Home to the Pirates, Grants has a boys' basketball program that is almost always in the state playoffs. The Pirates won 3A state titles in 1970 and 1986 and played in the 3A championship game in 1987, 2002, and 2006. As the city grew in more recent years, Grants has been bumped up two classification levels and reached the 5A state semifinals in 2015 and 2016 before losing to Gallup and Santa Fe Capital, respectively.

Boys' basketball games always draw a good crowd to the Grants gymnasium, which has the New Mexico state flag beneath an analog scoreboard on a baseline wall. Championship banners and "Go Pirates" signs dot the walls. "Grants" and "Pirates" are spelled out in the red bleachers along either sideline.

Basketball may be Grants's most popular sport, but the school's best program over its history has been boys' cross-country. The Pirates won five state championships between 1972 and 1983, with several individual champions. One of those individual champs was Phillip Castillo, who won a pair of New Mexico state titles before winning an NCAA Division II national championship for Adams State University in 1992. Castillo was a nine-time All-American for the Colorado university and was enshrined in the school's sports hall of fame in 2018. Castillo was also a part of the boys' track team that won a state title in 1990. The track teams share **Grants Pirates Field** with the football team. The stadium was built in 1958 and is a basic high school stadium with bleachers on either side to accommodate 2,000 spectators.

The Grants softball team won consecutive 3A state championships from 2004 to 2006, and the boys' golf team won a state title in 1994. The Pirates golf teams play at **Coyote del Malpais Golf Course**, which is just north of Route 66 as you enter Grants from the east. Tucked in the foothills of

Mount Taylor, Coyote del Malpais is one of the more beautiful courses you'll find on Route 66. The 18-hole course has a challenging 7,000-yard layout with 16 small lakes. It's a championship-level course that hosted the New Mexico state high school championships in 2005. The best part? You can play a round for under $20.

Stay at the **Sands Motel** for a couple nights and take in the scenic beauty of Grants. Hike El Malpais, play golf, and meet locals at a high school sporting event before driving the 62 miles to Gallup.

GALLUP

Gallup is a pretty narrow city located in a valley between two mountain ranges, and Route 66 cuts right through the center of it. The city of 21,000 is the last New Mexico city you'll pass through on Route 66 before entering Arizona. It's worth a couple of days or more. Gallup was once a popular location for Hollywood studios to film Westerns, and the historic **El Rancho Hotel** boasts it's the "home of the movie stars." The hotel has the "charm of yesterday" with the "convenience of tomorrow." The restaurant serves up tasty steaks, and the hotel's **49er Bar** frequently has live music to enjoy.

Another of Gallup's Route 66 attractions is **Red Rock Park**, a popular

Spend a few nights at historic El Rancho Hotel and go see a game or two in Gallup.

spot for hiking and camping just east of the city. The park is also home to a 5,000-seat arena that hosts concerts as well as summer rodeos. The arena has hosted the New Mexico High School Rodeo Association and holds the USTRC Red Rock Classic in early June. The crown jewel of rodeo at Red Rock is the annual Gallup Lions Club Rodeo, first held in 1948. The rodeo, which takes place in mid-June, begins with a parade and lures professional rodeo cowboys to Gallup. A month later, Red Rock hosts the Wildthing Championship Bull Riding, which Gallup has hosted annually since 1993.

Miyamura returns to postseason play year after year

Gallup has two public high schools—Gallup High and Miyamura High. Both are just off Route 66. If you decide to visit **El Morro National Monument** from Gallup while traveling down Route 66, you'll hang a left onto Boardman Drive. Less than a mile after you turn, you will pass **Hiroshi Miyamura High School**, which is named for a Gallup native and Congressional Medal of Honor recipient.

Miyamura has a solid baseball program, reaching the 4A state championship game in 2012 and 5A semifinals in 2017. The Miyamura softball team is usually in the thick of the postseason as well. The Miyamura Patriots also field competitive basketball programs, and their cross-country squads are usually strong. Both the baseball and softball teams play on artificial turf fields that have black and purple warning tracks. One cool thing about the school building itself is a colorful mural created by art students in 2012.

While cross-country is popular in Gallup, basketball is the draw. Longtime broadcaster Sammy Chioda said support for the Gallup basketball teams doesn't come from just the city of Gallup but also the nearby Zuni and Navajo Reservations. The fact that Miyamura had not won a basketball championship as of 2020 doesn't matter to the fans.

"It's an extended area, and there is a lot of great support for teams that go to Albuquerque," said Chioda, who was nominated for the New Mexico Sports Hall of Fame in 2018. The athletic field complex in Gallup was named **Sammy C. Chioda's Field** in 2015. The youth sports complex has three multiuse fields that can be used for baseball, softball, or soccer. One of the fields is surrounded by a track that can be used for recreational running or walking.

'Basketball is everything' at Gallup High

Gallup High School is located on the western side of the city, and its gymnasium walls are covered in banners recognizing district and state championship teams. Rarely does a year go by when either the Gallup boys or girls don't make a trip to The Pit for the state's elite eight. Since the Gallup girls won their first state championship in 1994 by upsetting powerhouse Eldorado in the 4A championship game, the Bengals have been in the state playoff hunt ever since. The girls' additional state titles came in 1997 (beating Santa Fe High), 2002, 2006, and 2011. The Bengals played in the championship game in 1998, 2000, 2015, and 2016. The boys were state runners-up in 1938, 2012, and 2015.

"Bengal basketball is everything," said Gallup athletics director Jessica Dooley. "Even before I moved here (in 2005), I already knew. It's the culture here. It's what makes this place hard to beat. It's the heartbeat. It's been very real for everybody, and everyone's just so invested in it.

"The girls have always been a powerhouse, but now both the boys and girls are top-five in the state every year," Dooley added. "Everyone here is a ball player. They start at the elementary school level with 25, 30 kids coming out for 12 spots on the team. It's just ingrained. They've been grown in basketball."

Angelo DiPaolo Memorial Stadium is shared by Gallup and Miyamura high schools.

When the Bengals play at the University of New Mexico, their fans nearly fill the 15,000-seat arena. Regular-season games at Gallup High draw standing-room only crowds of 3,500 fans. Basketball is year-round in Gallup, and the other sports suffer. The Bengals are not nearly as competitive in other sports but used to be a cross-country powerhouse when the state tournament was held at Red Rock Park. The Gallup boys won 18 state championships between 1983 and 2007, with the girls winning 14 during that stretch. The Bengals girls won 10 consecutive titles from 1996 to 2005.

The Gallup and Miyamura football and track teams share **Angelo DiPaolo Memorial Stadium**, less than a mile south of El Rancho. The 4,500-seat stadium has a concrete grandstand topped with a two-level press box overlooking the field. The stadium has an elevated perch in the residential neighborhood, providing excellent views of the valley.

Chioda has been the radio voice of Gallup sports for years and is also the owner of **Sammy C's Rock'n Sports Pub & Grille** in downtown Gallup, which has been recognized as one of the top sports bars in the country. Sammy C's opened in 2007 and has one of the most impressive collections of sports memorabilia you'll find anywhere, with more than 6,000 autographed items. Jerseys of Hall of Famers from every sport—many of them signed—adorn the walls of the 12,000-square-foot bar. There is also the "Floor of Fame" in

Just a few of the Green Bay Packers items on display at Sammy C's.

the center of the "Hall of Champions." The "floor" is a roped off section of the main floor and is painted to look like a small basketball court. The court, which covers a staircase to the basement, has been signed by myriad athletes and entertainers who have visited the establishment. Among the signatures are Joe Greene, Steve Garvey, Cliff Branch, Dick Vermeil, Dan Reeves, Ronnie Lott, Marv Levy, Jay Novacek, Ed McCaffrey, Ken Whisenhunt, Ron Jaworski, Kim Carnes, Dan Henderson, Nick Lowery, Juice Newton, Rick Trevino, Johnny Lee, Adriano Moraes, Cody Custer, Charlie Sampson, and Rasheed Wallace.

Chioda is a fan of the Green Bay Packers, so there are a lot of Packers jerseys like Brett Favre, Reggie White, Jordy Nelson, Dave Robinson, Randall Cobb, Eddie Lacy, Greg Jennings, Clay Matthews, Donald Driver, and Davon House, who has also signed the "Floor of Fame."

Because Gallup is in New Mexico, three Brian Urlacher Chicago Bears jerseys are the centerpiece of one wall though, as of 2020, the UNM alumnus and Pro Football Hall of Famer had never visited Sammy C's. But you can, and should.

A replica basketball court on the floor of Sammy C's is covered with autographs from celebrity visitors.

New Mexico Route 66 Points of Interest

BLUE SWALLOW MOTEL – 815 E. Rte. 66 Blvd., Tucumcari, NM 88401

MOTEL SAFARI – 722 E. Rte. 66 Blvd., Tucumcari, NM 88401

POW WOW RESTAURANT AND LIZARD LOUNGE – 801 W. Tucumcari Blvd., Tucumcari, NM 88401

MESALANDS COMMUNITY COLLEGE – 911 S. 10th St., Tucumcari, NM 88401

MESALANDS DINOSAUR MUSEUM – 222 E. Laughlin Ave., Tucumcari, NM 88401

QUAY COUNTY FAIRGROUNDS – W. Railroad Ave., Tucumcari, NM 88401

NEW MEXICO ROUTE 66 MUSEUM – 1500 U.S. Rte. 66, Tucumcari, NM 88401

TUCUMCARI HIGH SCHOOL – 1100 S. 7th St., Tucumcari, NM 88401

TUCUMCARI LAKE – 3899 Qr 64, Tucumcari, NM 88401

BLUE HOLE AND VISITOR CENTER – 1085 Blue Hole Road, Santa Rosa, NM 88435

PARK LAKE – 913 Blue Hole Road, Santa Rosa, NM 88435

SANTA ROSA LAKE STATE PARK – NM 91, Santa Rosa, NM 88435

SANTA ROSA HIGH SCHOOL – 1235 Mendocino Ave., Santa Rosa, CA 95401

ROUTE 66 AUTO MUSEUM – 2436 Historic Rte. 66, Santa Rosa, NM 88435

SANTA ROSA GOLF COURSE – Chuck N Dale Lane, Santa Rosa, NM 88435

MORIARTY HIGH SCHOOL – 200 Center Ave., Moriarty, NM 87035

MAGS INDOOR SHOOTING RANGE – 410 Cam Oriente, Moriarty, NM 87035

CLINES CORNERS TRAVEL DEPOT – 1 Yacht Club Drive, Clines Corners, NM 87070

WILDLIFE WEST NATURE PARK – 87 N Frontage Road, Edgewood, NM 87015

PECOS NATIONAL HISTORICAL PARK – 1 NM 63, Pecos, NM 87552

SANTA FE FLY FISHING SCHOOL – 79 Camino Rincon, Pecos, NM 87552

PECOS HIGH SCHOOL – NM 63, Pecos, NM 87552

EL FAROL RESTAURANT – 808 Canyon Road, Santa Fe, NM 87501

SANTA FE INDIAN SCHOOL – 1501 Cerrillos Road, Santa Fe, NM 87505

SANTA FE HIGH SCHOOL – 2100 Yucca St., Santa Fe, NM 87505

EL REY COURT – 1862 Cerrillos Road, Santa Fe, NM 87505

CAPITAL HIGH SCHOOL – 4851 Paseo del Sol, Santa Fe, NM 87507

BATAAN MEMORIAL BUILDING – 400 Don Gaspar Ave., Santa Fe, NM 87501

ST. MICHAEL'S HIGH SCHOOL – 100 Siringo Road, Santa Fe, NM 87505

FORT MARCY BALLFIELD – 490 Bishops Lodge Road, Santa Fe, NM 87501

MEOW WOLF – 1352 Rufina Circle, Santa Fe, NM 87507

MARTY SANCHEZ'S LINKS DE SANTA FE – 205 Caja Del Rio Road, Santa Fe, NM 87506

SANTA FE COUNTRY CLUB – 4360 Country Club Road, Santa Fe, NM 87507

NEW MEXICO DEPARTMENT OF GAME & FISH – 1 Wildlife Way, Santa Fe, NM 87507

SKI SANTA FE – 1477 NM 475, Santa Fe, NM 87501

BERNALILLO HIGH SCHOOL – 250 Isidora Sanchez, Bernalillo, NM 87004

NEW MEXICO SOCCER TOURNAMENT COMPLEX – 1001 Tamaya Blvd., Bernalillo, NM 87004

SANTA ANA STAR CASINO – 54 Jemez Canyon Dam Road, Bernalillo, NM 87004

ROUTE 66 OPEN SPACE – 14482 Interstate 40 Frontage Road E., Albuquerque, NM 87123

KIMO THEATRE – 423 Central Ave. N.W., Albuquerque, NM 87102

SAN FELIPE DE NERI CHURCH – 2005 N. Plaza St. N.W., Albuquerque, NM 87104

DOG HOUSE DRIVE-IN – 1216 Central Ave. N.W., Albuquerque, NM 87102

THE LIBRARY BAR & GRILL – 312 Central Ave S.W., Albuquerque, NM 87102

THE PIT – 1111 University Blvd. S.E., Albuquerque, NM 87106

SANTA ANA STAR FIELD – 1155 University Blvd. S.E., Albuquerque, NM 87106

ALBUQUERQUE CONVENTION CENTER – 401 2nd St. N.W., Albuquerque, NM 87102

UNIVERSITY OF NEW MEXICO GOLF COURSE – 3601 University Blvd. S.E., Albuquerque, NM 87106

ISOTOPES PARK – 1601 Avenida Cesar Chavez S.E., Albuquerque, NM 87106

ALBUQUERQUE HIGH SCHOOL – 800 Odelia Road N.E., Albuquerque, NM 87102

MILNE STADIUM – 1200 Hazeldine Ave. S.E., Albuquerque, NM 87106

SANDIA PREPARATORY SCHOOL – 532 Osuna Road N.E., Albuquerque, NM 87113

SANDIA HIGH SCHOOL – 7801 Candelaria Road N.E., Albuquerque, NM 87110

MANZANO HIGH SCHOOL/WILSON STADIUM – 12200 Lomas Blvd. N.E., Albuquerque, NM 87112

HIGHLAND HIGH SCHOOL – 4700 Coal Ave. S.E., Albuquerque, NM 87108

ELDORADO HIGH SCHOOL – 11300 Montgomery Blvd. N.E., Albuquerque, NM 87111

ALBUQUERQUE ACADEMY – 6400 Wyoming Blvd. N.E., Albuquerque, NM 87109

PETROGLYPH NATIONAL MONUMENT – Western Trail N.W., Albuquerque, NM 87120

THE DOWNS RACETRACK AND CASINO – 145 Louisiana Blvd. N.E., Albuquerque, NM 87108

SANDIA PEAK TRAMWAY – 30 Tramway Road N.E., Albuquerque, NM 87122

SANDIA PEAK SKI AREA – NM 536, Sandia Park, NM 8704

DUKE CITY BMX – 1011 Buena Vista Drive S.E., Albuquerque, NM 87106

INTERNATIONAL BALLOON MUSEUM – 9201 Balloon Museum Drive N.E., Albuquerque, NM 87113

SANDIA MOTOR SPEEDWAY – 100 Speedway Park Blvd., Albuquerque, NM 87121

ALBUQUERQUE COUNTRY CLUB – 601 Laguna Blvd. S.W., Albuquerque, NM 87104

LOS ALTOS GOLF COURSE – 9717 Copper Ave. N.E., Albuquerque, NM 87123

BOXING BEAR BREWING – 10200 Corrales Road, Albuquerque, NM 87114

ROUTE 66 CASINO HOTEL – 14500 Central Ave. S.W., Rio Puerco, Albuquerque, NM 87121

RIO PUERCO BRIDGE – 14311 Central Ave. N.W., Albuquerque, NM 87121

66 PIT STOP – 14311 Central Ave. N.W. I-40, Exit 140, Albuquerque, NM 87121

LAGUNA-ACOMA HIGH SCHOOL – NM 23, Casa Blanca Road, Casa Blanca, NM 87007

EL MALPAIS VISITOR CENTER – 1900 E. Santa Fe Ave., Grants, NM 87020

GRANTS HIGH SCHOOL – 500 Mountain Road, Grants, NM 87020

COYOTE DEL MALPAIS GOLF COURSE – 2001 George Hanosh Blvd., Grants, NM 87020

SANDS MOTEL – 112 McArthur St., Grants, NM 87020

EL RANCHO HOTEL – 1000 E. Hwy. 66, Gallup, NM 87301

RED ROCK PARK – 825 Outlaw Road, Church Rock, NM 87311

HIROSHI MIYAMURA HIGH SCHOOL – 680 Boardman Ave., Gallup, NM 87301

GALLUP HIGH SCHOOL – 1055 Rico St., Gallup, NM 87301

ANGELO DIPAOLO MEMORIAL STADIUM – 916 S. Grandview Drive, Gallup, NM 87301

SAMMY C'S ROCK'N SPORTS PUB & GRILLE – 107 W Coal Ave., Gallup, NM 87301

ARIZONA

The Arizona segment of Route 66 begins and ends in the desert, but between Holbrook and Oatman, you'll discover pine-covered mountains, an NCAA Division I university, multiple rodeo venues, an elite ski resort, and dynastic high school cross-country, wrestling, and football programs.

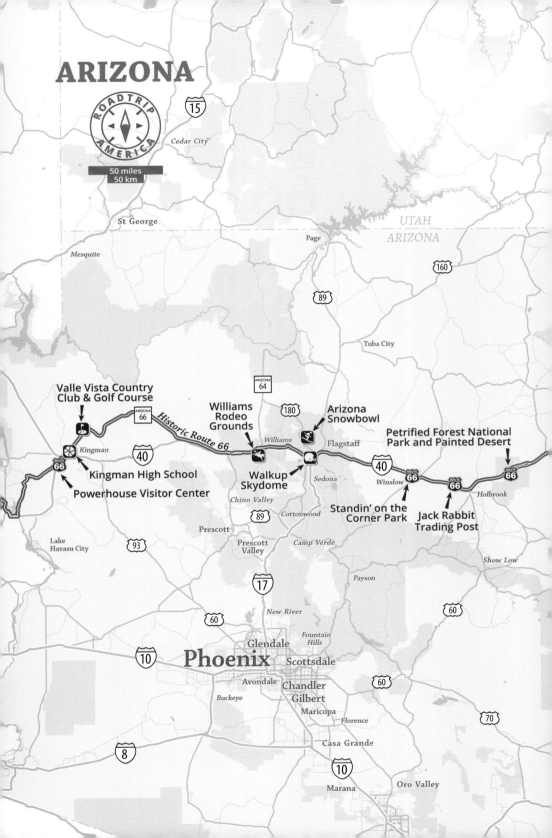

ARIZONA

ROADTRIP AMERICA

50 miles
50 km

Cedar City

St George

UTAH
ARIZONA

Page

Mesquite

160

89

Tuba City

ARIZONA
64

Valle Vista Country Club & Golf Course

ARIZONA
66

Historic Route 66

Williams Rodeo Grounds

180

Arizona Snowbowl

Petrified Forest National Park and Painted Desert

Williams

Flagstaff

Kingman

40

ROUTE
66

ROUTE
66

Kingman High School

Powerhouse Visitor Center

40

ROUTE
66

ROUTE
66

Walkup Skydome

Sedona

Winslow

Holbrook

Chino Valley

Standin' on the Corner Park

Jack Rabbit Trading Post

Lake Havasu City

93

89

Cottonwood

Prescott

Camp Verde

Show Low

Prescott Valley

17

Payson

60

60

New River

Fountain Hills

10

Glendale

Phoenix

Scottsdale

Avondale

Chandler
Gilbert

60

70

Buckeye

Maricopa

Florence

8

Casa Grande

10

Marana

Oro Valley

HOLBROOK

As you cross into Arizona from New Mexico on Interstate 40, you will immediately see your first Route 66 stop—the **Tee Pee Trading Post**. The large shop set at the base of red cliffs has a plethora of Route 66 and Native American souvenirs. The trading post has a Lupton address, but the tiny town of 25 residents is a half mile southwest. Sanders and Chambers are a little farther down the I-40 corridor before you get to Holbrook, which is the gateway community to **Petrified Forest National Park**.

The Petrified Forest, with its Painted Desert, is located about 30 miles east of Holbrook and hosts the annual Petrified Forest Marathon every October. The race begins and ends inside the park, which is the only national park through which Route 66 passes. Holbrook is worth a few nights' stay for Route 66 travelers. During one of your days there, you should explore the national park.

The TeePee Trading Post is just across the New Mexico-Arizona border.

Petrified Forest National Park is the only national park through which Route 66 directly passes.

Holbrook is the seat of Navajo County, and the city of 5,000 residents has a storied Native American legacy. The **Navajo County Courthouse**, built in 1898, is on the National Register of Historic Places, as are several area bridges. Another site listed on the historic register is the famed **Wigwam Motel**, where visitors can sleep in a modified teepee.

A five-minute walk north of the motel will take you to **Holbrook High School**, where the Roadrunners have built a powerhouse wrestling program. Holbrook won 11 state championships through 2020, most recently in 2014. Meets against rival Winslow, also a wrestling power, are saturated with energy and emotion. Holbrook's 11 championships are tied with Winslow for second-most in the state.

As much success as the Holbrook wrestling program has had, the gymnasium in which the Roadrunners compete is named for a former

Holbrook's Roadrunner Stadium is a unique venue set into the side of a rocky hill.

Holbrook basketball player. The Holbrook gym bears the name of NBA coach and Holbrook High School graduate Mike Budenholzer, who guided the Milwaukee Bucks to the NBA's best record in the 2018–19 and 2019–20 seasons. He was the NBA coach of the year in 2015 while leading the Atlanta Hawks, and then again in 2019 and 2020. Budenholzer was also an outstanding golfer and was on the basketball and golf teams at Pomona College in Claremont, California, also along Route 66.

While at Holbrook, Budenholzer played for his father, Vince. The elder Budenholzer was inducted into the Arizona Interscholastic Association (AIA) Hall of Fame in 2005 in honor of his more than 20 years at Holbrook.

Holbrook's soccer, track, and football teams play at **Roadrunner Stadium**, a unique venue set into the side of a rocky hill.

Before you leave Holbrook, enjoy an excellent meal at the **Mesa Italiana Restaurant**. Route 66, or Navajo Boulevard, again merges with Interstate 40 on its western path toward California.

JOSEPH CITY

As you approach Exit 277 on I-40 at Joseph City, you will see a large building with the words "A Tradition of Excellence" scrawled across the top of it. That is **Joseph City High School**, where the Wildcats have excelled in baseball, basketball, football, wrestling, and golf. The football field is directly in front of the school to the east.

The Joseph City football team was unbeaten in 1978 en route to a 1A state championship. They were led by Hall of Fame coach Charlie Esquivel, who also led Joseph City to a state golf title in 1979. That 1979 title was particularly impressive because the Wildcats did not have a home course on which to compete or practice. There still isn't a golf course in Joseph City. The nearest course is **Hidden Cove Golf Course** in Holbrook, 10 miles east of Joseph City and 2 miles north of Route 66.

Joseph City's 1978 football team won the first of six state championships for the Wildcats. Joseph City has a population under 1,400, and the high school has just over 100 students. Because of the small enrollment, the

Wildcats compete in eight-man football and were undefeated in 2009 and 2011.

Joseph City has two state wrestling championships, coming consecutively in 1997 and 1998. Those teams were led by legendary Hall of Fame coach Bob Crosswhite, who came out of retirement after leading Winslow to six championships in the 1980s. One of Joseph City's best wrestlers was Sam O'Connell, who was a three-time state champ. O'Connell, who died in 2017 at the age of 60, once held the Arizona state high school records for fastest pin and still owns the record for most consecutive pins with 45.

The gym used by the wrestling team is also home to the basketball squads, who have been successful in their own right. The boys' basketball team won a 1A state championship in 2003, and the girls won four straight championships from 1976 to 1979 with added titles in 1988 and 2001. Both squads are still regularly in contention to reach the state championships in Phoenix.

Because the **Jack Rabbit Trading Post** is 2 miles down the road from Joseph City, the small town can be easily bypassed by Route 66 travelers. But do yourself a favor and spend some time in the municipality that was founded in 1876 by Mormon settlers. Visit **Ella's Frontier Store** and see a Wildcats game before taking that selfie in front of the "Here It Is" sign.

The "Here It Is" sign next to the Jack Rabbit Trading Post.

WINSLOW

After standin' on a corner in Winslow, Arizona, take it easy by checking out a Winslow High School Bulldogs game or wrestling meet. **Winslow High School** can be seen from I-40 and is in between the modern Route 66 and the Old Highway 66 through the city center. The school is less than a mile from the historic **La Posada Hotel**. The stunning hotel was built in 1929 and is on the National Register of Historic Places. The upscale hotel now includes an Amtrak platform, restaurant, art gallery, and gift shop. It is considered *the* place to stay for Route 66 travelers, and Winslow is definitely worth spending a night or two.

The Winslow Bulldogs are a wrestling powerhouse, winning 11 of the school's 31 state championships. The highlight of Winslow's wrestling season is the annual Doc Wright Wrestling Invitational, which was first held in 1965. The tournament has grown into a two-day January event with wrestlers from more than 40 Arizona high schools. Not surprisingly, the two teams

Historic La Posada Hotel in Winslow.

that have won the most Doc Wright tourneys are Holbrook and Winslow.

Winslow also has a strong football tradition. The Bulldogs won three state championships under AIA Hall of Fame coach Emil Nasser. The 2,000-seat football stadium at Winslow High is named for Nasser, who led the team from 1947 to 1983. He came out of retirement in 1999 and led Joseph City to state titles in 1999 and 2002. Nasser also won a state baseball title at Winslow and coached the Bulldogs track-and-field teams as well.

The Bulldogs have multiple state championships in cross-country as well. A school with a good cross-country team usually fields a competitive track team as well. Winslow is no exception. Cranston "Cranny" Hysong coached the Winslow track-and-field teams for 31 years before retiring in 2001. Hysong's teams won 60 percent of their meets, and he led the Bulldogs to five state championships with a slew of individual champs. One of those individual champs was Nick Hysong, the coach's son. Nick Hysong was a

"Standing on a Corner in Winslow, Arizona" an Illusionary mural by John Pugh based on the Jackson Browne's song "Take it Easy"

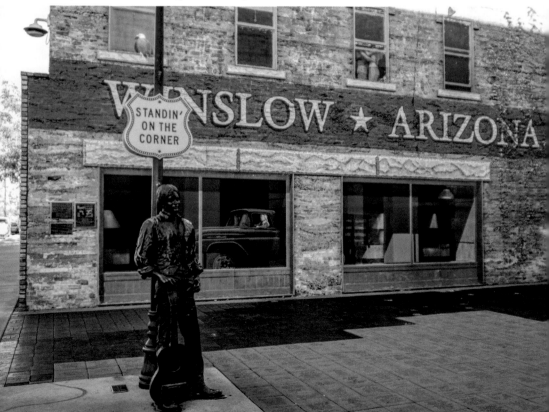

Winslow pole vaulter who went on to win a gold medal at the 2000 Olympic Games in Sydney.

The Winslow basketball, wrestling, and volleyball teams compete inside **Don Petranovich Gymnasium**, named for the AIA Hall of Fame girls' basketball coach who won 8 state championships in 16 title-game berths. Petranovich won more than 800 games over 30 seasons, and the Bulldogs regularly competed in front of standing-room-only crowds. "Petro" was the national coach of the year in 2011, two years after he was inducted into the National High School Athletic Association Hall of Fame.

When you're done exploring Winslow, continue west on Third Street before again merging with Interstate 40. Be sure to stop at the **Meteor Crater** and the ghost towns of **Two Guns** and **Twin Arrows** before arriving in Flagstaff. Two Guns was once home to a small community with a gas station, RV park and campground, and small zoo on the edge of Canyon Diablo. Twin Arrows, across I-40 from a Navajo casino with the same name, used to be home to a gas station, diner, and trading post. Both are now graffiti-riddled mélanges of abandoned structures, but they're havens for photographers.

FLAGSTAFF

There are a handful of "Muffler Man" statues along Route 66, but only "Louie the Lumberjack" is on a college campus. **Northern Arizona University** boasts a pair of Giant Lumberjack statues, both outside the **Walkup Skydome**. One is at the main entrance on the east side of the dome, which is home to the NAU

Louie the Lumberjack is the only "Muffler Man" statue you'll find on a university campus.

Welcome to Flagstaff.

football and basketball teams. The other, located at the west entrance, used to be inside the stadium until a new scoreboard was installed in the west end zone in 2018 and the statue had to be moved. It was placed in storage for a year before being installed at the student tailgate area adjacent to the parking lots. NAU employees are often asked to take pictures of visitors standing in front of the iconic statues, and they usually oblige.

The Skydome's electric atmosphere

Even before you enter the Skydome for a football game, you'll experience a fun atmosphere. Tailgating in the adjacent parking lots is a longstanding tradition. The smell of burgers, hot dogs, and chicken roasting over burning charcoal is ubiquitous. Music fills the air as fans eagerly await the team walking through the crowd, led by cheerleaders and members of the marching band. High fives and pats on the back are accompanied by words of encouragement.

"The community support is phenomenal," said Mitch Strohman, who has been the NAU play-by-play announcer since 1991. "It's a university-dominated community in Flagstaff. NAU has played such a big part of what Flagstaff has been for over 100 years. That intimate relationship between the city of Flagstaff and NAU builds a passion. When the teams are winning, this community comes out in droves. It's so cool to watch. It's a big part of what makes Flagstaff."

The Skydome was the world's largest wood-span structure of its kind when it opened in 1977. Covering six acres, the 500-foot-tall arena originally could host up to 15,000 people, but the remodel and addition of suites reduced the capacity to about 12,000. Championship banners for basketball, volleyball, tennis, and football hang from the rafters above the press box. Streamers for titles won by the track and cross-country teams hang on the opposite side.

A quote from Abraham Lincoln can be seen on a couple of walls inside the Walkup Skydome: "Give me six hours to chop down a tree and I will spend the first four sharpening the ax."

The most electric atmosphere Strohman experienced at the Skydome was a 1996 homecoming game against rival Weber State. Archie Amerson scored seven touchdowns in the game and was later inducted into the NAU Athletics Hall of Fame, which is also inside the Skydome.

An NAU sign in the concourse of the Walkup Skydome at Northern Arizona University.

Northern Arizona University gets down to business in Flagstaff

"I could hardly hear myself in my headset because the ambient sound from the crowd was so deafening," said Strohman. "Wherever you could put a body in this building, there were bodies. It was a game I'll never forget."

The NAU Lumberjacks compete at the NCAA Division I level. The football team was in the FCS playoffs six times between 1996 and 2017 but only made it out of the first round in 2003. Besides Amerson, another notable NAU football alumnus is College Football Hall of Famer Rex Mirich, who had a seven-year pro career with the Oakland Raiders, Denver Broncos, and then-Boston Patriots.

The NAU men's basketball team has qualified for the NCAA Tournament twice (1998 and 2000), and the women went to the Big Dance in 2006. NAU has three national championships, all in cross-country. Those titles came consecutively from 2016 to 2018.

A Personal Connection to Route 66

NAU play-by-play announcer Mitch Strohman is a Kansas City native with kinship ties to Southern California. When his family would travel west to visit relatives, they often traveled down the Mother Road.

"When I was a kid and we'd go visit family in California, we'd drive this route," Strohman recalled. "I can remember traveling down old Route 66 between Seligman and Kingman before the interstate was completed. We would get off at Seligman and take the old Mother Road through Peach Springs and Valentine and some of those great communities along that stretch of Route 66.

"I can remember even today, as a little kid, how cool it was winding through those beautiful hills on a two-lane highway off the big interstate. It was just so fun. Even now, there are so many people who live in Flagstaff, myself included, who enjoy exploring the old sections of Route 66.

"Route 66 and Flagstaff have an intimacy that is very deep," Strohman continued. "It goes so far back in American history and Flagstaff's history ... It's one of the things that makes Flagstaff a special part of that expansion west in history. We know that millions of people passed through here, slept here, ate here, gassed their cars here, and ended up living here.

"As Route 66 has become a nostalgic thing for so many, it reminds us of the days when we were moving to the West," Strohman added. "Route 66 was the main artery for so many, and people discovered towns like Flagstaff, Kingman, Winona, Oatman ... We've developed a love affair with Route 66 in Flagstaff. [The city of] Williams also has a huge passion for Route 66. We embrace the history and nostalgia of it, and it's become part of our identity.

"Route 66 is something we use to draw people to our community. Come visit us."

Flagstaff cross-country makes strong showing

Flagstaff is a city nestled on the slopes of the San Francisco Peaks. It is an ideal location to hike the mountains, including **Humphrey's Peak**, the tallest point in Arizona. It only makes sense that **Flagstaff High School** would have a strong cross-country program with a combined 10 state championships between the boys and girls teams as of 2020. The Eagles boys' and girls' teams swept the state championships five straight seasons from 2015 to 2019, becoming the first Arizona high school to accomplish such a feat. After several top-three finishes since the first state meet was held in 1968, the 2015 championship was the first for the Flagstaff boys.

Inside Flagstaff High School's War Memorial Gym.

The girls, however, had won three straight titles from 2011 to 2013, having their streak broken with a second-place finish in 2014. The Eagle ladies also won state championships in 1980, 1990, five straight from 2000 to 2004, and again in 2008.

Flagstaff High—or "Flag High"—is less than a mile from the city's visitor center on Route 66. The school resembles something more like a mountain hunting lodge than it does a school; brick pillars support timber-covered entrances. To the left of the school's front doors is the entryway to **War Memorial Gymnasium**. The "Home of the Eagles" hosts Flagstaff's basketball, wrestling, and volleyball teams, and each is regularly competitive.

The home of the Eagles baseball team is **Gil Corona Baseball Complex**, named for the AIA Hall of Fame coach who won 72 percent of his games between 1953 and 1984. Corona was a World War II pilot who was shot down and spent two years as a prisoner of war. The baseball complex was renamed in Corona's honor in 2016 before a Flagstaff victory over Winslow.

Bundle up for a November Flagstaff football game and enjoy a view of snow-capped mountains.

One notable player to come out of the Flagstaff baseball program was second baseman George Grantham, a Route 66 product through and through. Grantham was born in Galena, Kansas, but his family moved to Flagstaff when he was young. He graduated from Flagstaff High before playing baseball at Northern Arizona University. He made his MLB debut with the Chicago Cubs in 1922, beginning a 13-year MLB career that saw him help the Pittsburgh Pirates win the 1925 World Series. Following his baseball retirement, Grantham moved to Kingman, where he died in 1954 at the age of 53.

Get active on the golf course, ski slopes, and hiking trails

A pair of golf courses are just south of Route 66. **Continental Golf Club**, which hosted the 2007 Arizona high school state championships, is 2.5 miles south of the Mother Road along Country Club Drive. The 18-hole Continental course includes a variety of trees, small lakes, and sand bunkers situated in the middle of a golf community. It's a picturesque setting perfect for casual play, but only for members and their guests.

A half mile east of Continental is **Aspen Valley Golf Club**. Aspen Valley golfers can take in panoramic views of the San Francisco Peaks while teeing off down fairways lined with Ponderosa pines. Nonmembers can play at Aspen Valley, though greens fees are rather expensive.

While most Route 66 visitors travel during the summer, don't rule out the colder months. With an elevation of 7,000 feet, Flagstaff is a winter destination for many. Flagstaff boasts one of the Southwest's best ski resorts. The **Arizona Snowbowl** is located 14 miles north of the city in the San Francisco Peaks. At nearly 10,000 feet above sea level, the Snowbowl offers breathtaking views of the city below and is a haven for skiers and snowboarders of all levels. The Snowbowl is also popular in summer because

Coconino High School is nestled into a neighborhood at the base of the San Francisco peaks.

of its views, and the ski resort has a challenging disc golf course that is the highest such course in the United States.

Another disc golf course is at **Thorpe Park** near the tri-intersection of Santa Fe Avenue, Thorpe Road, and West Mars Hill Road. The latter takes you to the famed **Lowell Observatory**, where Pluto, now classified as a dwarf planet, was discovered in 1930. Flagstaff is a designated dark-sky community, and there is no better place to view the stars than from the observatory atop Mars Hill. Even during the day, Lowell Observatory has frequent visitors who want to hike the adjacent trails.

The Flagstaff area has innumerable hiking trails through the **Coconino National Forest**. One recommended spot is **Walnut Canyon National Monument**, where visitors can hike trails along ancient cliffside dwellings. The canyon rim elevation is 6,690 feet, and a mile-long loop descends 200 feet toward the canyon floor. Native Americans are believed to have lived in the cliff dwelling during the 12th and 13th centuries before mysteriously abandoning the area around 1250.

If you're just looking for a sports bar along Route 66 in Flagstaff, **Majerle's Sports Grill** is a good spot. The downtown pub, owned by former Phoenix Suns player Dan Majerle, has a plethora of televisions, a full bar, and a variety of bar food with pizzas, wings, and burgers.

Another spot to watch a game would be the **Museum Club**, colloquially known as The Zoo. While the televisions around the bar are usually tuned to sports programming, The Zoo is a Route 66 icon and a must for those wanting to see live music. The Zoo has a regular rotation of local artists, and has drawn national acts like Willie Nelson and Wanda Jackson.

On your way out of Flagstaff, Route 66 briefly merges again with Interstate 40. Taking Exit 178 will get you back on Old 66 and soon at the **Parks in the Pines General Store**. The store has a few souvenir items and small grocery section, but also a tiny diner that serves up a wonderful breakfast. After leaving Flagstaff's verdant landscape of Ponderosa pines, you'll find yourself back in the Arizona desert.

WILLIAMS

Six miles west of the general store, Route 66 forces you back onto I-40, but only for 5 miles. Exit 165 will take you by the **Bearizona Wildlife Park** and then to the city of Williams.

There is more to Williams than just the **Grand Canyon Railway**, which has been taking visitors to Grand Canyon National Park since 1901. The railway has been added to the National Register of Historic Places, and **Williams Station** is in the city's historic downtown district. That six-block district includes the **Williams Visitor Center**, which should be the first stop for Route 66 travelers. You can get your passport stamped there but also gain a wealth of information about the city and what to do and see. The visitor center includes a scale model of the city, which has a population around 3,000.

Route 66 is the main artery through Williams, and the Mother Road is lined with gift shops, eateries, bars, and nostalgic gas stations. If businesses in Williams don't have a Grand Canyon theme, they have a Route 66 theme. The **Williams Route 66 sign** is four blocks east of the visitor center, and a large Route 66 mural adorns a building to the west.

A great spot for hunting, fishing, and rodeo competitions

But Williams also has plenty for sports fans. The **Williams Aquatic Center** and **Cureton Park**, which has several baseball fields, are right along Route 66. The Williams area is also a popular destination for hunters and fishermen. **White Horse Lake** southeast of the city has plenty of trout, bass, sunfish, and catfish for those wanting to catch their own dinner or just catch-and-release for sport. **Santa Fe Lake**, a reservoir a half mile south of downtown Williams, is stocked with the same fish as well as yellow perch and crappie.

As with other southwestern Route 66 cities, Williams has a thriving rodeo scene. The city hosts one professional event each year with a couple of major amateur events during the summer. The Professional Rodeo Cowboys Association (PRCA) has taken over the **Williams Rodeo Grounds** every Labor Day weekend since 1993. One of the biggest amateur events

Pete's Gas Station on Route 66 in Williams.

is June's annual Cowpunchers Reunion Rodeo. Cowpuncher is an informal synonym for cowboy, and the rodeo highlights the "working cowboys" with competitive calf roping, team tying, bronc riding, steer riding, wild horse racing, ribbon roping, and even cow milking.

Williams community backs the Vikings

If there's one thing that gathers the community together, it's Williams High School athletics. **Williams High School** is a half mile south of Route 66 on the west side of town. The Williams Vikings have tremendous community support with grandparents, parents, siblings, cousins, friends, and neighbors showing up to cheer on the athletes.

The Vikings are highly competitive in several sports, but football reigns supreme. Williams plays eight-man football and won its fourth state championship in 2019, which was a front-page story in the local *Williams-Grand Canyon News*. The football title was the second in three years for the Vikings. The boys' basketball program won a state championship in 1980.

One of the best athletes to come out of Williams was roundballer Billy Hatcher, who set a state record with 20 assists in a game in 1978. While a superb prep basketball player, Hatcher excelled on the diamond. He once pitched an 11-inning no-hitter and was drafted by the Chicago Cubs in 1981. Hatcher spent 12 seasons in the big leagues with seven different teams and was a member of the 1990 Cincinnati Reds team that won the World Series. Three years after his retirement in 1995, he was hired by the Tampa Bay Rays as a coach before joining the Reds in 2006. He remained with the Reds through 2018 and was hired by the Miami Marlins as their first-base coach in 2020.

Williams identifies itself as the Gateway to the Grand Canyon, which is about 60 miles to the north. So spend a few nights in Williams to see the Grand Canyon and check out a rodeo or Vikings game after dining at **Rod's Steak House**.

ASH FORK

Less than 20 miles west of Williams is the community of Ash Fork. While the small town has just about 300 residents, Ash Fork has a rich history. The community was established in 1882 as a stop for the Santa Fe Railroad and has several sites listed on the National Register of Historic Places. Included on that list is the **Copperstate Motel**, where you can still get a room. Among Ash Fork's Route 66 attractions is **Desoto's Salon** that was originally a Texaco station and has a Desoto Chrysler purportedly once driven by Elvis Presley on its roof.

Ash Fork High School is also right on Route 66. While the current

The Ash Fork Grill.

enrollment is only about 60 students, the school was larger before the town's population dwindled. Ash Fork's only state championship was won by the 1969 baseball team, which was undefeated that season, and the baseball field is Route 66 with the Mother Road creating a short porch in right field.

SELIGMAN

Arizona's "Birthplace of Route 66," Seligman has all sorts of sites to see for Route 66 travelers: the **Delgadillo's Snow Cap** drive-in, **Black Cat Bar**, **The Road Kill Cafe**, **Westside Lilo's Cafe**, and **Seligman Sundries**. Angel Delgadillo and his family have operated a barber shop in Seligman since 1950. Credited with founding the Arizona Route 66 Association, Delgadillo has

Above: Return to the 50s Gift Shop in Seligman. Below: Lots of artifacts in Seligman.

become a Route 66 icon and is known as the "Guardian Angel of Route 66." Seligman is but a shadow of its former self but clings to the past as nearly every business in the town of 450 residents has a Route 66 theme to it.

Seligman High School is located three blocks north of Route 66, and its Antelopes athletics teams pay homage to the herds of ruminants that roam Aubry Valley west of the city. The Seligman Antelopes have a long history of athletics excellence. AIA Hall of Fame coach Henry Lennox led the 'Lopes to state football and baseball championships in 1958, '60, and '61. His football teams had an astounding 164–3 record from 1948 to 1963. Seligman also won a state championship in 1990, but recent teams have not have much success as the enrollment has shrunk to just 50 students. Seligman's football team lost a game in 2004 by a score of 108–8 and eventually dropped the program.

It's easy to look at Seligman and imagine it during the glory days of Route 66. The town holds a certain charm that makes it one of the more endearing communities along America's Main Street. Attending an Antelopes game may give visitors an opportunity to be regaled with stories of what once was. Do yourself a favor and spend a night or two in Seligman. You can stay at the **Stagecoach 66 Motel**, famous for its Americana-themed rooms like the Elvis Presley, Marilyn Monroe, U.S. Marines, and Harley-Davidson rooms.

Between Seligman and Kingman is the longest uninterrupted section of Route 66. The Mother Road turns north from Interstate 40 to Yampai, the Grand Canyon Caverns, and Peach Springs. Route 66 then winds south through Truxton, Crozier, Valentine, Hackberry, and Hualapai before reuniting with I-40 at Kingman.

Between Hackberry and Kingman is the **Valle Vista Country Club & Golf Course**. The golf course is less than 2 miles west of

This Dino at the Grand Canyon Caverns in Peach Springs has been attracting tourists for many years

Route 66 and not far from **Stetson Winery**. Valle Vista has an 18-hole championship course nestled between the Cerbat, Hualapai, Peacock, and Music Mountain ranges. Bountiful trees along the fairways and a few water hazards make the 5,704-yard (white tees) course challenging for players of any skill level.

Hackberry General Store.

KINGMAN

Flagstaff is the only Arizona city on Route 66 larger than Kingman. With a population around 30,000 people, Kingman is the last real city through which you'll travel before reaching California. There is a lot to do in Kingman, which has excellent museums and plenty of Route 66 history.

Visitors can book a room at **El Trovatore Motel**, which has the longest Route 66 map anywhere on an exterior mural. Kingman's twin waters towers are painted to recognize the city as the "Heart of Historic Route 66," as well as its railroad history. **Lewis Kingman Park** honors the city's namesake and is on Route 66. Kingman's portion of the Mother Road is Andy Devine Avenue, named for the character actor known for his raspy voice and roles in early Western films and as Danny McGuire in the original 1937 production of *A Star Is Born*. A colorful sign in front of Kingman Park directs you to some of Kingman's attractions. The small park also includes the Kingman Route 66 sign and a Route 66 shield painted on the pavement.

Another Route 66 passport stop is the **Powerhouse Visitor Center**, across the street from **Mr. D'z Diner**. The Powerhouse center includes the **Arizona Route 66 Museum** and is a must-see for Route 66 travelers.

Arizona Route 66 Museum in Kingman.

Mr. D'z Diner on Route 66 in Kingman.

Exhibits include unique race cars and a tribute to the 1928 Bunion Derby. The purchase of a ticket at the Powerhouse center will also gain you admission to the **Mohave Museum of History and Arts**, where Route 66 takes a sharp turn south toward Cool Springs and Oatman.

Kingman is the seat of Mohave County and was a one-high-school town at the turn of the century. **Kingman High School** is located 6 miles north of the Powerhouse Visitor Center. Originally called Mohave County Union High School, Kingman High opened in 1917. The school added a gymnasium in 1936, and that gym was added to the National Register of Historic Places in 1986. The Kingman Bulldogs have had some success in that building too. The Kingman boys' basketball team played its way to the state championship game in 1977, a year after the girls did the same.

While Kingman's football program hasn't been the most consistent, a Bulldogs player did set one impressive record. Gabe Lumas recorded seven interceptions during a 2011 game against Flagstaff. That is an Arizona state record that will likely never be broken. Mention Gabe Lumas at a Kingman football game, and you're likely to hear stories of his feat. Lumas went on to play collegiately at the University of La Verne in California. And, yep, that's another Route 66 city.

As Kingman High School grew, the district opened a second campus a few miles south. That campus eventually became its own school. **Lee Williams High School** opened in 2012. The campus is separated from the Mother Road only by **Kingman Veterans Memorial Park** across the street from the Powerhouse center. Each high school now has roughly 500 students.

The Lee Williams Volunteers had yet to win a state championship in their first eight years, but the Volunteers basketball teams have emerged as regular postseason participants. Part of the school's football field and one section of the stadium bleachers are located on the site of the old Pioneer Cemetery. Some graves were moved to accommodate construction of the stadium.

Kingman is also home to the **Arizona Route 66 Motorsports Park**, on the north side of town. The raceway is along Route 66 opposite the Kingman airport. The dirt track opened in 2012 and hosts motocross and hot rod drag racing competitions on the national, regional, and local levels.

For those wanting to get out and hike, **Hualapai Mountain Park** has miles of trails southeast of the city. Kingman also has the **Cerbat Cliffs Golf Course** off of Gates Avenue. Located 3 miles east of the Powerhouse visitor center, Cerbat Cliffs is a public, 18-hole championship course that can be played for less than $30. Bent grass greens are at the end of the fairways that are lined with trees, streams, and sand bunkers.

The Giganiticus Headicus is another unexplained oddity on Route 66 in Kingman.

OATMAN

From Kingman, Route 66 winds through the Black Mountains, complete with switchbacks, past Cool Springs before arriving in Oatman, where wild burros roam the streets.

The meandering road heads west from Oatman toward the California border. Before crossing the Colorado River into the eighth and final state of the Mother Road, fishermen may want to stop in Topock. The small community is home to the **Route 66 RV Park** and the **Topock Marina Resort**. The river and adjacent Topock Marsh are part of the **Lake Havasu Wildlife Refuge**, which is a bird-watcher's paradise. The wetlands are also full of catfish and bass.

Say hello to the wild burros roaming the streets of Oatman.

On the edge of the living ghost town of Oatman.

Arizona Route 66 Points of Interest

TEE PEE TRADING POST – Grant Road, Lupton, AZ 86508

PETRIFIED FOREST NATIONAL PARK AND PAINTED DESERT – 1 Park Road, Petrified Forest National Park, AZ 86028

NAVAJO COUNTY COURTHOUSE – 100 E. Arizona St., Holbrook, AZ 86025

WIGWAM MOTEL – 811 W. Hopi Drive, Holbrook, AZ 86025

HOLBROOK HIGH SCHOOL – 455 N. 8th Ave, Holbrook, AZ 86025

MESA ITALIANA RESTAURANT – 2318 Navajo Blvd., Holbrook, AZ 86025

HIDDEN COVE GOLF COURSE – 1500 Golf Course Road, Holbrook, AZ 86025

JOSEPH CITY HIGH SCHOOL – 4629 2nd N., Joseph City, AZ 86032

JACK RABBIT TRADING POST – 3386 U.S. Rte. 66, Joseph City, AZ 86032

ELLA'S FRONTIER STORE – 4720 Main St., Joseph City, AZ 86032

STANDIN' ON THE CORNER PARK – Kinsley & E. 2nd St., Winslow, AZ 86047

WINSLOW HIGH SCHOOL – 600 E. Cherry St., Winslow, AZ 86047

LA POSADA HOTEL – 303 E. 2nd St., Winslow, AZ 86047

METEOR CRATER – Interstate 40, Exit 233, Winslow, AZ 86047

NORTHERN ARIZONA UNIVERSITY – 1899 S. San Francisco St., Flagstaff, AZ 86011

WALKUP SKYDOME – 1705 S. San Francisco St., Flagstaff, AZ 86001

HUMPHREY'S PEAK – Humphreys Summit Trail, Flagstaff, AZ 86001

FLAGSTAFF HIGH SCHOOL – 400 W. Elm Ave., Flagstaff, AZ 86001

CONTINENTAL GOLF CLUB – 2380 N. Oakmont Drive, Flagstaff, AZ 86004

ASPEN VALLEY GOLF CLUB – 1855 N. Continental Drive, Flagstaff, AZ 86004

ARIZONA SNOWBOWL – 9300 N. Snow Bowl Road, Flagstaff, AZ 86001

THORPE PARK – 10 N. Thorpe Road, Flagstaff, AZ 86001

LOWELL OBSERVATORY –1400 W. Mars Hill Road, Flagstaff, AZ 86001

COCONINO NATIONAL FOREST – Lake Mary Road, Flagstaff, AZ 86001

WALNUT CANYON NATIONAL MONUMENT – 3 Walnut Canyon Road, Flagstaff, AZ 86004

MAJERLE'S SPORTS GRILL – 102 E. Historic Rte. 66, Flagstaff, AZ 86001

THE MUSEUM CLUB – 3404 E. Rte. 66, Flagstaff, AZ 86004

PARKS IN THE PINES GENERAL STORE – 12963 Old Rte. 66, Parks, AZ 86018

BEARIZONA WILDLIFE PARK – 1500 E Rte. 66, Williams, AZ 86046

GRAND CANYON RAILWAY – 235 N. Grand Canyon Blvd., Williams, AZ 86046

WILLIAMS VISITOR CENTER – 200 W. Railroad Ave., Williams, AZ 86046

WILLIAMS AQUATIC CENTER – 320 W. Railroad Ave., Williams, AZ 86046

CURETON PARK – 601 N. Grand Canyon Blvd., Williams, AZ 86046

WHITE HORSE LAKE – White Horse Lake, Arizona 86046

SANTA FE LAKE – S. Perkinsville Road, Williams, Arizona 86046

WILLIAMS RODEO GROUNDS – 750 Airport Road, Williams, AZ 86046

WILLIAMS HIGH SCHOOL – 440 S. 7th St., Williams, AZ 86046

ROD'S STEAK HOUSE – 301 E. Historic Rte. 66, Williams, AZ 86046

COPPERSTATE MOTEL – 101 Lewis Ave., Ash Fork, AZ 86320

DESOTO'S SALON – 314 Lewis Ave., Ash Fork, AZ 86320

ASH FORK HIGH SCHOOL – 46999 N. 5th St., Ash Fork, AZ 86320

DELGADILLO'S SNOW CAP – 301 AZ 66, Seligman, AZ 86337

BLACK CAT BAR – 114 Chino St., Seligman, AZ 86337

THE ROAD KILL CAFE – 22830 W., AZ 66, Seligman, AZ 86337

WESTSIDE LILO'S CAFE – 22855 AZ 66, Seligman, AZ 86337

SELIGMAN SUNDRIES – 22405 AZ 66 Scenic, Seligman, AZ 86337

SELIGMAN HIGH SCHOOL – 54170 N. Floyd St., Seligman, AZ 86337

STAGECOACH 66 MOTEL – 21455 W. Interstate 40 Business Loop Exit 123, Seligman, AZ 86337

STETSON WINERY – 10965 Moonscape Way, Kingman, AZ 86401

VALLE VISTA COUNTRY CLUB & GOLF COURSE – 9686 Concho Drive, Kingman, AZ 86401

EL TROVATORE MOTEL – 1440 E. Andy Devine Ave., Kingman, AZ 86401

LEWIS KINGMAN PARK – 2201 E. Andy Devine Ave., Kingman, AZ 86401

POWERHOUSE VISITOR CENTER – 120 W. Andy Devine Ave. #2, Kingman, AZ 86401

MR. D'Z DINER – 105 E. Andy Devine Ave., Kingman, AZ 86401

MOHAVE MUSEUM OF HISTORY AND ARTS – 400 W. Beale St., Kingman, AZ 86401

KINGMAN HIGH SCHOOL – 4182 N. Bank St., Kingman, AZ 86409

LEE WILLIAMS HIGH SCHOOL – 400 Grandview Ave., Kingman, AZ 86401

KINGMAN VETERANS MEMORIAL PARK – 310 W. Beale St., Kingman, AZ 86401

ARIZONA ROUTE 66 MOTORSPORTS PARK – N. Avenida Verde, Kingman, AZ 84601

HUALAPAI MOUNTAIN PARK – 6250 Hualapai Mountain Road, Kingman, AZ 86401

CERBAT CLIFFS GOLF COURSE – 1001 Gates Ave., Kingman, AZ 86401

DOWNTOWN OATMAN – 181 Main St., Oatman, AZ 86433

ROUTE 66 RV PARK – 13021 S. Water Reed Way, Topock, AZ 86436

TOPOCK MARINA RESORT – 14999 W. Historic Rte. 66, Topock, AZ 86436

Get your kicks on the wide-open spaces.

CALIFORNIA

On your way to the edge of the continent where Los Angeles has teams in each of the major four professional sports leagues, you'll also find major league soccer clubs, minor league baseball teams, iconic venues like the Rose Bowl and Dodger Stadium, famed horse racing, numerous golf courses, and elite high school and college sports programs.

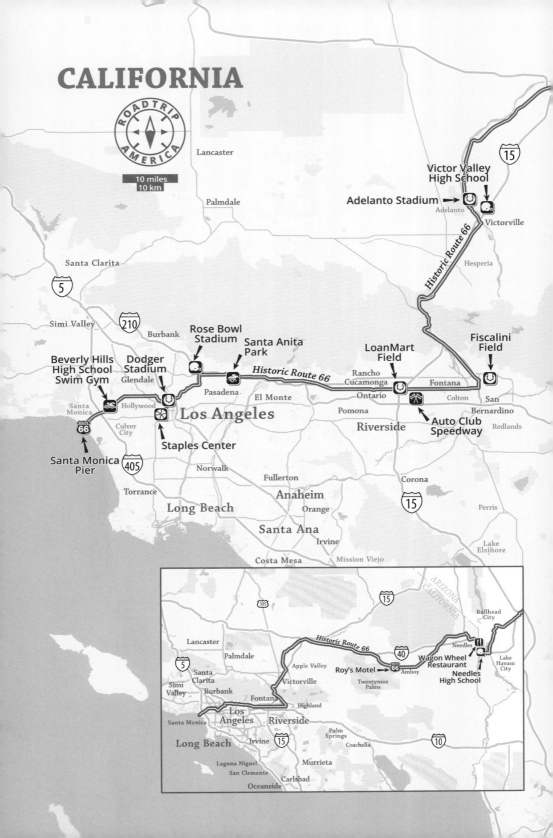

CALIFORNIA

ROADTRIP AMERICA

10 miles
10 km

Lancaster

Palmdale

Santa Clarita

5

Simi Valley

210

Burbank

Victor Valley
High School

15

Adelanto Stadium

Adelanto

Victorville

Hesperia

Rose Bowl
Stadium

Santa Anita
Park

Beverly Hills
High School
Swim Gym

Dodger
Stadium

Glendale

Hollywood

LoanMart
Field

Fiscalini
Field

Historic Route 66

Historic Route 66

Rancho
Cucamonga

Fontana

Pasadena

El Monte

Ontario

Colton

San
Bernardino

Santa
Monica

ROUTE
66

Santa Monica
Pier

405

Staples Center

Los Angeles

Culver
City

Norwalk

Torrance

Long Beach

Fullerton

Santa Ana

Anaheim

Orange

Irvine

Pomona

Riverside

Auto Club
Speedway

Redlands

Corona

15

Perris

Lake
Elsinore

Costa Mesa

Mission Viejo

ARIZONA
CALIFORNIA

395

Lancaster

Palmdale

15

Bullhead
City

Historic Route 66

40

Needles

5

Santa
Clarita

Apple Valley

Victorville

Roy's Motel

66

Amboy

Wagon Wheel
Restaurant

Lake
Havasu
City

Simi
Valley

Burbank

Fontana

Los
Angeles

Highland

Twentynine
Palms

Needles High
School

Santa Monica

Riverside

Long Beach

Irvine

15

Palm
Springs

Coachella

10

Laguna Niguel

Murrieta

San Clemente

Carlsbad

Oceanside

NEEDLES

Needles is the first California city you'll come to after crossing the Colorado River. The city of 4,900 residents has been mentioned in songs, movies, and books—most notably *The Grapes of Wrath* when the Joad family stopped there while traveling west on Route 66. When you enter Needles today, you're greeted by an old wooden wagon with the city's name scrawled across its side. A half mile later, you'll wind up at the iconic **Wagon Wheel Restaurant**. The Old West-style eatery is a great place to begin your day with a cowboy skillet for breakfast or end it with pot roast for dinner. If you're in an RV, Needles is a perfect spot to unhook your tow vehicle and take it to Oatman.

The remote location of Needles creates a unique situation for the **Needles High School** sports teams. Needles is one of five California high schools that competes in the Nevada Interscholastic Activities Association (NIAA).

The Wagon Wheel Restaurant is an iconic old-west eatery in Needles.

The other schools are Coleville, North Tahoe, South Tahoe, and Truckee.

Needles left the CIF and joined the NIAA in 1985. After winning a handful of CIF titles in the 1950s and '60s, the Mustangs have had quite a bit of success competing against Nevada schools. Needles won an NIAA 2A football championship in 2007 and advanced to the title game in 2018. The Mustangs played in their first Nevada state championship game in 1987. The Needles basketball programs each had four Nevada state titles as of 2020. Needles teams have had the most success on the diamond. The Mustangs baseball team won eight Nevada state championships between 1990 and 2009. The Needles softball team has been a veritable dynasty since 1989 with 12 state championships as of 2020.

Although there are some travel difficulties when Needles has to play a team from northeastern Nevada, for the most part, being part of the Nevada association has become the norm.

Needles High Stadium seats 1,200 and is a modest venue with a blue-and-white grandstand topped with a press box and bleachers on the opposite side. The Needles gym is not that big, with a capacity of about 800, but is usually packed when either basketball team is playing.

Nevada is often a side trip for Route 66 travelers who want to press their luck at Laughlin or Las Vegas casinos. Laughlin is less than 30 miles from Needles. If you want a taste of the Silver State that won't break your bank, spend a night or two in Needles and watch a Nevada high school team play the Mustangs before moving on.

"We have a lot of grandparents whose kids are long gone, and they still go to the games," said Bill Darrow, who has been the Needles athletics director since 1984 and sits on the NIAA board of control. "They still love watching the games. If someone were to talk with them, they could tell you a lot about the history of the town. There are a lot of interesting stories."

Through the largely abandoned communities of Goffs, Essex, Amboy, Bagdad, Siberia, and Ludlow, there are several Route 66 stops to see but nothing in terms of sports until you get to Barstow. The **Ludlow Cafe** is a great spot to grab a bite, and an evening drive through Amboy will allow you to see the **Roy's Motel and Cafe** sign lit up after being dark for years.

If the Roy's store is open, be sure and stop and pick up a Route 66 Rootbeer!

BARSTOW

Route 66 takes the form of the I-15 Business Loop in Barstow, and the city's two high schools are on either side of the Mother Road. **Barstow High School** is less than a mile south of the Double Six, while **Central High School** is a half mile to the north. But only Barstow High has an athletics program, with Central students augmenting the Aztecs teams.

Barstow High opened in 1915 and was moved to its current location on South First Avenue in 1938. The school is just seven blocks off Route 66 and has a park with a pair of ball fields on its north side. A separate baseball field is on the west side of campus, next to **Barstow High Stadium**. The Calico Mountains provide a scenic backdrop for spectators at the 3,880-seat stadium. The Aztecs have a proud football tradition with a CIF championship in 1969 and a long-standing rivalry with Victor Valley High from Victorville.

One Barstow mural depicts a landscape setting featuring travelers passing the Beacon Hotel.

The two teams have played annually since 1932, the second-longest high school football rivalry in the state. The winner of the game keeps "The Axe"—a ceremonial trophy axe—for the rest of the year.

Barstow High Stadium is also home to the soccer and track teams. The Aztecs have very strong track-and-field and cross-country programs. One complements the other, and Barstow's boys' cross-country teams were state champions six times between 2001 and 2008.

The Barstow basketball, wrestling, and volleyball teams compete inside **Bilsborough Gymnasium**. The 1,300-seat gym is named for Don Bilsborough, who was the Barstow athletics director from 1956 to 1986.

Barstow is home to a Marine Corps logistics base and is welcoming to the Marines stationed there. The city also takes pride in its Route 66 identity. Historic Main Street is lined with stone columns topped with cutouts of classic cars. Murals adorn the exterior

Classic cars top stone pillars that line Route 66 in Barstow.

walls of several buildings. The high-desert city is worth a couple of days to see all it has to offer. Stay at the **Desert Inn Motel** or the classic **Route 66 Motel**, shop and dine at **Barstow Station**, or eat at **Roy's Cafe**—named for the defunct restaurant in Amboy—and take in a game or two.

VICTORVILLE

Route 66 follows the intermittent Mojave River south from Barstow, past **Elmer's Bottle Tree Ranch**, to Victorville. The **California Route 66 Museum** on D Street is a must-stop for any Mother Road traveler. Right around the corner from Old Town Victorville, the Route 66 Museum contains a treasure trove of Mother Road nostalgia.

Victorville does have plenty for sports fans. There is minor league soccer and a high school that is part of the second-longest football rivalry in the Golden State.

The California Route 66 Museum has a large mural on an exterior wall.

Adelanto Stadium opened in 1991 as a minor league baseball stadium but is now home to the High Desert Elite Football Club, which plays in the National Premier Soccer League (NPSL). The NPSL is a semi-pro developmental league with clubs across the country—including Route 66 cities such as St. Louis, Tulsa, and Los Angeles. High Desert FC had its inaugural season in 2019 and was an immediate hit with the community. The first game drew more than 1,200 fans, and attendance remained steady.

Just a few miles from Victorville is Adelanto Stadium, which has hosted minor league baseball and semi-pro soccer teams.

Victor Valley High School is walking distance from the Route 66 Museum. The hilltop campus overlooks the Mother Road through Old Victorville. Victor Valley's Jackrabbits have a storied athletics history. The Victor Valley football team plays Barstow in an annual "Axe" rivalry game that dates back to 1932. Victor Valley has another trophy rival. The Jackrabbits and Sun Devils of Apple Valley High School have played for "The Bell" every year since 1969. The atmosphere during rivalry games is always fun with plenty of energy from fans, who often volley playful taunts across the field.

The Jackrabbits play at **Ray Moore Stadium**, which has the Victorville "V" on an adjacent hill to mark the location of Victorville's original high school. A new track and artificial turf were installed in 2018 to give the Jackrabbits one of the better playing surfaces in the region. A small grandstand with bleachers painted in sections of alternating green and white lines the home side.

While the Jackrabbits football team isn't quite what it once was, the school boasts a competitive basketball program. Next to the football stadium is the **Keith Gunn Gymnasium**, named for a longtime Victor Valley football coach and principal. The gymnasium floor is named for former basketball coach Ollie Butler, who retired as the winningest coach in San Bernardino County history. Butler had a record of 602–251 with 13 conference championships and consecutive berths in the CIF Southern Section 2A championship game in 1977 and '78. Former NBA player Greg Hyder played for Butler in

The Victor Valley Jackrabbits have a storied athletics history that includes two long-standing rivalry football games.

the 1960s.

Victor Valley also has strong baseball, track-and-field, wrestling, and tennis programs. More than a dozen baseball players have been selected right out of VVHS in the MLB Draft. Several Jackrabbits have claimed individual CIF championships in tennis and track-and-field over the years. Wrestling may be Victor Valley's best sport with eight overall CIF team championships between 1987 and 2019. Longtime head coach Sam Gollmyer is in the California Wrestling Hall of Fame. Former UFC fighter and Olympic wrestler Dan Henderson placed second at state in 1987 while helping to lead the Jackrabbits to the team title.

Another notable Victor Valley graduate is John W. Henry II, who owns both the Boston Red Sox and Liverpool Football Club.

Though not a sanctioned CIF sport, fencing is also offered to Victor Valley students. Victor Valley's fencing team won six straight California High School Championships from 2006 to 2011.

Victor Valley is one of two high schools in Victorville, with the other being **Silverado High School**, which opened in 1996 and is located 9 miles west of Route 66. Retired UFC fighter Joe Stevenson was standout wrestler at Silverado and remains close to the community. He opened his own mixed martial arts gym in Victorville in 2008 and resides in nearby Hesperia.

SAN BERNARDINO

As Route 66 leaves Victorville, it merges with Interstate 15. The highway skirts Hesperia as it heads toward San Bernardino, where the Los Angeles-area urban sprawl really begins. From here, one municipality turns into the next and into the next, and so on, without any sort of recognizable boundaries. San Bernardino is a city of more than 200,000 residents, and it has sports teams at the high school, collegiate, and professional levels.

Before you get to the city itself, Route 66 winds through Cajon Pass and by the **Route 66 Shooting Sports Park** for those wanting a little target practice. When Cajon Boulevard begins to run parallel with Interstate 215, you can see **Shandin Hills Golf Club** on the west side of the freeway. Nestled in the rolling San Bernardino hills, Shandin Hills has a par-72, 6,517-yard championship course that is open to the public. Tall trees line the rolling fairways that lead up to emerald greens.

The I-215 corridor of Route 66 also takes you by **Al Guhin Park**, which hosts the Little League World Series West Region championships every August. The winner of the West Region tournament heads to Williamsport, Pennsylvania, for the annual Little League World Series.

Men's basketball, women's volleyball represent Cal State San Bernardino at NCAA tourneys

One street that intersects Cajon Boulevard in San Bernardino is University Parkway, which heads north to **California State (Cal State) University, San Bernardino (CSUSB)**.

The Cal State San Bernardino Coyotes compete at the NCAA Division II level and are members of the California Collegiate Athletic Association (CCAA). The Coyotes have competitive baseball, golf, soccer, and softball programs and superb basketball and volleyball teams.

CSUSB's baseball team is a postseason regular with eight CCAA championships and three NCAA tournament West Region titles as of 2020. The Coyotes play at historic **Fiscalini Field**, which opened in 1934 and seats 3,500 people following a 1993 renovation. The stadium is on East Highland Avenue, 7 miles southeast of the campus.

Coussoulis Arena is the featured sports venue on the CSUSB campus. Located on the east end of campus, the 4,140-seat Coussoulis Arena has hosted concerts, WWE events, and Harlem Globetrotters games. It's also home to CSUSB's most prominent teams. The men's basketball team made 13 NCAA Tournament appearances between 1999 and 2014, while the women had five tourney berths from 1994 to 2011. The women's volleyball team qualified for the NCAA Division II tournament every season between 2000 and 2019, culminating in the program's first national championship in 2019 under longtime coach Kim Cherniss.

Former Coyotes golfer Scott Householder won an individual national championship in 1997 when he set an NCAA Division II record by shooting a 273 over 72 holes. Gene Webster Jr. is another PGA golfer who played collegiately at CSUSB. The Coyotes sent golfers to the NCAA tournament eight times between 1992 and 2009.

Cajon holds many CIF titles

Before former MLB player Aaron Brooks pitched for CSUSB, he was a standout player at **Cajon High School**. The Cajon High campus abuts the southeast end of the CSUSB grounds. The school serves the community of Devore and parts of San Bernardino.

The Cajon Cowboys have a solid baseball program with multiple conference championships and CIF playoff berths. Cajon's softball program is even better and won a CIF championship in 2006.

The Cowboys are competitive in nearly every sport and have several CIF titles. Cajon's football team had undefeated seasons in 1995 and 2010. The 2010 squad included cornerback Damontae Kazee, who played collegiately at San Diego State and was a fifth-round draft pick of the Atlanta Falcons in 2017. Kazee led the NFL in interceptions the following season.

Cajon Cowboy Stadium was renovated in 2017 to install a new turf field with a gold star at midfield and "CAJON" and "COWBOYS" in either end zone. The stadium isn't that big, but like everything real estate, it's all about location. Cajon Cowboy Stadium offers picturesque views of the San Bernardino Mountains.

Cajon's boys' and girls' basketball teams have also been very good. The

Cajon girls won three CIF titles between 2008 and 2016. Lou Kelly, who went on to star at the University of Nevada, Las Vegas, is Cajon's all-time leading scorer and averaged nearly 39 points per game in the 1996–97 season while leading the Cowboys to the CIF Southern Section quarterfinals.

The Cajon wrestling program has been solid, regularly sending grapplers to the state meet in Bakersfield; the program produced mixed martial arts fighter Saad Awad.

San Bernardino High preps athletes for the big leagues

Cajon is one of three San Bernardino high schools near Route 66. **San Bernardino High School** was the city's first high school and opened in 1891. The campus is five blocks north of the **Original McDonald's Restaurant and Museum** and just east of the I-215–Highway 259 junction. Even though San Bernardino High is blocks from the first McDonald's, SBHS graduate Glen Bell founded the Taco Bell franchise.

The SBHS gymnasium boasts multiple Cardinals championship banners, including one for the 1989 boys' basketball team that won a CIF Southern Section championship. That squad was led by former NBA player Byron Russell, who has returned to his high school alma mater to hold camps.

An extremely detailed mural is on the wall of the original McDonald's location in San Bernardino.

NFL running back Alexander Mattison was another standout athlete for the Cardinals. He won several league titles in track and wrestling and rushed for more than 2,000 yards in his final two seasons at SBHS. He played collegiately at Boise State University and was a third-round pick by the Minnesota Vikings in the 2019 NFL Draft.

Former MLB first baseman Dee Fondy, who played for the Chicago Cubs, Pittsburgh Pirates, and Cincinnati Reds in the 1950s, got his start in San Bernardino. Following his retirement as a player, Fondy worked as a scout and is credited with signing future Hall of Famer Paul Molitor while working for the Milwaukee Brewers.

SBHS has excellent facilities, including its own swim complex. The football stadium, which also houses the soccer and track-and-field teams, had a new artificial turf installed in 2019 as part of a $1 million renovation.

Baseball stars get their start in San Bernardino

Before Fiscalini Field was home to the CSUSB baseball team, it hosted several minor league teams and was even the spring training home for the Pittsburgh Pirates from 1938 to 1952, and the St. Louis Browns (now the Baltimore Orioles) in 1948 and 1953. Fiscalini Field, named for former minor league player and San Bernardino High School alumnus John Fiscalini, last hosted a minor league team in 1995 with the San Bernardino Spirit. That doesn't mean San Bernardino doesn't have professional baseball today.

The Inland Empire 66ers, the Single-A affiliate of the Los Angeles Angels of Anaheim, play at **San Manuel Stadium**. The team takes its name from the Mother Road, and its 8,000-seat stadium is 4 miles east of the famed Wigwam Motel. The stadium's exterior resembles an old Spanish mission. The 66ers were founded in 1993 as the Spirit, but the name was changed to the Stampede in 1996 before 66ers was adopted in 2003. The franchise won six league championships between 1995 and 2013 and were previously affiliated with the Seattle Mariners and Los Angeles Dodgers before aligning with the Angels in 2011.

Baseball Hall of Famer Ken Griffey Jr. once donned a San Bernardino uniform, as did All-Stars Adrian Beltre, Asdrúbal Cabrera, Del Crandall, Rafael Furcal, Kenley Jansen, Mike Hampton, Orel Hershiser, Paul Konerko,

Ted Lilly, Omar Vizquel, Tim Wallach, Devon White, and C. J. Wilson. Minor league baseball is always fun, and it seems only logical to see the 66ers play while traveling Route 66.

San Bernardino's **Wigwam Motel** is one of two on Route 66, the other being in Holbrook, Arizona. Spend a few nights in a wigwam and take in all that San Bernardino has to offer.

San Bernardino's Wigwam Motel on a rainy November day.

RIALTO

Though Rialto is only 8 miles long and 4 miles wide, there are 100,000 crammed into the city, and Rialto High is one of two public high schools to serve Rialto's residents. Just after the Wigwam Motel is the Rialto city limits, and less than 2 miles south of the teepee complex is **Rialto High School**.

The Rialto Knights compete at high levels in football, baseball, basketball, soccer, wrestling, golf, cross-country, and track-and-field. The Rialto football, soccer, and track teams use **Rialto High School Sports Stadium** as their home. The stadium, which underwent renovations in 2002, can seat up to 4,500 spectators and has a large grandstand topped with a press box accessed by an elevator.

Rialto has multiple professional athletes among its alumni, including former MLB pitcher Ricky Nolasco. Also included is former WWE wrestler

Lisa Marie (Sole) Varon, who was first a track athlete and cheerleader at Rialto High. Olympic speed skater Derek Parra, who won a gold medal at the 2002 Salt Lake City Games, is another Rialto graduate.

Rialto High is separated by only 5 miles from **Eisenhower High School** at the intersection of Lilac Avenue and Baseline Road. Just a mile and a half north of Route 66 and 3 miles west of the Wigwam Motel, Eisenhower High boasts a Pro Football Hall of Famer among its alumni.

Former San Francisco 49ers safety Ronnie Lott got his start at Eisenhower, where he led the Eagles on the basketball court as well. Lott attended a 2018 ceremony to unveil the renovated stadium that now bears his name. **Ronnie Lott Stadium** underwent a $7 million remodel to install a new synthetic turf, add LED stadium lights, update the sound system and scoreboard, and bring the overall capacity up to 5,000 spectators. There were track-and-field updates to the venue as well, including the addition of separate shot put and discus fields. The new stadium brought with it some good luck. The Eisenhower football team played for a Division 3A CIF championship in 2018, but fell to the Kaiser Catamounts of Fontana.

Lott was part of four Super Bowl championship teams with the 49ers and was selected to 10 Pro Bowls during a 15-year career that included stints with the Oakland Raiders and New York Jets. He isn't the only NFL player to come out of Eisenhower. Running back David Lang graduated from Eisenhower in 1986, and offensive lineman Ryan Clady was in the class of 2004. Both players were on Super Bowl-winning teams, Lang with the Dallas Cowboys in 1995 and Clady with the Denver Broncos in 2015.

When Eisenhower played for a CIF Division 1 championship in 1991, more than 33,000 people made the trip to Anaheim Stadium to watch the Eagles fall to Santa Ana's Mater Dei High School. The Eagles avenged the loss two years later in the CIF championship game against Mater Dei to complete a perfect 14–0 season. Eisenhower's football prominence dates back to 1959 when the Hawks appeared in their first CIF championship game.

Eisenhower is part of the San Andreas League, which includes Arroyo Valley and Rialto. The Eagles have won multiple football and basketball league championships, but also several baseball titles. The Eisenhower baseball program has its own famous alumnus. Jeff Conine, who helped the Florida

(Miami) Marlins win World Series titles in 1997 and 2003 and was the MVP of the 1995 MLB All-Star Game, got his start at Eisenhower.

The Eagles also have outstanding track and wrestling programs with a plethora of individual champions over the years.

FONTANA

Fontana has a font of options for sports fans—pun intended.

Just before you get to **Bono's Historic Orange** on Route 66, turn south on Citrus Avenue. **Fontana High School**, home of the Steelers, is 2 miles down the road. The Steelers, appropriately, have a very strong football program.

Coach Bruich led Fontana, Kaiser football programs to hundreds of wins

Under now-retired coach Dick Bruich, the Steelers qualified for the playoffs in each of his 22 seasons at Fontana. Bruich led Fontana to a 1987 national championship, 2 state championships, 2 CIF championships, 1 CIF runner-up, 4 CIF semifinal appearances, and 12 Citrus League titles. Bruich left Fontana in 1999 to take over at **Henry J. Kaiser High School**, which opened that year.

At Kaiser, Bruich continued his coaching success. He led the Cats to a Division 3A state championship in 2008, two CIF championships, one CIF runner-up, two CIF semifinal appearances, eight Sunkist League titles, and eight consecutive playoff berths before retiring in 2009. Bruich helped send several former Fontana and Kaiser players to the NFL.

Fontana High School Football Stadium has been the host site for multiple CIF Southern Section championship games and, when the Steelers are playing well, can be a fun place to watch a football game.

Basketball, soccer are top programs at Fontana

The Steelers take their name from the Kaiser Steel plant that opened in 1943. The massive plant has been used in several movies—most notably the climactic showdown scene at the end of *Terminator 2: Judgment Day*.

Fontana also has excellent basketball and soccer programs. The Steelers were CIF 4A runners-up in 1986, when they were led by future NBA player Sean Rooks. Fontana won another CIF title in 1995, a year before NBA player Corey Benjamin garnered state player of the year honors. The Fontana girls won a CIF basketball championship in 1984 and were 5 AA runners-up in 1989.

Fontana's boys' soccer team was CIF runner-up in 1991, 1993, and 2011. The 1991 squad was led by future MLS player Ante Razov, who joined the Los Angeles FC coaching staff in 2018. Razov began his MLS playing career with the LA Galaxy in 1996 after playing at UCLA. Mexican footballer Jonathan Suárez Cortés also played at Fontana.

Fontana has produced several individual champions in track-and-field and wrestling. The baseball program is also solid and produced MLB player Gregg Colbrun, who won a World Series with the Arizona Diamondbacks in 2001.

If you're a music fan, former Van Halen lead singer Sammy Hagar is also among the Fontana alumni. Eddie Van Halen formed the group with his brothers in 1972 while living in Pasadena, another Route 66 city.

Kaiser Cats on the prowl for another championship

The Kaiser Cats have remained a football power even after Bruich retired in 2009. The Cats won eight straight Sunkist League titles under Bruich and then added two more in 2012 and 2013. The Cats were CIF Central Division champions in 2012 and then won the Division 8 championship in 2018. Kaiser's college-like stadium has all the modern amenities fans would want. It's also home to the school's soccer, track-and-field, and lacrosse teams.

Kaiser High School is located on Almond Avenue 5 miles south of Route 66 on Cherry Avenue. Driving there will take you by **Auto Club Speedway**, a 2-mile oval track that has hosted a NASCAR race annually since 1997. Much of the Kaiser Plant was demolished to make way for the speedway. Jeff Gordon won the first Auto Club 400 in 1997 and again in 1999 and 2004. Gordon is one of four three-time winners of the event. Matt Kenseth, Jimmie Johnson, and Kyle Busch also had three victories at the track as of 2020. Busch picked up his third Auto Club victory in 2019. The 2020 race was won by Alex Bowman, whose only previous victory came in 2019 at Chicagoland.

Fontana has a third high school near Route 66—**A. B. Miller High School** north of Foothill Boulevard, just off the 210.

Former NFL linebacker Nick Barnett, who was born in Barstow, graduated from Miller before attending Oregon State. He then spent 11 seasons in the NFL and was part of Green Bay's Super Bowl championship team in 2010, his eighth and final season with the Packers. Barnett is part of a proud athletics program at Miller, where the Rebels have had success across multiple sports, notably baseball, girls' basketball, and wrestling.

RANCHO CUCAMONGA

Young players new to the Los Angeles Dodgers organization often get their start in Rancho Cucamonga. The Rancho Cucamonga Quakes are the Single-A affiliate of the Dodgers and play at **LoanMart Field**, which is just a block south of Foothill Boulevard. The Quakes have called the stadium inside the **Rancho Cucamonga Epicenter Entertainment & Sports Complex** home since 1993 and have outstanding community support. The 6,600-seat stadium is often sold out, and the Quakes have set and then broken attendance records.

The Quakes won a California League title in 1994 and were in the championship series again in 1998 and 2010. They claimed two more California League titles in 2015 and 2018. The team has had several MLB alliances over the years. They were the High-A affiliate of the Anaheim Angels from 2001 to 2010 before the Dodgers took control in 2011. There have been plenty of future MLB All-Stars and MVPs whose professional careers began in Rancho Cucamonga. Cody Bellinger, the 2019 National League MVP; Howie Kendrick, the 2019 NL Championship Series MVP; three-time American League MVP Mike Trout; pitchers Jered Weaver, Ervin Santana, and Walker Buehler—each of whom has thrown a no-hitter; six-time All-Star reliever Francisco Rodriguez; pitcher Bobby Jenks; first basemen Derrek Lee and Mike Napoli; shortstop Corey Seager; and outfielders Yasiel Puig and Joc Pederson have all donned a Quakes uniform.

The San Gabriel Mountains provide a scenic backdrop for a Quakes game at LoanMart Field in Rancho Cucamonga.

LoanMart Field is a gorgeous setting for baseball. Tall pine trees tower over the left-field wall with the San Gabriel Mountains as the distant backdrop. The best thing about minor leagues games is that ticket prices are affordable and, because the stadiums are smaller, it's impossible to pick a bad seat. One of the visible mountains is **Cucamonga Peak**, the tallest of the San Gabriels at 8,862 feet. It is a popular hiking destination for those wanting a challenge. A wilderness permit is required to hike the mountain.

LoanMart Field is surrounded by several baseball fields and a youth soccer training facility, so the Epicenter is almost always bustling with activity.

Rancho Cucamonga alums win Super Bowl rings

Rancho Cucamonga has three high schools near Route 66. **Rancho Cucamonga High School** is right off the 210 and has one of the area's best football programs. The RC Cougars have sent multiple players on to NCAA Division I universities and even the NFL. One of the most notable former RC players is Patrick Chung, who was part of three Super Bowl championship teams with the New England Patriots. Another RC graduate is Terrell Thomas, who won Super Bowl XLVI with the New York Giants, beating Chung's Patriots.

Rancho Cucamonga's football, soccer, and track teams compete at **Cougar Stadium**, a bowl-like venue that opened in 2016. Cougar Stadium can seat up to 5,000 spectators, who can take in a wonderful view of the San Gabriel Mountains. The field is surrounded by a gray, nine-lane synthetic track; a 7,000-square-foot field house is at the east end zone. Rancho Cucamonga is also known for the traditional Haka dance performed after home games. The Haka is a Māori ceremonial dance that has been performed to welcome guests and celebrate noteworthy achievements.

Rancho Cucamonga's football, boys' basketball, girls' soccer, softball, track-and-field, and wrestling teams have all competed for CIF championships. Michael Johnson Jr., the son of the Olympic gold medalist sprinter, won CIF Southern Section triple jump titles in 2003 and 2004 before joining the UCLA track team.

Los Osos teams make regular showings in postseason

Rivalry games are always fun. Rancho Cucamonga's biggest rival is **Los Osos High School**, which is on the other side of Highway 210. The Los Osos campus is surrounded by athletics fields to the north and east, Banyan Street to the south, and Milliken Avenue on the west side.

The Los Osos Grizzlies also have proud, successful athletics programs. Los Osos teams are postseason contenders, no matter the sport. Rancho Cucamonga and Los Osos are both members of the Baseline League, which includes nearby Upland.

Los Osos teams won nearly 80 Baseline titles and played for 18 CIF titles as of 2020. NFL players Tony Washington and Victor Bolden Jr. are products of the Los Osos program. Bolden was also a standout hurdler, placing second at the CIF state meet in 2012.

The Los Osos football stadium, also home to the soccer and track teams, is a 4,000-seat venue on the north side of campus. The Los Osos softball and baseball fields comprise the eastern border of the huge campus. The Los Osos girls soccer team won a CIF championship in 2012. The Grizzlies have had several individual champions in track-and-field, swimming, and wrestling.

The California Interscholastic Federation held its first water polo tournament in 1996, and Los Osos has become a power. The Grizzlies played for a CIF girls' title consecutively from 2009 to 2014, winning three championships. The Los Osos boys won titles in 2008, 2012, and '13 and were runners-up in 2009, '14, and '18. Nick Bell was the state player of the year before competing for the USA National Team.

Rocky Long, Eric Weddle hail from Alta Loma

Another Rancho Cucamonga high school is a couple of miles west on Base Line Road between Foothill Boulevard and Highway 210. **Alta Loma High School** has a gorgeous campus in the shadow of the San Gabriel Mountains. The school opened in 1963 and has since won several CIF titles while producing quite a few professional athletes.

Former NFL safety Eric Weddle was a three-sport athlete at Alta Loma, lettering in football, basketball, and baseball before attending the University of Utah. Weddle spent 2019 with the Los Angeles Rams but retired after the

The Rancho Cucamonga Service Station is a good spot to begin your exploration of the city.

season to end a 13-year NFL career. He was a six-time Pro Bowl selection and led the NFL with seven interceptions in 2011. Another pro player to come out of the Alta Loma football program was Rocky Long, who played for the British Columbia Lions of the Canadian Football League in 1970s before starting a long coaching career.

Long has definitive Route 66 ties. He was hired by the University of New Mexico in 2020 as the program's defensive coordinator. Long played collegiately at New Mexico and was the program's head coach from 1998 to 2008. His wife, Roxanne, is the former women's basketball program head coach at Rogers State University in Claremore, Oklahoma.

Just south of Alta Loma is the famous **Route 66 Cucamonga Service Station**, which is now a visitor center and a stop for a Route 66 Passport stamp. A little farther down the road are the iconic **Sycamore Inn** and **Magic Lamp Inn**. In the same area are the Route 66 hiking trailhead at **Red Hill Park** and the private **Red Hill Country Club** golf course.

Rancho Cucamonga's Magic Lamp is a good spot for photos and dining.

UPLAND

Upland's iconic **Madonna of the Trail Statue** stands at the corner of Euclid and Foothill Boulevard. A half mile west is **Upland High School**, at the intersection of Foothill Boulevard and San Antonio Avenue. The football field faces Foothill Boulevard, and "Home of the Scots" is visible on the stadium press box. The Upland teams are officially the Highlanders, and they've been pretty darn good in just about every sport.

Highlander Stadium is home to Upland's football, soccer, and track teams. The stadium underwent a $1 million renovation in 2017 to install new field and track surfaces. Like other venues along Foothill Boulevard, Highlander

Madonna of the Trail statue on Route 66 in Upland.

Stadium has a picturesque setting with the mountains as its backdrop.

The best-known Upland graduate is Baseball Hall of Famer Rollie Fingers, who was the first relief pitcher to win both the MVP and Cy Young Award in the same season. He did that in 1981 with the Milwaukee Brewers and then helped the Brewers reach their only World Series in 1982. The Brewers lost, but Fingers did win three World Series crowns with the Oakland Athletics from 1972 to 1974. Fingers, with his famous mustache, was a seven-time All-Star and was the relief pitcher of the year four times. He led the league in saves three times, and his number 34 has been retired by both the A's and Brewers.

CLAREMONT

The **Claremont Colleges** are a group of seven private schools near Route 66. Among them, **Harvey Mudd College** is right on Foothill Boulevard (Route 66). Harvey Mudd combines with **Scripps College** and **Claremont McKenna College** to compete at the NCAA Division III level as the CMS Stags (for male teams) and Athenas (for female teams). Claremont Mudd Scripps (CMS) is in the Southern California Intercollegiate Athletic Conference (SCIAC) and fields teams for each of the major sports. CMS teams have won several SCIAC titles.

The football and lacrosse teams play at **John Zinda Field at Fritz B. Burns Stadium**. It's a small venue that resembles a high school stadium, but the student section is always full for football games.

CMS teams began competing in 1947, but the Stags and Athenas had to wait a while for sustained success. An NAIA men's swimming championship in 1967 was the school's first national championship. The men's tennis team won an NCAA Division III title in 1981 and again in 2015. The 2017 CMS volleyball team won an NCAA Division III national championship, the first by any CMS women's team. That title was quickly followed by national championships by the women's golf and tennis teams. While CMS had just seven overall national championships as of 2020, the programs had combined for 48 individual titles.

Robert Pavilion is the home to the basketball and volleyball teams. The men's basketball team has qualified for the NCAA D-III tournament 14 times but got out of the first round just four times.

The baseball team plays at **Bill Arce Field**, named after the former CMS coach who was the program's first athletics director. One of Arce's former players, Wes Parker, went on to have a nine-year MLB career with the Los Angeles Dodgers. He was part of the 1965 World Series championship team and won six Gold Gloves at first base. The pitch at **John Pritzlaff Field** is used by the men's and women's soccer teams. **Matt M. Axelrood Pool** is the CMS natatorium and home to the successful swimming program.

If you're going to attend a CMS game, try to see the Stags or Athenas when they're playing rival Pomona College. The Sixth Street Rivalry brings out the best (or worst) in the students and alumni.

Just past the colleges and a few blocks north of Route 66 is **Claremont High School** on Indian Hill Boulevard. The school is just a half mile from **Wolfe's Market Kitchen and Deli**—appropriate since the Claremont sports teams are the Wolfpack. Claremont High includes actress Jessica Alba among its alumni.

Claremont has won several CIF titles across all sports, including consecutive football championships in 1984 and 1985. Those teams were led by quarterback Dan McGwire, who was the state's offensive player of the year in 1985. McGwire, whose brother is former MLB slugger Mark McGwire, played collegiately at San Diego State before a five-year NFL career with the Seattle Seahawks and Miami Dolphins.

LA VERNE

One of Claremont High School's bigger rivals is **Damien High School** in La Verne, where Mark McGwire was a standout baseball player at Damien before his record-setting MLB career.

Soccer players leave Damien prepped to play with the pros

Damien is off of Arrow Highway a few blocks south of Route 66, just before the Mother Road crosses the 210 at **Mr. D's Diner**. Damien is an all-boys Catholic school that opened in 1959, and the Spartans have been a sports powerhouse ever since. Spartans teams consistently compete for championships in the Baseline League that includes Upland, Los Osos, and Rancho Cucamonga.

The Spartans have won multiple CIF championships over the years. Hurdler Geoff Vanderstock, who once held the world record in the 400-meter hurdles, graduated from Damien when it was a co-ed school called Pomona Catholic.

McGwire may be the best-known professional athlete to come out of Damien, but he's not the only one. Several MLB and NFL players were groomed at Damien. McGwire set a then-MLB record with 70 home runs in 1998 and finished his career with 583 homers. The Damien baseball team calls **Tom Carroll Stadium** home. It's named in honor of the longtime athletics director who convinced McGwire to stick with baseball when he wanted to quit the team to play golf. Good advice, don't you think?

The Damien football stadium was named after former coach Dick Larson in 2010. Larson was the coach for both CIF championships and won 174 games in 19 seasons at Damien, which won CIF titles in 1977 and 1982.

Sports agent Bill Duffy, who was the 1977 CIF basketball player of the year and a 1982 draft pick of the Denver Nuggets, is also a Damien graduate. Childhood friend Ronnie Lott, a Rialto Eisenhower alum, helped Duffy land his first client—former NFL wide receiver and two-time Pro Bowler Webster Slaughter. Duffy has since focused on NBA players and his client list is impressive: Steve Nash, Yao Ming, Rajon Rondo, Joakim Noah, Luka Dončić, Tacko Fall, Frank Kaminsky, Deandre Ayton, and Hamidou Diallo among them. Basketball is strong at Damien, where the 2,500-seat gymnasium is almost always filled to capacity for Spartans games.

Soccer has been the Damien's most consistent sport, with two CIF titles and four runners-up finishes. The program has produced numerous professional players like Chukwudi Chijindu, Brian Dunseth, Joe Franchino, Mike Hunter, and U.S. National Soccer Hall of Famer Rick Davis. Dunseth, Franchino, and Davis were all members of the U.S. National Team.

University produces football, baseball, golf greats

Between Damien and Bonita lies the campus of the **University of La Verne**, where the Leopards compete at the NCAA Division III level. La Verne has been a D-III power with multiple national championships across several sports.

La Verne's women's volleyball team is a perennial contender with national championships in 1981, '82, and 2001. The men's volleyball team claimed a national title in 1999.

La Verne's baseball, football, golf, softball, and track-and-field teams are also highly competitive. The football team, which had an undefeated regular season in 2015, is a regular postseason participant. The Leopards program produced former NFL kicker Joaquin Zendejas, and a pair of coaches who held jobs at the college and pro levels. Larry Kernan had a 50-year coaching career that included a 13-year tenure as the executive director of the NFL Coaches Association. Steve Ortmayer was a longtime assistant coach with the Oakland Raiders before becoming the general manager of the San Diego Chargers and St. Louis Rams—before both teams moved to Los Angeles. The Leopards play at **Ortmayer Stadium**, a classic small-college venue that underwent a makeover in 2012. The renovations included a new scoreboard, resurfaced track, and installation of artificial turf on the field also used by the soccer teams.

La Verne's baseball program won national championships in 1972 and 1995. The 1972 team included Dan Quisenberry, whose "submarine style" of pitching became legendary. Quisenberry, who was only 45 when he died of brain cancer in 1998, was a three-time All-Star for the Kansas City Royals. He led the American League in saves five times and was the closer for Kansas City's 1985 World Series championship team.

La Verne's golf program produced PGA player Kelby Scharmann, who won an individual national championship in 2015. There are a pair of La Verne golf courses just north of Route 66. The **San Dimas Canyon Golf Course** and **Marshall Canyon Golf Course** flank the Sierra La Verne Country Club, which closed its golf course in 2019. Where Sierra La Verne was a private course, both San Dimas and Marshall are open to the public. San Dimas has a 6,400-yard, par-72 course with tree-lined fairways of Kikuyu grass and Poanna grass greens. With affordable prices, it's an ideal place for the casual golfer to play a round. Marshall Canyon can also be played while on a budget. The 6,100-yard 18-hole course with Kikuyu grass can be a fun, challenging course for players of all levels. Both courses have driving ranges and offer stunning views of the San Gabriel Mountains.

As Route 66 continues out of La Verne, it skirts **San Dimas Canyon Park**, a popular hiking area, before going past the Glendora Country Club.

GLENDORA

The **Glendora Country Club** has a 6,597-yard course along the foothills of the San Gabriel Mountains. The picturesque fairways feature undulating hills, various water features, numerous trees, and well-manicured greens for the club's members and their guests. The country club has been open since 1956 and includes a restaurant that's open to the public. It hosted the 1982 CIF boys state championships and the 1983 girls' tourney.

Nearly abutting the golf course and just three blocks north of Route 66 is **Glendora High School**. Oak trees surround the school, which opened in 1959. The school's first graduating class voted on a mascot for the sports teams, and Tartans won the vote.

Since Glendora's opening, several future pro athletes have walked across the stage to receive their diplomas. Tennis player Lea Antonoplis; NBA players Casey Jacobsen and Tracy Murray; NHL goalie Collin Delia (who played for the Amarillo Bulls from 2012 to 2014); and MLB players Brian Cooper, Ed Kirkpatrick, Adam Plutko, and 2007 All-Star and two-time World Series champion Aaron Roward all graduated from Glendora.

With multiple MLB players as part of its alumni, it shouldn't be a surprise that the Tartans' baseball program is pretty darn good. Glendora won a CIF Division 2 championship in 2010 and is consistently in the postseason hunt. Roward was the 1995 California state player of the year. Plutko took those honors while leading the 2010 championship team.

Glendora's basketball program reached the CIF 4AA championship game in 1989 but fell to Menlo-Atherton from the San Francisco Bay area. Glendora won the championship game the following season led by coach Mike DeLuc. The Tartans added CIF titles in 1992, 1998, and 2001 with second-place finishes in 1996 and 1999. Glendora's girls' basketball won a 2A state championship in 2018 after finishing second in 2017. Glendora's gym can get packed for basketball games, even with two levels of bleachers on either side of the floor.

Jacobsen was the state player of the year in 1998 and '99. Murray was the CIF player of the year in 1989, when he averaged better than 44 points per game and set a state record for most points scored in a single season with

1,505. Glendora home games would sell out more than three hours before tip-off that season because Murray was such a huge draw.

"It's always special when you can coach players who end up going to the NBA," DeLuc said. "Casey and Tracy were both great players and just great people. I've coached a lot of great players who I'm proud of. You don't have to play in the NBA. We've had a lot of guys who have gone on to have a lot of success."

Under DeLuc, the Tartans won 702 games over 29 years with four CIF Southern Section championships and 15 league titles. DeLuc left Glendora in 2015 to become the head coach at Damien, where he previously coached from 1979 to 1986 and won 124 games in eight seasons. DeLuc picked up his 900th career victory in 2018 with fewer than 240 losses.

AZUSA

Continuing west on Route 66 will take you right by **Azusa Pacific University**, an NCAA Division II school with a proud athletics history. Despite being a D-II school, Azusa Pacific has produced an impressive number of professional athletes and Olympians.

As of 2020, 14 APU alumni had competed in the Olympics, including 2008 decathlon gold medalist Bryan Clay. Fellow decathlete Dave Johnson took bronze in the Barcelona Games and is a 1986 APU graduate. Nigerian Davidson Ezinwa ran for APU before claiming a silver medal in the 400-meter relay at the 1992 Olympics. His brother, Osmond, donned a silver medal in the same event at the 1997 World Championships in Athens. Innocent Egbunike was a bronze medalist at the 1984 Olympics and still holds the Azusa Pacific record for the 400-meter dash.

Azusa Pacific draws several students from Nigeria. The most famous would be former Kansas City Chiefs running back Christian Okoye, who was known as the "Nigerian Nightmare" because of his size and bruising running style. At 6-foot-1 and 260 pounds, Okoye was difficult for any one defender to bring down by himself. Okoye would run through a would-be tackler instead of avoiding hits. That resulted in a short career from 1987 to '92, but he was a two-time Pro Bowler and led the NFL with

1,480 rushing yards and 12 touchdowns in 1989.

Another APU alumnus had a much longer NFL career. Offensive tackle Jackie Slater spent his entire 20-year career with the Rams—19 in Los Angeles and the 1995 season in St. Louis. Slater was a stalwart on the Rams' line, helping Eric Dickerson rush for an NFL-record 2,105 yards in 1984. Slater was selected to seven Pro Bowls and enshrined in the Pro Football Hall of Fame in 2001. The Rams retired his number 78 after the 1995 season. After his playing career, Slater got into coaching and tutored offensive linemen at his alma mater from 2011 to 2018. Slater's son, Matthew, has been a special teams ace for the New England Patriots with eight Pro Bowl selections and three Super Bowl championships. Matthew played his college football up the road for UCLA at the Rose Bowl in Pasadena.

The APU Cougars play at **Citrus Stadium**, a 10,000-seat venue that is also the home to the Glendora, Covina Gladstone, and Azusa high school football teams. Azusa Pacific's baseball program boasts several pro players. All-Star catcher Steven Vogt, former outfielder Kirk Nieuwenhuis, and pitchers Jeff Robinson and Ruben Niebla all played on the Cougars' baseball field that faces Route 66 at Alosta Avenue. Nieuwenhuis led the Cougars to consecutive NAIA World Series appearances in 2007 and '08.

Former pro soccer player Steven Lenhart was an NAIA All-American in 2007 while leading Azusa Pacific to a national championship. Azusa Pacific also has a solid basketball program that has former Harlem Globetrotters player Kevin Daley as part of its alumni. The APU basketball and volleyball teams play inside the 3,500-seat **Felix Event Center**, which is also a frequent host for the CIF basketball championships.

Less than a mile southwest of the APU campus is **Azusa High School** on North Cerritos Avenue. Azusa's biggest rivals are the Gladstone Gladiators from West Covina, 2 miles to the south. Attending rivalry games is always fun, especially when the schools are so close and share a stadium.

The Azusa Aztecs have a few CIF championship and several individual champions in wrestling, track-and-field, and golf. One of those champs was golfer Lizette Salas, who won the CIF golf tournament in 2006 after placing second a year earlier. She made her LPGA debut in 2012 and won the 2014 Kingsmill Championship in Williamsburg, Virginia.

DUARTE

As you enter the city of Duarte, you'll go right by the **Rancho Duarte Golf Course**. It's an ideal spot to get in a quick round with just nine holes laid out along the foothills of the San Gabriels. The first hole can be tricky off the tee because it's only 68 yards long. The entire par-31 course is short at just 1,635 yards. The longest hole is number three, a par-4 at 329 yards.

Across the street from the golf course is the **Justice Brothers Racing Museum** on East Huntington Drive. The museum is a must for gear heads.

MONROVIA

Monrovia High School is a mile west of the iconic **Aztec Hotel** that was added to the National Register of Historic Places in 1978. The hotel closed in 2011, but plans to reopen were initiated in 2019.

The Monrovia Wildcats have a long and storied sports tradition dating back to their first appearance in the CIF football championship game in 1935. That team was led by quarterback Roy Zimmerman, who went on to lead San Jose State University to an undefeated season in 1939. Zimmerman was a two-time All-Pro during a nine-year NFL career and helped the Washington Redskins win the 1942 NFL championship. Also on that 1935 Monrovia team was Johnny Lindell, who was a three-sport standout in football, track, and

The historic Aztec Hotel was added to the National Register of Historic Places in 1978.

baseball. Lindell won the 110-meter hurdles at the 1935 CIF state meet and was third in the long jump. Lindell's primary sport was baseball, and he was signed by the New York Yankees in 1936. He made his MLB debut in 1941 to begin a 14-year MLB career that saw him win three World Series championships and get selected to the 1943 All-Star Game.

The Wildcats football team was again state runner-up in 1951 and 1959. A member of the 1951 squad was lineman Hardiman Cureton, who led UCLA to a national championship in 1954 and then was a five-time All-Star in the Canadian Football League and helped the Hamilton Tiger-Cats win the Grey Cup in 1963. Several more CIF title game appearances followed for Monrovia, which spawned the professional careers of multiple NFL players. Among them are defensive back Chris Hale and running back Keith Lincoln, who was a five-time American Football League All-Star and helped the San Diego Chargers win the 1963 AFL championship. Hale was also a two-time CIF Southern Section long jump champion in 1983 and '84.

Monrovia High was established in 1893 and has a gorgeous campus with 100-year-old oak trees around historic buildings of neo-Spanish architecture. A $45 million bond was passed in 2006 to upgrade all of the school's athletics facilities. As with the other schools along Foothill Boulevard, outdoor sporting events offer spectators glorious views of the San Gabriel Mountains.

ARCADIA

Less than a mile south of the Santa Anita Avenue-Colorado Street intersection is **Santa Anita Park**, which is one of the more well-known horse tracks in the country.

Visit a Breeders' Cup track

Santa Anita is a regular host of the Breeders' Cup, hosting the event eight times between 2003 and 2019. The Breeders' Cup is just one of several prestigious events the track has hosted since the first Santa Anita Handicap was held in 1935. The Handicap, held every March, is a Grade 1 Thoroughbred race for horses aged 4 years or older. Hall of Fame jockey Bill Shoemaker is

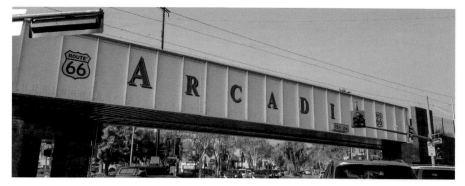

Welcome to Arcadia, California.

the all-time wins leader of the Handicap at 11. A life-sized bust of Shoemaker, who died in 2003, is at the track.

Game On Dude, ridden by Canadian jockey Chantal Sutherland, has the most wins by a horse with victories in 2011, '13, and '14. Game On Dude retired at age 7 after the 2014 season. The legendary Seabiscuit won the 1940 Handicap in his final race and now has a full-sized statue at Santa Anita. Triple Crown winners American Pharoah and Justify trained at Santa Anita before going on to win the Kentucky Derby, Preakness, and Belmont Stakes. Justify, a descendant of Secretariat, won the 2018 Santa Anita Derby and joined Seattle Slew that year as the only undefeated Triple Crown winners. The Santa Anita Derby, held annually since 1935, is one of the final races before the Kentucky Derby and has a purse of $400,000.

Santa Anita has everything you'd expect from a major horse track—year-round racing, restaurants, betting windows, gallery viewing, and live wagering for races at other tracks. The art deco facade gives the track a throwback feel as you enter. The track itself is a mile and a quarter with a downhill turf that was added in 1953. The long grandstand can seat up to 26,000 spectators with room for another 50,000 on the track infield. The Handicap and Derby regularly draw Hollywood stars, so maybe you'll rub elbows with a few celebrities while watching the horses run.

Next to the track is **Arcadia County Park**, which houses the **Santa Anita Golf Course**. The course opened in 1938 and occupies the space that was once used for a U.S. Army air field. The 126-yard, par-3 fourth hole is where the hangars used to stand. Today, the course is a 6,090-yard, par-71

Entrance to Santa Anita Park in Arcadia.

(men's white tees) with a superb view of the San Gabriels from any tee or green. The undulating fairways are lined by tall oaks and pines and dotted with sand bunkers. A round of golf is very affordable, and after playing, you can grab a bite or just have a drink at the **Finish Line Bar & Grill**.

Runners find their groove at Arcadia High

Across the street on the park's south end is **Arcadia High School**, which opened in 1952. The Arcadia Apaches are regular CIF playoff participants in every sport and consistently compete for championships in the Pacific League, which includes Pasadena High School and Pasadena Muir.

Arcadia has proud cross-country and track-and-field traditions. The Apaches consistently send runners to the CIF state meet and have regularly placed in the top 10 as a team since 2005.

Arcadia has hosted the nation's most prestigious prep track meet every April since 1968. The Arcadia Invitational has drawn high school athletes from across the United States and even runners from Canada, Mexico,

Breeders Cup race in 2008 at Santa Anita Park in Arcadia.

Ireland, Australia, and New Zealand. At least 25 high school records have been set at the Arcadia Invitational, which has produced more than 150 Olympians. Gold medalists Steve Lewis, Danny Everett, Quincy Watts, Gail Devers, Valerie Brisco-Hooks, Carmelita Jeter, Allyson Felix, Monique Henderson, Cathy Freeman, Michael Marsh, Stephanie Brown Trafton, and Ashton Eaton and NFL players Jahvid Best and Steve Smith all competed at the Arcadia Invitational while in high school.

Notable NFL, MLB players have come from Arcadia

The Apaches also have strong football and baseball programs. While the Apaches had not won a CIF football championship through 2020, they have produced a few NFL players—most notably Pro Football Hall of Famer Bruce Matthews and his older brother Clay, who was a four-time Pro Bowler for the Cleveland Browns. Bruce Matthews anchored Arcadia's 1977 and '78 teams and is one of the best offensive linemen to ever play in the NFL. He was selected to the Pro Bowl 14 times over a 19-year career all spent with the Houston Oilers/Tennessee Titans franchise. Former NFL punter Mike Saxon and kicker Mike Lansford are also Arcadia products. Between their time at Arcadia and their NFL careers, Lansford and Saxon both played at Pasadena City College.

While a CIF title has eluded Arcadia's football team, the Apaches baseball team did win a CIF title in 1965 and was runner-up in both 1964 and 1978. Arcadia's baseball program has also produced multiple professional players, notably 1979 MLB All-Stars Bruce Bochte and Steve Kemp. One of the best baseball players to play at Arcadia was Bill Seinsoth, who was drafted five times by MLB teams but chose to play at the University of Southern California. He was the CIF player of the year in 1965 and then led USC to a national championship in 1968, when he was named the tournament's MVP. He played just one year in the minors before a fatal car accident took his life at the age of 22. Seinsoth's family received a letter of condolence from then-California Governor Ronald Reagan.

Arcadia High is also the site of the CIF Southern California badminton championships every May. Olympic badminton players Iris and Rena Wang came out of the Arcadia program. Arcadia has been home to very good golf teams as well. The Apaches are regularly represented in the CIF meet, and Arcadia's golf program produced LPGA players Amy Hung and Angel Yin.

The Apaches volleyball program produced John Speraw, who was the CIF player of the year in 1990 before leading UCLA to a pair of NCAA national championships. He then coached UC-Irvine to three national titles between 2007 and 2012. Speraw was an assistant coach on the USA men's national volleyball team that won a gold medal at the 2008 Olympics and head coach for the group that took the bronze in 2016.

PASADENA

There isn't a more iconic sports venue along Route 66 than the **Rose Bowl**. It can be reached by taking Colorado Boulevard west through Old Pasadena and then briefly north on Orange Grove Boulevard before turning west on Holly Street. Legendary broadcaster Keith Jackson called the Rose Bowl the

The facade of the famed Rose Bowl.

"Mecca" of college football.

"This is the mansion at the end of the Yellow Brick Road," the late Jackson said in a quote commemorated on a plaque near elevators that take media members up to the press box that now bears his name. "For everybody who's a college football fan, this is where you want to come—the Rose Bowl in sunny Pasadena.

"It's just the aura, the ambiance, particularly when it's full. And then you've got the broad-shouldered San Gabriel (Mountains) sitting there, looking down on all of this."

Not to be missed: The Rose Bowl

The Rose Bowl is one of just four college football stadiums on the National Register of Historic Places. The others are the Yale Bowl, Harvard Stadium, and the Los Angeles Coliseum. The Rose Bowl, built in 1922, was modeled

The "broad-shouldered" San Gabriel Mountains add to the aura of the Rose Bowl.

after the Yale Bowl, which opened in 1914. The Rose Bowl's original 1922 locker room is now used as a museum accessible to the public with the purchase of a stadium tour.

The Rose Bowl, with a capacity around 100,000, has hosted five Super Bowls, three World Cups, and two Olympic Games with another on the way in 2028. Brian Brantley, the director of advancement for the Rose Bowl Legacy Foundation, said "America's Stadium" is the primary landmark for the city of Pasadena.

"We're very proud of that," Brantley said. "It is a special place, not only in the community but in the country."

The Rose Bowl is home to the "granddaddy" of college bowl games. The first Rose Bowl game was in 1902, and it has been played every year since 1916. All but two of these contests were held in Pasadena. The first exception was in 1942 when the game between Duke and Oregon State was moved to Durham, North Carolina. In 2021 it was played in Arlington, Texas. The game grew out of the annual Tournament of Roses Parade held every New Year's Day.

Future Pro Football Hall of Famers like Bob Griese, Dick Butkus, Troy Aikman, Randall McDaniel, O. J. Simpson, Lynn Swann, Warren Moon, Orlando Pace, and Peyton Manning played at the Rose Bowl during their respective college careers.

The Rose Bowl is also the home stadium for UCLA football, which has a proud tradition that includes a national championship in 1954 and more than 40 All-American players. UCLA has called the Rose Bowl home since 1982 and played in the Rose Bowl game five times since. The red and green colors of the rose marquee above the main gate change to blue and gold for UCLA games.

The Rose Bowl facade lights change from red and green to blue and gold for UCLA football games.

The 2010s decade was not kind to the Bruins, with four straight losing seasons from 2016 to 2019. Even when the football isn't great, the UCLA band still puts on a wonderful halftime show. The stadium may not be near capacity when the Bruins aren't playing well, but the band gives it its all, and the UCLA fans in attendance are a passionate bunch.

The Rose Bowl is a vibrant place to see a game, and its storied history is chronicled by plaques and photos at every turn. Statues of Keith Jackson, Brandi Chastain, and Jackie Robinson stand in

Brandi Chastain's iconic celebration at the 1999 World Cup is immortalized in bronze in front of the Rose Bowl.

front of the stadium. Robinson was a four-sport athlete—baseball, football, basketball, and track—at UCLA before his pioneering MLB career. Chastain is forever frozen in her iconic 1999 World Cup celebration.

"It is a place of passion, strength, tradition, honor," ESPN broadcaster Kirk Herbstreit says in a video played inside the locker room museum. "When you walk onto the field and hear nearly 100,000 people cheering so loud that you can hardly hear yourself think, that's when you know you're in America's stadium. That's when you know you're in the Rose Bowl."

The Rose Bowl is surrounded by **Brookside Golf Club** inside **Arroyo Seco Natural Park**. Brookside has two pristine 18-hole courses, separated by the Arroyo Seco channel. Both Brookside courses, designed by William P. Bell, are open to the public and have hosted various PGA and LPGA events.

Jackie Robinson tops the list of Pasadena City College greats

Less than 4 miles east of the Rose Bowl complex is **Pasadena City College**, where Jackie Robinson's stardom was born. The Jackie Robinson statue at the Rose Bowl depicts Robinson in a PCC football uniform. PCC's athletics program has an impressive list of alumni.

Robinson led the Lancers football team to an undefeated season in 1938. The Lancers were also unbeaten in 1936 when they were led by the versatile Grenny Landell, who was a running back, quarterback, punter, kick returner, and safety. Landell was selected 10th overall in the 1940 NFL Draft and is still the highest draft pick of any former PCC player. PCC

A statue of Jackie Robinson stands centered in the Rose Bowl plaza.

The artsy entrance to Pasadena City College.

won another junior college national championship in 1977 with future NFL kicker Mike Lansford setting a single-season scoring record. PCC also won a junior college national title in 1953, led by four-sport athlete Larry Ross. Former Cleveland Browns running back Jerome Harrison, who recorded the third-highest single-game rushing total in NFL history with 286 yards in 2009, set several PCC rushing records during the 2002 and '03 seasons.

In his two years at PCC, Robinson set several school records that stood for more than 60 years. The PCC Lancers baseball, softball, and football teams all play at venues named for Robinson. The baseball team calls **Jackie Robinson Field** home while the football team plays at **Robinson Stadium**—jointly named for Jackie Robinson and brother Mack Robinson, who was a standout track athlete at PCC and silver medalist in the 200-meter dash at the 1936 Berlin Olympics. The PCC softball team plays at **Robinson Park** on North Fair Oaks Avenue.

Jackie Robinson broke baseball's color barrier when he made his MLB debut with the Brooklyn Dodgers on April 15, 1947. He was the National

League Rookie of the Year and then had a legendary 10-year career, all with the Dodgers. Robinson endured racism throughout his career yet was a six-time All-Star and led the NL in batting in 1949. He was enshrined in the Baseball Hall of Fame in 1962, and his number 42 was universally retired by all MLB teams in 1997.

Other notable PCC alumni

Jackie Robinson Field is at **Brookside Park** next to the Rose Bowl. Robinson isn't the only Baseball Hall of Famer who played for the Lancers. St. Louis native Dick Williams also played for the Brooklyn Dodgers and was a teammate of Robinson from 1951 to 1954 and in '56. Williams had a 14-year MLB playing career, but he made his mark as a manager. He got his first managerial job with the Boston Red Sox in 1967 and later led the Oakland Athletics to World Series championships in 1972 and '73. He also led the San Diego Padres to the World Series in 1984. Williams is in the team halls of fame for both the Red Sox and the Padres and was enshrined in the National Baseball Hall of Fame in 2008.

One of Williams's assistant coaches on his World Series championship teams was Irv Noren, a teammate of Williams at both Pasadena High School and PCC. Noren had an 11-year MLB career and played in four World Series between 1952 and 1956 as a member of the New York Yankees. The Yankees won three of those Series, and all four of Noren's World Series appearances came against the Robinson-led Dodgers.

Before Darrell Evans was a two-time MLB All-Star and a World Series champion with the 1984 Detroit Tigers, he was smashing home runs for the PCC Lancers. While at PCC, Evans led both the baseball and basketball teams to California championships and is the only junior college athlete to captain state championship teams in two sports in the same school year. Evans, who led the American League in home runs with 38 in 1985, is also the answer to a trivia question. He was on base when Hank Aaron hit his record-breaking 715th career home run for the Atlanta Braves in 1973.

The PCC Lancers basketball, volleyball, and badminton teams play inside **Hutto-Patterson Gymnasium**, adjacent to Robinson Stadium. PCC's women's basketball and volleyball teams have been nationally ranked. Dionne

Pounds, a member of Finland's national women's basketball team, was PCC's first 1,000-point scorer. Her father is former NBA player Larry Pounds, who also got his collegiate start at Pasadena City College.

Before Michael Cooper was a standout at the University of New Mexico in Albuquerque, he was a star at Pasadena Community College. Cooper went on to have a 12-year NBA career and won five NBA championships with the Los Angeles Lakers. He was named the NBA's Defensive Player of the Year in 1987. Cooper later got into coaching and led the Los Angeles Sparx to WNBA championships in 2001 and 2002.

George Trapp is another former PCC basketball star and played for legendary coach Jerry Tarkanian, who led the Lancers for three seasons before winning a national championship at the University of Nevada, Las Vegas in 1990. "Tark" led four UNLV teams to the NCAA Final Four. Trapp's brother, John, also played at PCC before a five-year NBA career that included a league title in 1972 while a member of the Lakers.

Charles Paddock, who was known as the world's fastest human when he won a gold medal in the 100-meter dash at the 1920 Olympics, ran track for PCC after graduating from Pasadena High School. Other PCC alumni who participated in the Olympics were diver Carol Fletcher (1924 Paris Games), discus thrower MayBelle Reichart (1928 Amsterdam Games), gymnast George Greenfield (1972 Munich Games), and sprinter Edino Steele (2012 London Games).

Former tennis pro and PGA golfer Ellsworth Vines, who was inducted into the International Tennis Hall of Fame in 1962 and later the Southern California PGA Hall of Fame, was a standout PCC athlete from 1927 to 1929. Vines was once ranked as the world's top tennis player and won the 1931 U.S. Open. Twenty years later, he had a top-four finish at the PGA Championship. Vines was a two-time high school state champion for Pasadena before arriving at PCC.

Dave Freeman, considered the greatest American badminton player of all time, was a star tennis player at PCC in 1938. Freeman was the first American inducted into the International Badminton Hall of Fame in 1997. Hugh Stewart also played tennis at PCC and won national championships at the junior college and NCAA levels before a long pro career that included round of 16 finishes at Wimbledon and the U.S. Open.

PCC has also been home to the annual "Bandfest" before the New Year's Day Tournament of Roses Parade. "Bandfest" features high school and college marching bands from around the country.

Basketball is tops at Pasadena High

Many PCC student-athletes have come from **Pasadena High School**, just a few blocks north of Colorado Boulevard (Route 66). Pasadena High opened in 1891 and was originally on the Pasadena City College campus. The high school moved to its current location on Sierra Madre Boulevard in 1960. The school's spacious parking lots are used as a post-parade staging area for the Rose Bowl parade floats.

Baseball has been strong at Pasadena since the program played for a CIF title in 1919. The program has spawned MLB players like the late Irv Noren and Lee Walls. Basketball has arguably been Pasadena's best program. Long before Noren went on to play in four World Series with the New York Yankees as part of an 11-year MLB career, he was the CIF state basketball player of the year in 1942.

The Pasadena basketball team was the CIF state runner-up in 1972 and '73, led by future NBA star Michael Cooper. The Bulldogs won their first two CIF titles in 1977 and 1978. The 1977 team was even awarded a mythical national championship. The Bulldogs claimed a 2 AA title in 1995 and another in 2007. Pasadena won another CIF championship in 2012 and also produced former NBA players Jim Marsh and Michael Holton.

The gymnasium at Pasadena High is named for Tom Hamilton, who was the school's longtime head football coach and athletics director. Hamilton was a star athlete at both Pasadena City College and USC before he got into coaching. The Bulldogs won 16 league titles during Hamilton's 24 years as their coach.

Pasadena's 58,000-square-foot athletics complex, which includes **Hamilton Gymnasium**, underwent a $19 million remodel in 2019. The renovation included new air conditioning, lighting, floors, upgraded sound systems, bleachers, a lobby with concession stand, and new entries. The gym is used by Pasadena's basketball and volleyball teams. The Bulldogs won a

CIF 2 A volleyball crown in 2006.

Pasadena's first state championship came in football when the Bulldogs walloped Whittier, 50–0, in the 1915 championship game. The Bulldogs won additional CIF titles in 1924 and 1933 and have been runners-up six times. The Pasadena program has produced several NFL players, including three-time Pro Bowl cornerback Chris McAlister, who helped the Baltimore Ravens win Super Bowl XXXV.

One of the biggest games on the Pasadena schedule is the annual Turkey Tussle against rival **John Muir High School**. The game has been played at the Rose Bowl every Thanksgiving weekend since 1947. Muir High is not far from the Rose Bowl, on the north side of the 210. It's also the high school alma mater of Jackie and Mack Robinson. The Victory Bell goes to the Tussle winner, which has been Muir for two-thirds of the rivalry. Muir won its fourth straight Tussle game in 2019.

Not far from Pasadena High is **Eaton Canyon Golf Course**, a nine-hole, par-35 public course. The municipal course opened in 1962 and is an affordable way to get in a quick round while taking in the majesty of the San Gabriel Mountains.

Legendary rock band Van Halen was formed in Pasadena with the Van Halen brothers attending Pasadena High and David Lee Roth graduating from Muir. They met while students at Pasadena City College. Jam out to a little "Jump," "Panama," "Poundcake," "Right Now," "You Really Got Me," and "Eruption" while cruising the City of Roses. Before leaving Pasadena, be sure to see the **Colorado Street Bridge**, historic **Rialto Theatre**, and all of the Arroyo Seco icons before heading to downtown Los Angeles.

LOS ANGELES

Just as Route 66 begins in sports-rich Chicago, it ends in another metropolis that boasts *two* teams in each of the four major professional leagues. The Los Angeles area has MLB teams the Dodgers and Angels of Anaheim, the NHL's Los Angeles Kings and Anaheim Ducks, and the NBA's Clippers and Lakers and now has two NFL teams with the Chargers and Rams moving

The Staples Center in downtown Los Angeles.

into **SoFi Stadium** in Inglewood near the LAX airport. LA also has two MLS teams with the Galaxy and LAFC, and a pair of Division I universities in UCLA and USC.

About 140 high schools are located in the CIF Los Angeles City Section; however, most are not along the Route 66 corridor. The focus in Los Angeles will be on the many major professional and collegiate teams that call the City of Angels home. Three of them play at the downtown **Staples Center**.

The course of Route 66 through Los Angeles may seem confusing, but just take the 110 south to the 101 and head west. Then exit at Santa Monica Boulevard and go west.

Dodger Stadium worth the stop (and the traffic headache)

The **Dodger Stadium** exit is just before California Highway 110 merges with U.S. Highway 101 and right near the **Figueroa Street Tunnels**. The venerable stadium sits atop a hill that has incomparable views of Chavez Ravine, Elysian Park, and downtown Los Angeles. Although it's a traffic nightmare to get in and out of the stadium, it's been home to one of baseball's most revered franchises since 1962. With teams at every level along America's

Main Street, the Los Angeles Dodgers are undeniably the baseball kings of Route 66.

Jackie Robinson may have never played for the LA Dodgers, but the stadium at Chavez Ravine has hosted its share of MLB legends. Large baseballs outside the right-field entrance feature signatures of each of the franchise's Cy Young Award winners: Don Newcombe, Don Drysdale, Sandy Koufax (three times), Mike Marshall, Fernando Valenzuela, Orel Hershiser, Eric Gagne, and Clayton Kershaw (three times). Koufax was also the National League MVP in 1963, and Kershaw was named the 2014 NL MVP. They are two of six players to be named MVP since the team moved. Former Dodgers shortstop Maury Wills was the 1962 NL MVP in their first LA season. First baseman Steve Garvey was the 1974 MVP; outfielder Kirk Gibson took home the 1988 NL MVP; and outfielder Cody Bellinger was named the 2019 NL MVP. Gibson's famous home run in the 1988 World Series helped the Dodgers win their sixth World Series title. The Dodgers next reached the World Series in 2017 and 2018 but fell to the Houston Astros and Boston Red Sox, respectively. However, the Dodgers won the 2020 World Series.

The home stadium of the LA Dodgers is located just north of downtown Los Angeles.

The Dodgers also had one of the best broadcasters to ever grace a press box. The incomparable Vin Scully called his first Dodgers game in 1950, eight years before the team left Brooklyn. He was enshrined in the Baseball Hall of Fame in 1982 and called his final Dodgers game on October 2, 2016. In addition to calling baseball games, Scully was the voice of NFL games for CBS and called tennis matches and golf tournaments as part of his legendary career. No one has called more MLB games for the same team as long as Scully did with the Dodgers, and the organization honored him with a large circular plaque at Dodger Stadium in 2017. The plaque, unveiled by former pitcher Sandy Koufax and longtime manager Tommy Lasorda, is part of the stadium's Ring of Honor that honors former players who have had their respective numbers retired.

Lasorda's number 2 is also retired, and one of the more popular selfie spots at Dodger Stadium is in front of Lasorda's giant bobblehead statue in the right-field concourse. Lasorda led the Dodgers to World Series crowns in 1981 and 1988 and was inducted into the National Baseball Hall of Fame in 1997.

Dodger Stadium is unique among MLB parks because it sits on top of a hill with the field essentially dug into it. That means most of the people who attend Dodgers games enter the stadium at the upper level and make their way down to their seats.

If traffic prevents you from catching the first pitch at Dodger Stadium, fret not. You won't be alone.

"It is a running joke in Los Angeles that people arrive late for games and leave early," said California Historic Route 66 Association President Scott Piotrowski. "Look around Dodger Stadium at first pitch and with the walk-off home run and see how many seats are empty.

"Traffic in Los Angeles is notorious, and that accounts for some of it. But honestly, there's just a ton going on. I always say that I love living in Los Angeles because I can get or do anything within two hours of here. And that makes sports just one part of the big picture of Los Angeles.

"Yes, it's important to some. It's unimportant to others. I, for one, have passions outside of the Mother Road. The Los Angeles Football Club is one of them for me. I also support the Dodgers and their affiliates along the

Mother Road in Oklahoma City, Tulsa, and Rancho Cucamonga. I call them the Boys in Route 66 Blue, and I'm surprised it has not caught on more."

Lakers offer a fan experience like no other

Not many NBA teams have a more dynastic history than the Los Angeles Lakers. The Lakers entered 2019 with 16 NBA championships, and only the Boston Celtics had more with 17. Led by recent stars LeBron James and Anthony Davis, the Lakers tied the Celtics by winning their 17th NBA championship during the pandemic-interrupted 2019–20 season.

James, who left Cleveland to sign with the Lakers in 2018, is honored to play for such a storied franchise.

"When you look at the teams and players who have come through this franchise, you're talking about some of the best teams you've seen, or did not see but you've read about or seen clips of," James said. "And when you start to think about all the great players and coaches, the history of this franchise is unmatched. It's pretty cool when you're able to put yourself in the category of some of the greats.

LeBron James speaks with reporters following a Lakers win over the Wizards on Nov. 29, 2019.

"It's great to be a part of this franchise and this legacy."

Dwight Howard, who was with the Lakers for the 2012–13 season and rejoined the club in 2019, said "it's amazing" to wear the Lakers purple and gold.

"Every time we step on that court and put on that jersey, I feel like it's *Men in Black*—the scene in the movie when (Rip Torn) says, 'Are you ready to put on the last suit you'll ever wear?' That's how we feel every time we put on this uniform," Howard said.

Los Angeles is the entertainment capital of the world, and the Lakers understand that. Player introductions are a spectacle, and Lakers games regularly draw celebrity fans like Jack Nicholson, Arsenio Hall, Leonardo DiCaprio, Denzel Washington, Andy Garcia, Flea and Anthony Kiedis of the Red Hot Chili Peppers, and Ice Cube. Just as with the Dodgers, Randy Newman's "I Love L.A." plays after Lakers' victories. You can take in the "Lake Show" at Staples Center, where Howard said the atmosphere for a Lakers game is unrivaled among NBA venues.

"Every time we're on the road, we look forward to coming back home and playing at the Staples Center," Howard said. "We look forward to playing in front of our home crowd. They give us an energy like no other. We feed off them."

Players warm up on the court at Staples Center before a Nov. 29, 2019 game between the Lakers and Wizards.

Clippers have become regular playoff contenders

The Lakers aren't the only team to call Staples Center home. The 20,000-seat arena that opened in 1999 is also home to the NBA's Clippers and the NHL's Kings.

The Clippers do not have the storied success of the Lakers; in fact they were one of the worst teams in the NBA before and after their 1984 move from San Diego. That started to change in 1992 when the Clippers made the playoffs for the first time since 1976, when the franchise was the Buffalo Braves and led by Hall of Famer Bob McAdoo. The Clippers made the playoffs three times in the 1990s but never got out of the first round.

Things finally changed in 2006 when the Clippers advanced to the Western Conference Finals but fell to the Phoenix Suns in seven games. The Clippers were led by Elton Brand, who made his second All-Star Game that season. The Clippers were back in the conference finals in 2012, led by second-year player Blake Griffin. With the exception of the 2017–18 season, the Clippers qualified for the playoffs every year between 2012 and 2020. The Clippers have their own celebrity fan base that includes Billy Crystal, Jay Z and Beyoncé, Floyd Mayweather Jr., Rihanna, Kristen Bell, Frankie Muniz, and Serena Williams.

Gretzky brought the spotlight to hockey in LA

While the Clippers and Lakers both moved from other cities, the Kings are an original LA team. Of the teams in the four major professional sports leagues, the Kings are the only LA team that has never played elsewhere. The Kings joined the NHL in 1967 as one of six expansion teams, along with the St. Louis Blues, Minnesota North Stars (now the Dallas Stars), Philadelphia Flyers, Pittsburgh Penguins, and Oakland Seals, who moved to Cleveland in 1976 and folded in 1978.

The expansion brought the NHL from its original 6 teams to 12, and the Kings were in the Stanley Cup playoffs in each of their first two seasons. The Kings missed the playoffs the next four seasons but acquired Hall of Famer Marcell Dionne in 1975 and reached the playoffs the next seven seasons. Hockey still wasn't that popular in Los Angeles, however. They needed real star power and got it in 1988 when then-owner Bruce McNall orchestrated a trade that brought Wayne Gretzky to the City of Angels. Gretzky was already a superstar, named the NHL MVP eight straight seasons from 1980 to 1987 while leading the Edmonton Oilers to four Stanley Cup championships. Two hours after the Oilers won the Cup in 1988, news broke that "The Great One"

A frieze honoring the L.A. Kings' Stanley Cup championship teams is outside of Staples Center.

was getting shipped to LA. The deal was a steal for the Kings—trading two lesser-known players and three draft picks for Gretzky and fellow stars Marty McSorley and Mike Krushelnyski.

The trio joined future Hall of Famer Luc Robitaille, and the Kings got out of the first round of the playoffs for the first time since 1983. When rookie defenseman Rob Blake joined the squad for the 1990–91 season, the puzzle was complete. The Kings won their first division title that season and were in the Stanley Cup Final two seasons later. While the Kings fell to the Montreal Canadiens in the 1993 Final, hockey had finally caught on in LA.

With Gretzky, Blake, Robitaille, and McSorley, the Kings were now a draw, but the enthusiasm eventually waned when Gretzky was dealt to the St. Louis Blues in 1996 after the Kings missed the postseason in the four subsequent years after their first Stanley Cup Final berth. The team was saved from bankruptcy in 1995 and moved into Staples Center in 1999. It made the playoffs its first three seasons at the new arena, but then had another lull.

The 2010s were kind to the Kings, who had drafted goaltender Jonathan

Quick in 2005. Quick made his NHL debut in 2007 and became the team's fulltime goalie in 2008. He became the cornerstone of teams that won the Stanley Cup in 2012 and 2014. Quick was awarded the Conn Smythe Trophy as the playoffs MVP in 2012 when he had a goals-against average of 1.41 in 20 games. When the Kings dominated the New York Rangers in the 2014 Final, it was right winger Justin Williams who took home the Conn Smythe.

Despite qualifying for the playoffs in just two of the next six seasons, the fan support built during the championship seasons was still strong. Kings games are full of excitement and energy. The Kings may have the most impressive list of celebrity fans of LA teams. Taylor Swift, Justin Bieber, Tori Spelling, Demi Lovato, David and Victoria Beckham, Channing Tatum, Katy Perry, Will Ferrell, Will Arnett, Joshua Jackson, Chuck Lorre, Colin Hanks, Zac Efron, Elliot Page, Vince Vaughn, David Boreanaz, Eric Stonestreet, Alexander Skarsgård, and Tom Cruise are all regulars at Kings games. Whether you see the Kings, Lakers, or Clippers at Staples Center, there's a good chance you'll have a celebrity sighting.

The magic inside Staples Center

The employees at Staples Center deserve a ton of credit because they can transform the arena in mere hours. The arena is covered in purple and gold for Lakers games but switched to black and silver for a Kings game the next night. The basketball court is removed to uncover the ice beneath it. The floor is then returned and the signage switched to red, white, and blue for a Clippers game the following afternoon. Switch the order around, depending on team schedules, but the quick transformation is a marvelous feat and doesn't even factor getting the arena ready for concerts and conventions that may be held during the basketball and hockey seasons.

The interior walls of Staples Center are dotted with posters from the innumerable concerts the venue has hosted as well as memorable sports moments. Staples Center hosted the 2004, 2011, and 2018 NBA All-Star games, as well as the 2002 and 2017 NHL All-Star Games. It was also home to the 2009 World Figure Skating Championships. The arena hosts more than 250 events each year and is one of the most spectacular venues along Route 66. Staples Center's location is in the heart of a shopping and entertainment complex and mere blocks from the corner of Seventh Street and Broadway, which was the original terminus of Route 66 before it was extended to Santa Monica in 1936.

Visit UCLA to see where champions are made

With the exception of the Rose Bowl, the UCLA athletics facilities are centrally located on the **Westwood** campus. The UCLA football offices and practice field are right next to the tennis courts. Both complexes are adjacent to the famed **Pauley Pavilion**, which is home to UCLA basketball, volleyball, and gymnastics. Pauley Pavilion, also known as "The House that Wooden Built," was home to the glory days of UCLA men's basketball under legendary coach John Wooden. UCLA won an NCAA-record 88 straight games between 1971 and 1974 under "The Wizard of Westwood," who led the Bruins to 10 national championships over 12 seasons. Wooden's name—along with that of his wife, Nell—is on the court as well as in the halls of Pauley Pavilion. A statue of the late coach stands outside the arena while a bronze bust of him is just inside the main entrance atop his "Pyramid of Success."

Walking into Pauley Pavilion can give you chills when you see Wooden's likeness, displays of the program's history in the concourse, and the

UCLA plays San Jose State on Dec. 1, 2019, at Pauley Pavilion.

championship banners hanging from the rafters alongside retired jersey numbers of basketball Hall of Famers Kareem Abdul-Jabbar (Lew Alcindor), Bill Walton, Reggie Miller, Don Barksdale, Gail Goodrich, and Jamaal (Keith) Wilkes. The arena is drenched in history and is one of the most revered venues in all of college basketball.

UCLA has a slogan of "Champions Made Here" at Pauley Pavilion, and it's not just the men's basketball team that has won national titles. The men's volleyball team has nine national championships through 2020; the women have seven volleyball titles; and the gymnastics team also has seven national championships.

Pauley Pavilion isn't the only home to national champions on the UCLA campus. The men's soccer team is always a national contender and had four national championships as of 2020.

Outside of the men's basketball team, the women's softball is the most successful UCLA program. UCLA softball has 13 national championships—more than any other school in the country—as of 2020. The 13th title came in 2019 when the Bruins made their NCAA-record 29th NCAA Tournament appearance. The Bruins are well represented at the USA Softball Hall of Fame in Oklahoma City with former coaches Sharron Backus and Sue Enquist, and former pitcher Lisa Fernandez enshrined there. Former UCLA catcher Kelly Inouye-Perez took over the program in 2007 and had the Bruins in the NCAA Tournament every season through 2019. The 2020 tourney was canceled because of the COVID-19 pandemic. Inouye-Perez helmed national championship

A statue of legendary basketball coach John Wooden stands outside of Pauley Pavilion.

teams in 2010 and 2019. The Bruins play at the 1,300-seat **Easton Stadium** on Sunset Boulevard.

The UCLA baseball team plays at **Jackie Robinson Stadium** with his number 42 proudly displayed on the center field wall. Robinson Stadium has a seating capacity just over 1,800 and has been the home for Bruins baseball since 1981. UCLA did cram more than 2,600 fans into the stadium for a 2010 NCAA Tournament game against Louisiana State. The Bruins drew a record crowd of 2,914 for a 1997 game against cross-town rival USC. UCLA has a very strong baseball tradition that includes a national championship in 2013 and a runner-up finish in 2010. The program produced MLB All-Stars Trevor

---

Sports stops to consider as long as you're in the area

Stray a bit from downtown Los Angeles to see the area's other major sports teams. Anaheim, 27 miles southeast of LA, has the easily accessible **Angel Stadium**, home to the 2002 World Series champions and one of MLB's best players in three-time American League MVP Mike Trout. Angel Stadium is next to the ARTIC train station and across the street from **Honda Center**, home to the NHL's Anaheim Ducks. Both the Angels and Ducks were once owned by the Walt Disney Company, and **Disneyland** is minutes away.

The **Los Angeles Coliseum**, built in 1923 and added to the National Register of Historic Places in 1984, is 3 miles south of downtown. The Coliseum, with a capacity around 80,000, has hosted just about everything. It was the temporary home for the Dodgers from 1958 to 1961 before Dodger Stadium was ready. Three games of the 1959 World Series between the Dodgers and Chicago White Sox were played there. The Coliseum has hosted two Super Bowls, including the first one, and has been the home to the NFL's Rams. The venue is the permanent home for the USC football team, which has won 11 NCAA national championships and produced seven Heisman Trophy winners. With the addition of the 2028 Olympics, the Coliseum has hosted three Olympic games, and the stadium's torch is one of its signature features.

Next to the Coliseum is **Banc of California Stadium**, where the Los Angeles Football Club has taken the pitch since 2018. It was also a venue for the 2019 CONCACAF Gold Cup. The Coliseum and Banc of California Stadium are just off the 110.

A little farther south is **Dignity Health Sports Park** in Carson, where the MLS LA Galaxy club has called home since 2003. It was also the temporary home to the LA Chargers from 2017 to 2020. The 30,000-seat Carson stadium will be used for the 2028 Olympics and has hosted several FIFA, CONCACAF, and international friendly soccer matches. A new National Women's Soccer League team, Angel City, makes its debut in 2022.

Bauer, Chris Chambliss, Gerrit Cole, Jeff Conine, Brandon Crawford, Troy Glaus, Chase Utley, and of course, Robinson. MLB managers Ron Roenicke and Dave Roberts also played for the Bruins.

UCLA's 119 total national championships, as of 2020, were second-most in NCAA annals. Only Stanford, with 127, has more national titles. UCLA's athletics tradition is unrivaled by most, and a stroll through Westwood is like a walk through sports history.

HOLLYWOOD

Hollywood is synonymous with glitz and glamour, especially along Hollywood Boulevard just north of Route 66. Hollywood Boulevard has the **Hollywood Walk of Fame**, the **TCL Chinese** and **El Capitan theatres**, and the **Hollywood Wax Museum**. Route 66 is not left out of the Hollywood lore. The **Hollywood Forever Cemetery** is right on Santa Monica Boulevard and is the final resting place of celebrities like Chris Cornell, Johnny Ramone, Judy Garland, Estelle Getty, John Huston, and Mel Blanc.

A 15-minute walk north from the cemetery is **Bernstein High School** on North Wilton Place. The school, which opened in 2008, was used as the film set for the television show *Glee*.

A mile and a half west of Bernstein is **Hollywood High School**, where the glory days of athletics have long since passed. Hollywood's teams are called the Sheiks—taken from the 1921 Rudolph Valentino film of the same name. The high school was built in 1910 and added to the National Register of Historic Places in 2012. The school is surrounded by palm trees and adorned with colorful murals. Because of its beautiful campus, Hollywood High School is a popular filming location for movies and television shows.

Hollywood's football team is a perennial contender for Metro Conference championships. Its small stadium is parallel to Hollywood Boulevard and its oft-visited Walk of Fame. Spectators at a Sheiks game will have a direct view of the historic El Capitan Theatre and the **Hollywood Roosevelt Hotel**.

BEVERLY HILLS

If you ever wanted to feel like a cast member of *Beverly Hills, 90210*, be sure to check out **Beverly Hills High School** (BHHS) a few blocks southeast of Santa Monica Boulevard on Moreno Drive. The original buildings were created using the French Normandy style of architecture, which is why the BHHS athletics teams are called the Normans. It should be noted that *90210* was filmed at Torrance High School, not BHHS.

Beverly Hills High School has strong traditions in football, golf, and tennis, but the real athletics draw at BHHS is its gymnasium.

Called the "**Swim Gym**," the court used by the basketball and volleyball teams covers a 25-yard pool. The gym was designed by architect Stiles O. Clements in 1939 as a New Deal project. If you've seen the movie *It's A Wonderful Life*, you've seen the Swim Gym. BHHS was the site for the scene where George Bailey and Mary Hatch are participating in a Charleston dance contest before falling into the pool after the court is opened by a man whom Mary spurned.

The court is used by the Normans basketball, volleyball, and wrestling teams. The Swim Gym has been a frequent host of the CIF swim championships, which the Normans won six times between 1943 and 1960. Wally

Welcome to Beverly Hills.

Wolf, who won a gold medal at the 1948 Olympics, was a five-time state swim champ for the Normans between 1945 and 1947.

While BHHS has an array of famous alumni in the entertainment world, several pro athletes also graduated from BHHS—most notably Super Bowl champion Spencer Paysinger and 2004 MLB All-Star Ken Harvey.

The Beverly Hills football, lacrosse, soccer, and track teams compete at **Nickoll Field**, which is adjacent to one of several oil rigs on the BHHS campus. Up until 2017 those oil wells pumped about 10 gallons of oil per day generating $300,000 per year for the school. Despite the wealth, Nickoll Field is a small stadium. Spectators do have a nice view of the Century City skyline. One draw for BHHS football games is the world-renowned Beverly Hills High School marching band. The band has been invited to play at Disneyland several times and even traveled to London in 2016 to take part in the city's New Year's Day parade.

Golfers will notice various private country clubs around Beverly Hills, but Route 66 travelers can get a round in at the public **Rancho Park Golf Club**. The club includes a par-3 course as well as an 18-hole municipal course with Bermuda grass fairways and bent grass greens. The 6,879-yard, par-71 course has hosted several PGA and LPGA events. The 508-yard, par-5 ninth hole was the site of Arnold Palmer's infamous 12 at the 1961 LA Open. Rancho Park began as a private country club but has been a public course since 1947 and is available for those who want to boast they golfed among the glitz of Beverly Hills.

SANTA MONICA

Santa Monica Boulevard takes you right into the street's namesake and final city on Route 66. The city's welcome sign is 3 miles from the ceremonial end of Route 66 at the **Santa Monica Pier**, where a variety of bars and restaurants lines the boardwalk next to the **Pacific Park** roller coaster and Ferris Wheel. While the Santa Monica Pier may be the "End of the Trail," the official end of Route 66 is at the corner of Olympic and Lincoln boulevards near **Mel's Drive-In**.

Greetings from Santa Monica.

Santa Monica High develops Hall of Fame athletes

Santa Monica High School is a few blocks south of the Mother Road's official terminus. The school is famous for an alumni base that includes Brat Pack members Robert Downey Jr., brothers Emilio Estevez and Charlie Sheen, Rob Lowe, and Sean Penn. But the Santa Monica High School Vikings also have strong sports programs. *Lois & Clark* actor Dean Cain was a star football player at Santa Monica before playing collegiately at Princeton University.

The Vikings football program has multiple CIF championships to its credit and produced multiple NFL players, including 1960 All-Pro R. C. Owens, two-time Super Bowl champ Mel Kaufman, two-time All-Pro Glyn Milburn, and six-time Pro Bowler Dennis Smith. Smith was also a state high jump champion for the Vikings in 1977 and is enshrined in the Santa Monica High School Hall of Fame.

The baseball program has produced several pro players, though its most famous alumnus is Sheen, whose real name is Carlos Estevez. Sheen had aspirations of playing major league baseball someday but realized he wasn't a good-enough hitter and turned his attention to acting.

Faye Dancer, who played in the All-American Girls Professional Baseball League made famous by the 1992 movie *A League of Their Own*, was also a Santa Monica High School graduate. Dancer played six professional seasons and averaged more than 70 stolen bases per season. She was inducted into the National Women's Baseball Hall of Fame in 2002 and is featured in the Women In Baseball display at the National Baseball Hall of Fame in Cooperstown, New York. Dancer started out playing softball, and the Santa Monica team has had some recent success.

Santa Monica's track, swimming, and wrestling programs have also been superb and dotted with individual state champions. Parry O'Brien, who was a gold medal-winning shot putter at the 1952 and 1956 Olympics, was the CIF shot put champion in 1949. O'Brien also played for Santa Monica's state championship football team in 1948. O'Brien is credited with pioneering the modern shot put technique and was on the cover of *Sports Illustrated* in 1959. He was the U.S. flag bearer at the 1964 Tokyo Games and was enshrined in the National Track & Field Hall of Fame in 1974, U.S. Olympic Hall of Fame in 1984, and the USC Athletic Hall of Fame in 1994.

Laurence Jackson is also a Hall of Fame Santa Monica athlete. Jackson was a three-time state champion from 1984 to 1986 and inducted into the California Wrestling Hall of Fame in 2013. Another notable Santa Monica wrestler is Madison Tung, who was a national champion at the 2014 USA Girls Folkstyle championships in Oklahoma City and then became the first woman to wrestle for the Air Force Academy. A Rhodes Scholar, Tung graduated from the academy in 2019 and began service as an officer in the United States Air Force.

Pacific Park at the Santa Monica Pier.

Another noteworthy Santa Monica graduate is Phil Hill, who was the first American to win the Formula One World Drivers' Championship in 1961. Hill was inducted into the International Motorsports Hall of Fame in 1991.

One of Santa Monica's more prolific programs is volleyball. Both the girls' and boys' teams have been veritable powerhouses over the years. The Vikings excel at both indoor and beach (of course) volleyball. The programs have produced several Olympians and professional beach players like siblings Eric and Liane Sato, Jim Menges, Patrick Powers, and Liz Masakayan.

At the Santa Monica beach itself, you'll see plenty of people surfing and playing beach volleyball. There are outdoor courts at nearby Venice Beach, where pickup games can always be found. The famous outdoor weightlifting platform known as "Muscle Beach" was originally at Santa Monica before it was moved to Venice.

There is plenty to do and see in and around Santa Monica. So enjoy the fun and games of the area, and congratulations on making it to the "End of the Trail."

California Route 66 Points of Interest

WAGON WHEEL RESTAURANT – 2420 Needles Hwy., Needles, CA 92363

NEEDLES HIGH SCHOOL – 1600 Washington St., Needles, CA 92363

LUDLOW CAFE – 68315 National Trails Hwy., Ludlow, CA 92338

ROY'S MOTEL AND CAFE – 87520 National Trails Hwy., Amboy, CA 92304

BARSTOW HIGH SCHOOL – 430 S. 1st Ave., Barstow, CA 92311

CENTRAL HIGH SCHOOL – 405 N. 2nd Ave., Barstow, CA 92311

DESERT INN MOTEL – 1100 E. Main St., Barstow, CA 92311

ROUTE 66 MOTEL – 195 Main St., Barstow, CA 92311

BARSTOW STATION – 1611 E. Main St., Barstow, CA 92311

ROY'S CAFE – 413 E. Main St., Barstow, CA 92311

ELMER'S BOTTLE TREE RANCH – 24266 National Trails Hwy., Oro Grande, CA 92368

CALIFORNIA ROUTE 66 MUSEUM – 16825 D St., Victorville, CA 92395

ADELANTO STADIUM – 12000 Stadium Way, Adelanto, CA 92301

VICTOR VALLEY HIGH SCHOOL – 16500 Mojave Drive, Victorville, CA 92395

ROUTE 66 SHOOTING SPORTS PARK – 15810 Cajon Blvd., San Bernardino, CA 92407

SHANDIN HILLS GOLF CLUB – 3380 Little Mountain Drive, San Bernardino, CA 92405

AL GUHIN PARK – 3664 Little League Drive, San Bernardino, CA 92407

CAL STATE SAN BERNARDINO – 5500 University Pkwy., San Bernardino, CA 92407

FISCALINI FIELD – 1135 E. Highland Ave., San Bernardino, CA 92404

CAJON HIGH SCHOOL – 1200 W. Hill Drive, San Bernardino, CA 92407

SAN BERNARDINO HIGH SCHOOL – 1850 N. E St., San Bernardino, CA 92405

ORIGINAL MCDONALD'S RESTAURANT AND MUSEUM – 1398 N. E St., San Bernardino, CA 92405

SAN MANUEL STADIUM – 280 S. E St., San Bernardino, CA 92401

WIGWAM MOTEL – 2728 Foothill Blvd., San Bernardino, CA 92410

RIALTO HIGH SCHOOL – 595 S. Eucalyptus Ave., Rialto, CA 92376

EISENHOWER HIGH SCHOOL – 1321 N. Lilac Ave., Rialto, CA 92376

BONO'S HISTORIC ORANGE – 15395 Foothill Blvd., Fontana, CA 92335

FONTANA HIGH SCHOOL – 9453 Citrus Ave., Fontana, CA 92335

HENRY J. KAISER HIGH SCHOOL – 11155 Almond Ave., Fontana, CA 92337

AUTO CLUB SPEEDWAY – 9300 Cherry Ave., Fontana, CA 92335

A. B. MILLER HIGH SCHOOL – 6821 Oleander Ave., Fontana, CA 92336

LOANMART FIELD – 8408 Rochester Ave.; Rancho Cucamonga, CA 91730

RANCHO CUCAMONGA HIGH SCHOOL – 11801 Lark Drive, Rancho Cucamonga, CA 91701

LOS OSOS HIGH SCHOOL – 6001 Milliken Ave., Rancho Cucamonga, CA 91737

ALTA LOMA HIGH SCHOOL – 8880 Base Line Road, Rancho Cucamonga, CA 91701

ROUTE 66 CUCAMONGA SERVICE STATION – 9670 Foothill Blvd., Rancho Cucamonga, CA 91730

SYCAMORE INN – 8318 Foothill Blvd., Rancho Cucamonga, CA 91730

MAGIC LAMP INN – 8189 Foothill Blvd., Rancho Cucamonga, CA 91730

RED HILL PARK – 7484 Vineyard Ave., Rancho Cucamonga, CA 91730

RED HILL COUNTRY CLUB – 8358 Red Hill Country Club Drive, Rancho Cucamonga, CA 91730

MADONNA OF THE TRAIL STATUE – 1010 Euclid Ave., Upland, CA 91786

UPLAND HIGH SCHOOL – 565 W. 11th St., Upland, CA 91786

CLAREMONT MUDD SCRIPPS COLLEGES – 500 E. 9th St., Claremont, CA 91711

CMS ATHLETICS COMPLEX – 690 N. Mills Ave., Claremont, CA 91711

MATT M. AXELROOD POOL – 680 Claremont Blvd., Claremont, CA 91711

CLAREMONT HIGH SCHOOL – 1601 N. Indian Hill Blvd., Claremont, CA 91711

WOLFE'S MARKET KITCHEN AND DELI – 160 W. Foothill Blvd., Claremont, CA 91711

DAMIEN HIGH SCHOOL – 2280 Damien Ave., La Verne, CA 91750

MR. D'S DINER – 919 Foothill Blvd., La Verne, CA 91750

UNIVERSITY OF LA VERNE – 1950 3rd St., La Verne, CA 91750

SAN DIMAS CANYON GOLF COURSE – 2100 Terrebonne Ave., San Dimas, CA 91773

MARSHALL CANYON GOLF COURSE – 6100 Stephens Ranch Road, La Verne, CA 91750

SAN DIMAS CANYON PARK – 1628 Sycamore Canyon Road, San Dimas, CA 91773

GLENDORA COUNTRY CLUB – 2400 Country Club Drive, Glendora, CA 91741

GLENDORA HIGH SCHOOL – 1600 E. Foothill Blvd., Glendora, CA 91741

AZUSA PACIFIC UNIVERSITY – 901 E. Alosta Ave., Azusa, CA 91702

FELIX EVENT CENTER – 701 E Foothill Blvd, Azusa, CA 91702

AZUSA HIGH SCHOOL – 240 N. Cerritos Ave., Azusa, CA 91702

RANCHO DUARTE GOLF COURSE – 1000 Las Lomas Road, Duarte, CA 91010

JUSTICE BROTHERS RACING MUSEUM – 2734 E. Huntington Drive, Duarte, CA 91010

MONROVIA HIGH SCHOOL – 845 W. Colorado Blvd., Monrovia, CA 91016

AZTEC HOTEL – 311 W. Foothill Blvd., Monrovia, CA 91016

SANTA ANITA PARK – 285 W. Huntington Drive, Arcadia, CA 91007

SANTA ANITA GOLF COURSE – 405 S. Santa Anita Ave., Arcadia, CA 91006

ARCADIA HIGH SCHOOL – 4703 E. Indian School Road., Phoenix, AZ 85018

ROSE BOWL STADIUM – 1001 Rose Bowl Drive, Pasadena, CA 91103

BROOKSIDE GOLF CLUB – 1133 Rosemont Ave., Pasadena, CA 91103

PASADENA CITY COLLEGE – 1570 E. Colorado Blvd., Pasadena, CA 91106

JACKIE ROBINSON FIELD – 678 N. Arroyo Blvd., Pasadena, CA 91103

ROBINSON PARK – 1081 N. Fair Oaks Ave., Pasadena, CA 91103

BROOKSIDE PARK – 360 N. Arroyo Blvd., Pasadena, CA 91103

HUTTO-PATTERSON GYMNASIUM – 1570 E. Colorado Blvd., Pasadena, CA 91106

PASADENA HIGH SCHOOL – 2925 E. Sierra Madre Blvd., Pasadena, CA 91107

JOHN MUIR HIGH SCHOOL – 1905 Lincoln Ave., Pasadena, CA 91103

EATON CANYON GOLF COURSE – 1150 Sierra Madre Villa Ave., Pasadena, CA 91107

COLORADO STREET BRIDGE – 504 W. Colorado Blvd., Pasadena, CA 91105

RIALTO THEATRE – 1023 Fair Oaks Ave., South Pasadena, CA 91030

DODGER STADIUM – 1000 Elysian Park Ave., Los Angeles, CA 90012

STAPLES CENTER – 1111 S. Figueroa St., Los Angeles, CA 90015

SOFI STADIUM – 1000 S. Prairie Ave., Inglewood, CA 90301

PAULEY PAVILION – 301 Westwood Plaza, Los Angeles, CA 90095

EASTON STADIUM – 100 De Neve Drive, Los Angeles, CA 90024

JACKIE ROBINSON STADIUM – 100 Constitution Ave., Los Angeles, CA 90095

LOS ANGELES COLISEUM – 3911 Figueroa St., Los Angeles, CA 90037

HOLLYWOOD WALK OF FAME – Hollywood Blvd., Vine St., Los Angeles, CA 90028

TCL CHINESE THEATER – 6925 Hollywood Blvd., Hollywood, CA 90028

EL CAPITAN THEATRE – 6838 Hollywood Blvd., Los Angeles, CA 90028

HOLLYWOOD WAX MUSEUM – 6767 Hollywood Blvd., Los Angeles, CA 90028

HOLLYWOOD FOREVER CEMETERY – 6000 Santa Monica Blvd., Los Angeles, CA 90038

BERNSTEIN HIGH SCHOOL – 1309 N. Wilton Place, Los Angeles, CA 90028

HOLLYWOOD HIGH SCHOOL – 1521 N. Highland Ave., Los Angeles, CA 90028

HOLLYWOOD ROOSEVELT HOTEL – 7000 Hollywood Blvd., Los Angeles, CA 90028

BEVERLY HILLS HIGH SCHOOL – 241 S. Moreno Drive, Beverly Hills, CA 90212

RANCHO PARK GOLF CLUB – 10460 W. Pico Blvd., Los Angeles, CA 90064

SANTA MONICA HIGH SCHOOL – 601 Pico Blvd., Santa Monica, CA 90405

SANTA MONICA PIER – 200 Santa Monica Pier, Santa Monica, CA 90401

PACIFIC PARK – 380 Santa Monica Pier, Santa Monica, CA 90401

MEL'S DRIVE-IN – 1670 Lincoln Blvd., Santa Monica, CA 90404

Photo Credits

The author gratefully acknowledges the contributions of the following photographers on these pages:

Laurie Losh Babcock – 299

George Carey – 109

Jonathan Cole/Pendulum – 40

Chris Epting – 323

Ellen Levy Finch – 310

Jean Fruth – 114

Keith Growden – 266

Jlvsclrk – 311

Joey Kincer – 10, front cover

Rick Quinn – 252

Peter Thody – 68, 86, 128, 146, 147, 172–174, 183–185, 187, 195, 251, 263, 265, 267, 268, 271, 281

ACKNOWLEDGMENTS

This book was a labor of love but was definitely something I did not produce on my own. There are so many people to thank because without them, this book would not have been possible.

First, I'd like to thank Mark Sedenquist and Megan Edwards of Imbrifex Books for taking a chance on a guy who had a crazy idea about a topic that had never been written about before. They had a wonderful team in place to help me through the process. Special thanks go to book designer Sue Campbell and editor Vicki Adang, without whom I would have struggled to create the final product. The constant dialogue with Mark and Vicki was something I truly appreciated.

Most Route 66 books are written from the author's perspective, but I didn't want this book to have just my voice. I wanted readers to "hear" from people connected to the various places along the Mother Road. That idea came to fruition thanks to the assistance of the staffs at high schools, colleges, and professional teams. I want to thank the media relations staffs of the Chicago Blackhawks and Los Angeles Lakers; the sports information directors at Illinois State University, the University of Illinois Springfield, Missouri State University, Missouri Southern State University, the University of Tulsa, the University of New Mexico, Northern Arizona University, and UCLA; and the many high school administrators who helped provide information—especially in Hinsdale, Edwardsville, Maplewood, Wildwood, Stroud, Bushland, and Needles.

Most of all, I'd like to thank my wife, Patti, for her support along the way. We traveled the entirety of the Mother Road together from Sept. 25 to Dec. 2, 2019, and she provided invaluable input for the book. She was most instrumental in helping me trim the original manuscript to what you see now. As a writer, I have a hard time cutting things, but Patti's suggestions made sense, and I know Mark and Vicki were also grateful for them. Patti has been a partner in life and travel for years, and I'm grateful to have her by my side.

INDEX